THE F-CK LIST

Schahrzad Morgan

DEDICATION

This book is dedicated to you.

CONTENTS

PREFACE

I didn't come up with the idea of writing a book, much less a sex memoir. That credit goes to about five of my friends. They were amused and intrigued by the hookup stories I shared with them and on Facebook. The sex I described was hot, the situations I created were funny, my insights revealing, and my playfulness and comfort with my sexuality was captivating.

"You should write a book," they said.

I was flattered, but not at all interested. ...that is, until last summer. A man to whom I grew attached said he didn't want to be with me. For almost two months, as I cried over him, I searched inside and outside myself for a mission to bring more meaning into my life.

"You should write a book," my friend Jean Franzblau said.

That time, I listened. But, could I really write a book?

Yes.

I did have a story to tell. I went about sex in a different manner than other women. I met young men for coffee and hooked up with them. I saw sex as playful and lusty, and a gateway to intimacy and connection, not shameful. The men I met didn't think of me as a slut, but respected me. This was not what society or my parents had predicted would happen. At the same time, I was insecure about my sexual responsiveness. I thought it took me too long to come, and that getting me off was a chore. I needed to let that go. Those doubts were surely not unique to me. Surely other women had them too.

The more I talked about sex and my feelings and made myself vulnerable, the more other women and men were drawn to me. The more real I was, the more people liked me. So why didn't more people talk openly about sex?

The stories are true. The names are changed to protect the identity of the women and men in this book. They can come forward if they wish. It's not my place to do it on anyone's behalf. The pictures were taken with natural light and are not photo shopped. This book is about being real, flaws and all.

I say "come" in place of "cum", and "licking pussy" in place of "eating pussy". They are not typos.

Thank you for reading my story.

Schahrzad Morgan

May 25, 2015

CHAPTER 1

HOOKUP WITH 21-YEAR-OLD TOMMY

I sat outside at the Starbucks in San Diego, California, and waited for Tommy, a 21-year-old man I had arranged to meet from the online dating site. That encounter was a long way from my dissolved marriage of 25 years, and my life as a 51-year old mother of three grown children.

Tommy walked up with a confident gait. He was 5'11", lean and strong, with curly brown hair and sexy brown eyes. I was pleasantly surprised, because he was more handsome than his online dating profile pictures.

"Hi. Tommy?" I greeted him.

"Yes."

We shook hands and he beamed a wide smile at me. My heart jumped. Damn, he was good looking and charming! He sat down next to me.

"Do you want to get coffee?" I asked him.

"No."

His dimples showed when he smiled. I wanted to get to know him, to decide if I wanted to fuck him after the coffee.

"What do you like to do for fun?" I asked.

"I skateboard and I surf. I don't drink, and don't go to bars."

I liked that…a guy who liked the outdoors and didn't drink.

We talked for a few more minutes, and he told me about his new full-time job at the health food store.

"Do you like older women?" I asked.

He looked right at me and smiled.

"Yes."

That was hot! I liked younger men. I liked their hard bodies, their passion in the bedroom and in life, and their youthful energy.

Tommy's eyes were beautiful, the eye contact intense. God, I was getting so turned on knowing that he wanted me sexually for what I was, including my age. I felt warm and my clit was throbbing. I wanted to lie on him, our naked bodies pressed close together, and feel his hard cock inside me.

But first, I had to ask him about his sexual history and STDs. It didn't sound sexy, but it was important.

"I want to review our STD testing results. I was last tested for STDs two months ago. All my results were negative. I was tested for HIV, hepatitis B and C, chlamydia, gonorrhea, and syphilis. I was last tested for HPV in the spring of 2013 during my pap smear." I turned to him. "And you?"

He looked right at me and said without hesitation, "I haven't had sex in eight months. I was tested four months ago when I moved back to San Diego and I'm negative."

I believed him on the STD tests. He said it so smoothly, but it didn't matter, because I used a condom every time and I would be protected. I was surprised that a lusty good-looking young man had gone without sex for eight months. His fortunes were about to change.

I had my apartment to myself that evening. Before I set up our coffee date, I had checked my son's schedule to make sure he'd be out.

What time are u coming home? I had texted Wilson, my 17 year old son.

Going to a game. Around 10.

I'm having a guy over, don't come home before 10

I looked back at Tommy. He looked so sexy sitting there across from me.

"Do you want to come over?" I asked.

"Yeah!" His eyes lit up.

"I live about a mile away. Just follow me, and park anywhere not covered."

We walked to our cars, and he followed me to my apartment complex. I met him at his car.

"Did you bring condoms?" I asked, as we walked along the walkway.

"No," he smiled sheepishly.

"That's fine," I told him. "I always have condoms."

I liked to ask men if they brought condoms, because I was curious if the man used them, and also to let him know that it was his responsibility to have one. Most men did not bring condoms so I kept magnum size condoms at home. Magnum fit penises of all sizes. For smaller penises I just left more room at the tip.

We walked up the stairs to my apartment. He grabbed my ass on the way up, and I turned around and giggled. I unlocked the door and turned on the lights.

"I love your apartment!" he said, as soon as we walked in.

I went in the kitchen.

"Do you want something to drink, maybe some water or tea?"

"No."

I put on the Passenger station on Pandora and lit some candles. Tommy watched me the entire time. He wanted me. He walked over, pressed his body against mine, and put his hands around my waist. He leaned forward and his determined soft lips met mine. Wow. I kissed him back. I felt weak in the knees and

3

started moaning. I held my hands behind my back and leaned into his kiss. I turned myself on just with our kissing. My husband had never wanted to kiss me, and yet I loved kissing so much. I liked to use kissing to warm up sexually and start the connection.

Tommy's erect penis pressed against my groin. I pulled away a bit. I liked a man to warm me up with kissing, then finger fuck me or touch me in some way, before I touched his penis. I just liked to take my time that way. We kept kissing and then he reached his hand in the back of my jeans, inside my thong panties, and my slippery wetness. He slid his fingers deep inside, in and out, in and out.

"Oh my god, fuck, that feels soooooo good," I whimpered.

I felt weak in the knees and held on to him, as he kept finger fucking me. I moaned louder. *Please, don't stop, don't stop.* I didn't want to talk or think of words. All my attention went to the pleasure deep inside my body. Damn, he was so good with his fingers.

"Let's go in my bed," I suggested when I caught my breath.

We went in my bedroom and hurriedly took off our clothes. I gasped at the sight of his lean muscular body, especially his toned abs, and his gorgeous cock!

"Oh my god, you're so hard!"

His penis was so hard and erect that its tip almost touched his stomach. A hard penis was all I wanted. Hardness, not shape or size, was the most important factor, because hardness felt good. His penis was above average length, with a slight curve, and a thick rim around the head. I didn't look at it too long because I liked to admire a man's penis as part of my blowjob.

"Your body is amazing," I told him.

I just couldn't stop admiring him.

I had been used to looking at my 57–year-old husband's body. He was still fit, however over the years he had acquired more curves, padding, wrinkles and age spots. I didn't mind any of that. But what broke my heart was his declining desire for sex with me and his softening erections. It had been so long since I'd ridden a hard cock.

I couldn't wait for Tommy's hard cock inside me. I sat on my bed. Tommy got in bed with me. He kissed me tenderly and I whimpered at how gentle he was. I fell back on my pillows, and he got on top. My skin felt warm, and my cunt ached for him. I felt Tommy's head move down between my legs. He sucked my outer labia and then sucked and stretched my long inner labia, which was sexy as hell. Most men ignored my labia completely during oral. Then his tongue flicked across my clit, flicking and sucking. I was so wet and aroused. I spread my legs wide apart. He kept doing that. I was immensely grateful. I wasn't used to getting oral sex. My husband didn't like going down on me, and had not done it the first 22 years of our marriage. At the end of our marriage, he would do it as a favor but would always ask me to wash up first, which made me feel dirty and not valued as a woman. He had never made me come with oral sex.

"You're really good at that," I told him. "Do you like doing it?"

"Yeah." He had a huge smile on his face. "I love it!"

I wrapped my legs around his head and I let myself just lie there and enjoy myself. *I deserve this,* I repeatedly told myself. But I really didn't think I did, because I assumed it was unpleasant work, something I had learned from my husband. Also, in the interest of fairness, he deserved a turn at being pleasured.

"Here, come lay on your back," I invited him.

When he lay back, I held his penis in my hand and looked at it closely. To my delight, he had a curve at the base. I had seen penises curved at the base or top or middle, leaning in various degrees and directions.

"Oh my god, you have a curved penis!" I exclaimed. "I love curved penises!"

He looked at me in surprise, and maybe relief. Men with curved penises often told me they thought they were defective or they caused the curve by masturbating. Intercourse with a curved penis, even a very, very, small one, was the most intense pleasure I could imagine, and sent goose bumps up my spine.

I kissed Tommy's stomach and thighs. I licked his scrotum. He moaned. I inhaled deeply into his sweet musky smell.

"You smell good!" I whispered and looked at him.

I kissed his balls, and sucked on them ever so gently. I licked under his balls, on the side of them, and then ran my tongue on his perineum, and down to his ass. I circled my tongue around his asshole, a technique called *rimming*. He let out a deep breath and looked at me. Was he turned on by my boldness? It didn't really matter. I was having fun.

I knew he was eager to feel my mouth engulf his penis. I was too. I slid my tongue in one motion from his balls, up the shaft of his dick, and up to his thick rim and head. I looked him in the eyes as I circled the ridge of his head with my tongue. He looked back at me and watched. I nibbled gently with my lips around his ridge, circled all around, and licked his hard shaft all up and down again.

I sucked gently on the head of his penis. I imagined how good that would feel to him. I imagined his penis head was like my clitoris and sucking on his head felt like having my clit sucked. I didn't know what a man felt there, and if he really wished for me to go faster. I was just enjoying myself and I figured if I had pleasure in it, he would too. I gently played around some more, licking and gently sucking. Then I put some spit on my left hand, wrapped it around his shaft, and stroked him up and down with that hand while I sucked on his head at the same time. He gasped with pleasure.

I sucked hard and fast for a few strokes, then broke the intensity with gentle kissing on his balls. Back to sucking a few strokes. I looked at him. He was clearly in a land of faraway pleasure. I felt satisfied that I knew how to please a man. He was rock hard, even though I was old. Maybe I was sexier than I thought.

Handling his beautiful hard cock turned me on even more, and I just wanted to get on top of him. I reached into my nightstand for a condom and put it on him. We started fucking immediately. His penis sent waves of pleasure through my pussy. The pleasure wave filled my whole body and my moans became wails.

He was quiet. I was always surprised that men were so quiet during sex. I couldn't help but moan when the pleasure was intense. His cock filled me up in the most delicious places deep inside my body. My pussy got wetter and wetter and I felt so tight, as I gripped his cock. I moaned louder and louder. I thought the neighbors could hear me and I didn't care. I hoped our fucking would never end.

Tommy gently and firmly turned me over on my stomach. I liked submitting to a man and the positions he moved me into. He laid his muscular young body on top of my back and slid his penis inside me from behind.

"Fuck me slowly," I whispered. "Go slowly from this angle until I get warmed up."

He entered me gently, pushing me open with his cockhead. Then he came in all the way and pushed gently, pulsing deeply.

"Yeah, just like that…like that…wow, that feels sooo good."

He was younger than my eldest child, yet he handled me like a man. I was completely his. I let go and succumbed to him. His warm breath was in my ear, his warm body pressed on my back, and his hands were tenderly on top of mine, as he thrust his penis gently inside me, slowly and deeply. I stretched my arms out to my side, my hands near my head, and gave myself to him completely.

I was in a cocoon of unimaginable pleasure, safety, security, and tenderness. I got lost, in a place inside myself I had never been. I felt sexually and emotionally fulfilled more than anytime in my 25 year marriage. Tears rolled down my cheek as my heart welled up with love. So that was what it was like to make love!

My husband would get mad when I cried so I assumed all men got mad when a woman cried. I didn't want to make Tommy

7

uncomfortable, but I accepted if he was, because my main concern was allowing myself to feel.

"Don't worry, I'm fine, I just want to cry," I said softly.

He didn't ask me to stop. He whispered softly and slowly into my ear.

"Let it out....let it out...let it out."

My heart jumped and I felt warm in my body and heart as I welled up with emotion. He wanted me to cry and feel. I had dreamed of this type of love making for years!

I let out my feelings and got lost in his hard cock deep inside me. I lay there enveloped by tenderness, which was love, not really sure what would happen next. Tommy kept thrusting his hard cock deep inside me, pushing, thrusting, and going deep against my cervix, where I felt the pleasure reach maximum intensity. He flipped me over into the missionary position. He moved his body on top of mine and fucked me deeply.

"I'm close to coming," he said as he looked in my eyes.

"Where do you want to come?" I asked.

"In your mouth."

He got up and sat on the edge of my bed. He looked relaxed, so I knew he wasn't about to come right then, and I took my time. I kneeled on the carpet and licked his soft scrotum, and inhaled deeply.

"You smell good!" I told him again.

I kept licking him and looked up. He looked right at me. Slowly, while keeping my eyes on him, I licked the shaft of his beautiful hard cock, and circled my tongue around its ridge and head. He looked back at me, full of lust, wanting, and longing. At times he squinted in pleasure, or closed his eyes briefly, then he opened them again and looked at me. I was so turned on with us looking at each other as I gave him head. I sucked on his cock, as he grew harder and harder, and I knew he was about to orgasm.

"I'm going to come," he whispered as he looked in my eyes.

His eyes had a faraway look. His body tensed and his breathing quickened. He maintained his gaze on me. How daring of him to look at me while he was being brought to orgasm. I was incredibly turned on, and looked at him, as I continued to suck him, until, his eyes deeply lost in mine, he moaned and I felt a rush of warm liquid in the back of my throat, and a sweet taste on my tongue. I swallowed quickly. I wanted to love the taste of semen, but I really did not like the mucous-like texture so I always took it in the back of my throat and swallowed quickly.

My mind was spinning with what had just happened. He had looked at me during his entire orgasm! Nobody had ever done that with me. I had read about open eye orgasms just a few years earlier in a marriage book, and it turned me on incredibly every time I thought of trying it. I had kept my eyes open during orgasm on two occasions, but nobody had ever done that with me.

As soon as Tommy came, his body relaxed and he stopped looking at me. Our union was over. He looked around for his clothes and it seemed like he wanted to leave. Then he paused as if he suddenly realized that it wasn't fair for him to leave without me having an orgasm also. I was really horny.

"What about me?" I asked.

"Yes, right," he said in a flat voice.

He came back to bed.

I was disappointed. I didn't like disconnecting so quickly. I wanted to stay and cuddle after sex for at least a couple minutes. I also didn't like that Tommy couldn't hold the sexual energy for me after his orgasm, and that I was faced with the same predictable routine I had grown tired of during my marriage: intercourse as foreplay for masturbation. It meant I fucked with a man, he had an orgasm, and I masturbated afterward. I wasn't just bored though; I was hurt and felt less valued that I came last every time and that I gave myself my own orgasms every time. That wasn't a discussion to be had with a man who wanted to

9

leave. I needed to stay present to my body and get an orgasm so he could leave. So I masturbated to come while he eagerly watched. I had a regular orgasm that flowed and pulsed like a wave and when I looked at him I saw he was hard again. I felt happy and satisfied, and snuggled up to him.

"Will you spend the night next time?"

"Sure, I will," he said.

I fantasized that Tommy and I would start dating and maybe fall in love. I had dated older men when I was his age, so the age difference didn't seem a problem for me. I didn't know at the time that Tommy had just put on a show, that like many other young men he had an intense sexual attraction for older women, but that when it came to a relationship, he wanted a woman his own age.

I was completely smitten with Tommy. After we made love, everything seemed brighter. On my trail run the next morning, I noticed for the first time a large oak tree. Its leaves were silvery, and their fluttering in the breeze sounded like a symphony. Was the tree speaking of love, showing me I had finally found it? Or was I just high from the previous night's intoxicating hookup?

After my run, I sent Tommy a text message. *"Want to come over?"*
Minutes later, I received his reply: *"No."*

My heart sank. He didn't want to see me? That made no sense. Why would he say no? Maybe he thought I just didn't like him. Maybe he was afraid of the social stigma of dating an older woman. Maybe he feared our passion and intimacy. I knew just what to do: I would give him love and assurance. Affection and persistence worked in the past with my husband and teens. Certainly this should work for dating as well. I sent him several texts to tell him how wonderful he was, how great the sex had been, and how much I wanted to see him again. He didn't reply.

I was crushed. I longed for Tommy's touch, his embrace, his cock, and his kisses. Thinking about Tommy made my heart felt warm and my vagina hot. I was sure it had been hot for him also.

I replayed our love making over and over and over for weeks on end. He did not come back over, but would sometimes send me snapchats or text messages. He texted me that he couldn't come over because he had to spend time with his family, or he had work, or he was going skating or surfing.

I couldn't understand why he didn't come back to see me. The sex had been amazing. He had a high sex drive, and I was desirable and available to him. Why didn't he want to see me again? How could I be smitten with a 21-year-old man? Why was I crying over a man I met only once? I knew why. Tommy had opened my heart to an intoxicating flow of love. I didn't even know <u>him</u>. I didn't cry for him. I cried for how he made me feel and what he offered: tender loving passionate sex. At night, alone in bed, I cried. Sad songs on the radio called to my heart and passion and I cried. At work, I cried. It wasn't that I cried all day long, but sporadically throughout the day for probably ten minutes a day for over a month. And then time passed and I stopped thinking about him.

Tommy and I hooked up a few more times afterward. He told me more about himself each time. He was raised by his older sister and was uncomfortable with feelings and physical touch. Another time he admitted he changed how he had sex just for me.

"I didn't just read your dating profile. I studied it. You said you liked kissing, eye contact, and slow thrusting. I never had sex like that before, but I was horny and I thought I would try it." He paused. "Yeah, and I kinda like it."

He just gave me a performance. He didn't give himself. He wasn't comfortable with his own feelings, and lacked the capacity to handle my feelings or anyone else's. I had made the mistake of thinking the sex we had defined his capacity in a relationship.

Tommy never spent the night. He kept sending me snaps. Initially his snaps were hot, when they involved surfing or work, but later they were sillier, when he took pictures of his open mouth full of ice cream, or a silly face shot, or hanging out with kids his age at the skate park. The biggest turnoff was when he replied to my carefully crafted snaps with "stop bothering me." Then I saw Tommy no longer as a man, but as a child and I didn't want him anymore.

But I kept my appetite for young men.

CHAPTER 2
EARLIEST SEXUAL EXPERIENCES

I took off my panties and stood in front of my bedroom window in our townhome in Berenbostel, Germany. I had to climb a chair to do it. I was 5 years old.

I did it because I liked the warm tingly feeling between my legs when I exposed myself. After that, I experimented with more settings. I wore my favorite dress and went pantiless into the backyard and did summersaults, or I would hang from the monkey bars on the playground. I wanted men to see my pussy. It was intensely arousing. I never considered it anything but natural.

My parents never shamed me or anyone for our bodies or touching ourselves. I sometimes saw my cousin rubbing her legs together on the living room floor, and our parents said she was doing "sweaty sweaty" and we all just accepted it as normal. She was probably six or seven years old. I didn't know why she got all sweaty like that, but it all seemed fine. Nobody ever suggested she should go do that in the privacy of a bedroom. My dad said "bodies are beautiful," and we kids saw my mom naked in her bathroom until I was about twelve years old and we both became more modest.

Perhaps I was more open minded than others because I had moved from overseas. I was born in Düsseldorf, Germany in 1961 to my German mother and Persian father. My sister and brother came right behind. We lived in small towns as my father worked in the city and climbed the career ladder as a pathologist.

I had loving parents and I wasn't spanked except one time. I felt loved by my dad, but in a distant way, because we didn't spend much time together. He worked late hours, and asked my mom to have us in bed when he came home, so he could relax. He also didn't take us on vacation, so I got to spend a lot of time with my wonderful grandparents when I was younger. My dad taught me to speak Farsi, made sure we gave him hugs and kisses, made home movies of us on 8mm film, and took bubble baths with us children. I loved sitting on his lap when he sat in the living room with his Persian friends and they laughed and talked. I found their discussions interesting. My dad often talked about the value of family, discipline, and the importance of the Persian culture.

My mom stayed home to raise us. I got my love and most of my physical affection from my mom. She decided to give her children the love she herself never received as a child. She nursed all of us, and raised us on healthy food. She tucked us in at night, sewed clothes and felt storyboards for our bedroom walls, and made sure we were all reading by the time we went to kindergarten. I was left handed, and my mom took the time to teach me to write with my right hand. I was the best student in my grade every year. I was adventurous and for fun I rode my Kettcar and bicycle far beyond the one-block limit set by my mom. I didn't see any reason to stick so close to home.

When I was nine years old, my parents began to talk about something that had them excited. One day they shared it with us.

"We're moving to America," my mom said.

I had watched the western Bonanza on TV, and I wasn't really sure why my parents would take us to a desert with horses and no cars, but I trusted them and figured it would all work out. A few months later, we got off the plane in Omaha, Nebraska, and started our new life. We were barely settled into our new apartment, when my dad stopped coming home at night. He said he was tired and fell asleep at work. We found out there was a woman. My mom said he had cheated on her since their wedding night. I made a decision at the age of 9 to never cheat.

My parents divorced when I was 12 years old. My mom turned to Transcendental Meditation to fill the empty places in her heart that he left behind. She took me to learn TM and I was hooked on the deep silence within that filled me with radiance, peace, and strength. The following year, my mother went to a nine-month long TM teacher training course in Switzerland. I lived with my grandparents in Germany that year and attended the gymnasium.

A HAND-HELD SHOWER

A handheld shower in my grandparents' house gave me my first orgasm. I was thirteen years old. I was just holding the shower head to rinse soap off my stomach and vulva off and it felt good, so I kept holding it there, and it felt better and better, so I kept holding it there and it felt better and better, and then I came. Wow! I took a lot of showers after that.

After we got back to the States, I didn't have a handheld shower. I had to learn to masturbate without a showerhead. I learned how, using my fingers.

When I was walking to school in 5th grade, I saw a pile of Playboy magazines on the side of the road. I found myself very turned on by the female centerfold with her legs spread wide open. Between her legs were pink fleshy lips and crevices. Her pussy was beautiful. I was intrigued. I bought Playboy magazines and hid them in my bedroom. I'd pull out those Playboy centerfolds and stare at their pussies and clits while I masturbated.

I looked at women's pussies in Playboy centerfolds that I hid in my bedroom, or at my own pussy and clit I with a magnifying makeup mirror between my legs so I could watch myself. Seeing my own sex turned me on. I liked to use my fingers instead of vibrators. I watched my finger slide next to my clitoris, and got more and more aroused. I liked a very gentle soft touch. I used one or two fingers to rub my clit in circles or in up-and-down strokes, with my palm resting on my pubic bone. As my arousal built, I noticed my clitoris became engorged and swollen. I paid careful attention to my stroke, moving gently and softly, and touching different areas of my clit. I knew the clitoral area encompassed more than just the "bean". In fact, the most sensitive areas were on top just under my pubic bone, and the entire area under my outer labia was extremely sensitive, particularly to firm pressure. I wondered often why I didn't see more of the vulva touched in porn or in my own sexual encounters. I couldn't get excited about most porn, because it involved penises and women who never seemed to have an orgasm. I couldn't see why there wasn't more porn involving clitoral stimulation. I was definitely a clit girl.

Even my masturbation fantasies were all about clits. My favorite masturbation fantasy was being watched. I imagined a man was watching my swollen clitoris for the entire 15-30 minutes it took me to climax. And that made sense, because men were proud of their penises and probably wanted women to worship their cocks. I was proud of my clit. Same thing.

LOST MY VIRGINITY

My first longing for a man came at the age of 14. I met him at a one-month long summer course at Maharishi International University (MIU) in Fairfield, IA. He was 21 years old. I didn't know what I wanted, other than to be very close to him. He was attracted to me also, but because of our age difference, he did not pursue it. I cried over him for months.

That fall, I took the first half of the TM teacher training course at MIU. I turned 15 years old on the course, and I missed most of my first semester of high school. It was worth it. I gave some introductory lectures and checked some meditations. (I did not ever go to the second half of the training in Switzerland that was required to become a teacher of TM.)

After I returned, my dad married a wonderful woman. My mom never dated again. She said people should not need other people, and she disliked men because they were not as refined as women. She disliked sex too.

"Spiritual people don't have sex," she said. "Sex is for the earthly life. We seek detachment from all that comes of the earth."

That worried me greatly. I'd always been a sexual woman and masturbated regularly, yet I was so drawn to meditation and my inner silence. I was worried I'd never experience sex. My priorities were meditation, vegetarian cooking, juicing, fasting, and my education. I thought I would become enlightened and never want sex as my mom had predicted.

At the age of 16, I set out to experience sex before it was too late. I had sex with the first boy who showed interest in me in high school. It was painful and didn't feel good. Neither of us knew what we were doing.

After that, I sometimes had sex with men just because they wanted it and I didn't have the confidence to say no. I was shy about sex and my body. In all my hookups I had no orgasm.

My first boyfriend was a 21-year-old line cook at the restaurant where I worked. I was 17 years old. I wasn't in love with him. I knew we could never last because I wanted to marry a man with a college degree who could provide for me and our children. The sex was mediocre. I enjoyed being with him, but I didn't ever have an orgasm with him. I was shy to masturbate in front of him, and he didn't try to give me an orgasm either. Once when he asked me to get into a doggy style position I felt ashamed, as if I was in a dog position, which seemed inappropriate. I never cheated on him.

I was on the pill, but sometimes I forgot to take one. I missed a period. I was over two months pregnant. I did not want children until I had a college degree. My mom lent me the money for a D&C abortion. The second time I got pregnant with him, I had a suction abortion. Both times, I tried to make myself feel sad over it, because I read about girls who were so sad and struggled over their abortions, but despite looking at pictures of aborted fetuses, I could see no wrong in it. Any soul planning to enter the body of my fetus could enter it later in life when I was ready.

I never did have many feelings for him, so I ended it after about two years.

I liked men, but I didn't enjoy intercourse that much. Sex was mostly about an emotional connection and an attraction to a man. I sometimes had one-night stands when I was out drinking. I wondered if I would ever fall in love.

FIRST GIRL-GIRL SEX

I was intensely curious about sex with a woman, especially because I was so turned on watching those playboy centerfolds.

I had my first sexual experience with a woman when I was in high school. One night at a gay bar in Omaha, Nebraska called *The Stage Door*, a 35-year-old beautiful blond woman seated at the adjacent table made long eye contact with me and kept smiling at me. I was only 17 years old. The woman came over to my table, and sat down. Her name was Vera. She told me she was a lesbian and 35 years old, she kept leaning close and smiling. I was nervous, and her age intimidated me, however I was curious to experience her sexually. I didn't really know what to say about sex, or what to talk about with a woman so much older than I was. She leaned over to kiss me. Her lips felt soft. I'd never kissed soft lips like that. I became more curious about touching her body. I wanted the full sexual experience, so I invited her to come over to my dad's house, which is where I was staying while he and my stepmom were out of town. We took a bath in the large tub in my parents' master bathroom. We played around and flirted and kissed in the water. Then we dried off and lay on the bed in the guest room.

She lay on top of me. As we kissed, she ground her pelvis on top of mine. The bedroom door opened and my brother walked in. When he saw us in bed, he quickly shut the door. I wasn't embarrassed about that at all. I thought it was funny and she and I continued our sexual encounter. We kept kissing, but I wasn't aroused by her and I wasn't sure how and where to touch her. Would she be mad if I grabbed her someplace? Was there a certain order in which to touch a woman? Did she like my kisses? Should I be aggressive and more like a man, or soft? I wasn't really sure what I was doing. I was mostly curious about touching her body and her clit. We removed our clothes and she went down on me for a few minutes. I liked how her tongue felt on my clit, however it wasn't any different from how a man did it. She then used her fingers to bring me to a clitoral orgasm. I was excited at the idea of going down on her and touching her clitoris. I started to go down on her, and she stopped me before I touched her vulva area.

"Here, put your fingers in me," she said.

She lay on her back, placed my fingers inside her pussy, and moved my hands. She started to moan, and I was surprised. I had never wanted penetration as a preference to clitoral touch. I kept fingering her for about five minutes, all the way to orgasm.

I did not enjoy fingering her at all. It didn't turn me on and it made my wrist sore and also I was jealous she could have a vaginal orgasm and I never had one. Maybe I was deficient in some way after all, because she had a vaginal orgasm so easily.

My brother told everyone in my family what he had seen. Nobody in my family seemed to mind. The day after we had sex, Vera sent flowers to my home. My mom figured it out and asked why a woman would send me flowers. She just smiled and didn't say another word, so I figured she was glad I was having sex with a woman and not a man.

Vera and I hooked up again the following week. I had an orgasm each time. I had never had an orgasm with a man, because they didn't try to give me one, and I was embarrassed to ask them to, or to masturbate in front of them. I never faked it with them. They just didn't care if I came or not, or they didn't know how to do it, and we never talked about it. I felt used when I had sex with men, because it seemed they got all the pleasure. With Vera, I felt like the sex was about us, not just about a man getting off. Vera left for India to live in an ashram for six months. When she returned, she brought a woman, her new girlfriend. They were both celibate then.

After my first girl-on-girl encounter, I continued going to the gay bar and met more women. I was attracted to pretty butch lesbians. Tina was a slender brunette, my age, also 18 years old. She had a hip short haircut and wore makeup, and she wore a t-shirt underneath a man's shirt, jeans, and boots. So hot! She came over and asked me to dance. I liked how she moved on the dance floor and how she was dressed. We were both attracted to each other and wanted to hookup. We both lived at home and she couldn't have sex at her house, so I invited her to mine. I figured my mom wouldn't know, or wouldn't mind. My brother was away at college, so we went into his bedroom in the basement. We left the lights off, so it was dark.

She lay on the mattress and I climbed on top of her. We kissed. I liked kissing her soft lips and feeling her soft face against mine. It reminded me of kissing Vera. I was used to lying on top of men and feeling a hard bulge in a man's pants where I ground my hips. When I ground my pelvis on hers, there was no hard penis there, which I missed but I was going to have a clit to lick instead. I slid my hand into her jeans and she didn't stop me. I was glad. I still wasn't comfortable touching a woman. She wasn't saying anything or making any noises so I wasn't sure if she liked what I did. I moved my hand into her panties and all the way down to her pussy. Her panties were moist. I felt her vulva lips. They felt full and soft and warm. I became excited. I kept moving my hand in between her labia.

She didn't try to stop me. I was glad. I finally reached inside her inner lips and found a treasure trove of wet slipperiness. She was soaking wet. That's when it hit me how turned on she was. She was wet because of me! I felt desirable and sexy that I could make a woman so wet for me. I eagerly removed her pants and lay on top of her. I moved my fingers around her inner lips and folds to find her clitoris, but I didn't know where it was in the dark. I was a little embarrassed, because I thought I should know my way around a woman's body.

I finally found a hard spot which seemed like her clit, but I did not know how hard she wanted it touched, and how to move my fingers. Would she like to be touched in the same way and places I liked? She didn't make any sounds, and she didn't say anything. She seemed as inexperienced as I was. I moved my fingers around in that slippery wetness and eventually she started to breathe heavily and then she stopped and I think she had an orgasm. She fingered me a little bit and she wasn't making much progress and I was horny, so I stopped her and masturbated while she held and kissed me.

I saw her once more after that. I picked her up to go on a date to the gay bar, and when we left, she asked me to stop at an ATM. She withdrew some money, and took me to a hotel. We had sex and spent the night together but didn't have much to talk about. I think we both were a bit uncomfortable around each other because we didn't have anything to discuss. That was the last time I saw her. I wondered if I could ever meet a woman I'd want to date instead of a man.

A force just as strong as my sexual force was my spirituality. TM was my foundation. Through it, I felt innocent, pure, and connected to the universe. In the summer after I graduated from high school, my car was totaled in a rear-end collision. I used the entire $3000 I got from the insurance company to pay for the siddhis course, a series of about a dozen sutras for TM practitioners. The course was more valuable than any car I could buy. The siddhis deepened my experiences in meditation.

That fall, I turned 18 years old and enrolled at MIU. I loved the curriculum, food, and friends, but I didn't like all the rules, such as required attendance at every class and being in the dome for group meditation, so after one semester I left. I moved back home and enrolled at the University of Nebraska-Omaha. I was 18 years old.

CHAPTER 3
"I'M GONNA MARRY THAT GIRL"

*A*s *a little girl I dreamed of college, a husband who loved me and never cheated on me, a beautiful home, and raising my children. I got all that.*

I didn't dream about sex. I figured sex was just something that would keep happening and if two people loved each other and liked sex, the sex would be good…at least for the first two years while it was all new and exciting. So when it became boring, I thought it was normal.

I didn't dream about the things that I didn't know about, like intimacy and vulnerability. By the time I knew about it in my late 40's, it was all I wanted. I never got that.

I didn't dream about the kind of woman I would be for my husband, and whether he would be pleased with me and look forward to coming home. By the time he came home to the kids and not to me, I no longer cared if he came home at all.

I didn't dream about divorce.

I was 19 years old when we met. He was 24. We were in the same chemistry class at the University of Nebraska- Omaha. He told me later he had noticed me since the beginning of the semester. He came into class that spring morning, and sat in the empty chair next to me.

"Hi, I'm Rick," and he smiled at me.

I had never seen him before. He was 5'10", handsome and athletic, with curly blond hair, yet I had no interest in him at all.

He started a conversation about our class assignments. I thought he was annoying. The next day, he sat next to me again. He said something funny about what he had done at work the day before, and I laughed. I talked with him too, and I noticed his dimples. The next day, I didn't see him, and I wondered where he was. The following day, I came to class early and spotted him and my face turned red. I quickly grabbed the empty chair next to him.

We started dating, and we had lots of sex. Our sex started off rocky. The first time, he couldn't get hard. He said he wasn't nervous. I researched this for us. I read many books and articles and we talked about it and thought maybe he couldn't combine sex and love, that maybe he could get hard only for hookup sex. After the third time we had sex, that problem was gone. He had a beautiful large cock, and our love for each other made us insatiable. We had sex every chance we could. We both lived at home, so we often would splurge on a hotel room, or we had sex quietly in our basements while our parents were asleep. Our sex was mostly about experimenting with intercourse positions, me giving him blowjobs, and him giving me hand jobs.

I enjoyed his company, his humor, and what he was about. He was everything I wanted in a man. He was smart, driven, disciplined, and college educated. We studied together for hours everyday at the library. He showed me his engineering drawings for designs he wanted to build. We went out for drinks and talked about life and our futures. He was financially responsible and he had money to pay for us to go out, and that made me feel protected and cared for. He was affectionate and romantic. He played guitar and sang for me. We sat on his bed by candlelight, as he strummed his guitar and tenderly sang "Vincent". I had never felt so complete. I loved looking at his fit strong body. I admired his love of the outdoors, and that he was an avid runner and skier. I admired that he was mechanically inclined and could work on cars. He had a sporty MGB convertible and we drove around with the top down and it was fun. He showed me off to his friends and he learned to meditate because that was important to me. Our sex together was satisfying. My parents liked him.

"Mom, I'm gonna marry that girl," he told his mom.

That summer he took me on a vacation to Key West, Florida. He introduced me to his friends and we were happy together.

That fall, we both transferred to the University of Nebraska-Lincoln. We looked for apartments and moved in together. We were both in the engineering program. He was there to study, and I was too, except I also wanted to play housewife. I cleaned our apartment and learned to cook.

I was vegetarian since age 12, so I bought a vegetarian cookbook. My first recipe was for chilaquiles with mushrooms. The recipe called for one clove of garlic.

"Wow, it sure smells good in here," Rick said when he walked in one evening after school.

"I smelled garlic from half a block away."

He inhaled deeply and turned to me.

"How much garlic did you use?"

"One clove," I said and pointed to a bulb of garlic on the counter.

"You used a bulb, which is about 20 cloves at least!"

We both laughed. We sat down to dinner and we were happy to be together. I decided to become a better cook.

I had a part-time job as a nurse aid caring for elderly patients in their homes. He was on the GI bill and frugal, so his entire day was spent at school and on his studies.

Our sex life was good when we experimented. We gave mathematical names to our favorite sex positions, such as Pie/2, in which we were at a 90-degree angle to each other. We didn't connect emotionally during sex, and I didn't know that mattered, so the sex got boring quickly and I yearned for novelty. I wanted to have threesomes with a woman, go to strip clubs and sex shops, or watch porn together, but he wasn't interested so he told me no. I loved him and I couldn't fault him for wanting to be sexually monogamous, yet I started feeling unsatisfied.

I was 20 years old, and still enjoyed bars and drinking. He was 25 and wanted to study. When I got tipsy, I got moody and argued about anything. We had many unnecessary arguments late at night about how to spend our time, whose turn it was to clean up, or how loud I could play my music while he studied.

I thought he was boring to stay home and study all the time, and not be more sexually exciting, so after two semesters I left him and moved back to Omaha.

CHAPTER 4

CALL GIRL

Then I forgot all about him. In Omaha, I got a job as a nurse aid in a nursing home and changed my major to premed.

That year I met Zoe. I met her at a party when I was 19 years old, and she was 18. I was immediately attracted to her. Her blond hair, flawless skin, thin lips and turned-up nose, her curvy body and small breasts, the way she moved and talked, her love for home decorating and cooking, and her sexual energy, left me spell bound. I wanted to be close to her, and it wasn't just sexual. I had a huge crush. I asked her over, and she refused all my invitations. Then one day, Zoe and her boyfriend asked me to join them for a threesome. I put up with him so I could be with her. I had never kissed lips so soft. For some reason, although our kissing was tender and sweet, she wouldn't kiss me again. She said she didn't like kissing. I went down on her and gave her an orgasm, and then she did it too while her boyfriend watched. He saw how much we were into each other, and she told me later that made him jealous.

Sometimes we spent the night together. Sadly, we only had sex when she decided we would. She never wanted to have sex at night when we went to bed.

"Let's wait until morning," she would say.

"Let's wash up," she said when we woke up.

We both washed up and went back to bed. Then she went down on me until I came. That turned her on a lot, and she came quickly when I went down on her. I loved licking her clit and pussy. One time when I was licking her clit, I licked her asshole and put my finger in her pussy and her ass. She moaned harder and then she came.

"Wow, that felt so good! You were doing so many things to me," she said.

Zoe was the only person who could give me an orgasm every time. None of my boyfriends could do that. With them, I had to masturbate to come. She probably just did to me what felt good to her. Her technique was amazing. Mostly, I could sense she loved what she was doing, so I could fully relax and let go. Being with Zoe led me to believe that a woman wanted to lick another woman's clit, while a man was doing it out of duty or as a favor.

Sometimes Zoe let me go down on her too, other times she only let me use my fingers. My biggest problem with Zoe was that I had feelings for her and she avoided me. I'd ask many times to see her and she would usually say she was with her boyfriend. I couldn't understand why she would choose him over me.

I knew she liked me, because on her living room wall she hung a framed poster of two women, a blond and a brunette. She told everyone who came over, "that's me and Schaz."

Like me, Zoe was bisexual. She liked me, and sex with me, however her romantic and love interests were always men.

I preferred men also. I liked them for a relationship, and I didn't hook up. The exception was when I went to bars. When I drank, I picked up men. I must have done that more than other girls, because my sister's friend made a comment about it one night when we were out.

"You have sex with so many men, you might as well get paid for it," she said.

My mouth dropped open.

"Oh my god, you are brilliant!" I exclaimed.

I felt she was connected to the universe because she spoke of something that resonated deep inside me and felt right. That is exactly what needed to be done.

I became a call girl. It was the early 80's, and I was about 21 years old. I worked for an escort service that sent me to service businessmen in hotels. A married couple ran the escort service from their home. They required us girls to be sober and take our outbound phone calls from their home. The wife was also an escort. She gave me some advice.

"Lick their balls to death before you suck their cocks. It makes them come faster," she said.

I started licking men's balls from that day forward.

"Use a warm washcloth to wash off their penis after they come," she said.

I did it, and the men liked it.

"On the nights you work, you must be sober and at our house. If you drink or do drugs while you're on call, you're fired," her husband told us.

We girls sat around, smoked cigarettes, played cards, and talked, and waited for calls to come in. He answered the phone, verified the client's identity, sent us out on calls, and handled the credit cards and payments to us. We used a portable credit card swiper, and a business name of T&S Advertising. The clients paid us $180 for 20 minutes, and $250 for 30 minutes. We gave the agency $50 and kept the rest. I made about $8,000 per month. The year was 1982.

The men were handsome and dressed in business suits, which was a huge turn on. They were nice, and I dated a few of them. I liked that the men paid me for sex. I was in power and I got attention. I couldn't understand why prostitution was illegal, but I was glad because it meant we could charge more money.

In that year I worked for the escort service, I had lots of sober sex with strangers. Having sober sex with strangers was easy for me, because I loved sex, kissing, showing off my body, and pleasing men. In my mind, I was the beautiful madam who gave them love and sex and affection they craved and didn't get at home. I didn't have orgasms with them. I was there just to provide a service. The men mostly wanted blowjobs. I used a condom every time for intercourse. The men were so horny by the time they called for an escort, they usually climaxed in just a couple minutes.

I decided that when I got married, I would please my man so he didn't need to seek sex and blowjobs elsewhere.

I liked my job, but the problem was, I kept getting arrested. The police officer would pose as a client in a hotel, ask for sex, and arrest me when I asked for money. I paid a lawyer to take care of the charges the first time. And the second time.

One of my clients, a man twice my age named Drew, introduced me to cocaine. I liked the cocaine high, and enjoyed Drew's company. Drew would call me to service him, but be too high to want sex, so we sat in his hot tub and snorted cocaine. A few weeks later when I came over, he was injecting it and I watched with fascination. I refused to go that far. We became friends and took cocaine constantly. We both started freebasing while he kept injecting. The cocaine habit made me paranoid, and I needed to do it every ten to fifteen minutes to avoid the discomfort of coming down off the cocaine. I was up for days on end and lost my appetite. My habit had already started to interfere with my prostituting job. It was harder to look men in the eye because I was paranoid, and my tongue was numb and it was harder to give blowjobs. I wondered if the men's' penises got numb too, but I was afraid to ask.

My cocaine habit and paranoia made it harder to leave the house. I really couldn't function well enough to keep going to school or get a different job. I stopped going to school and failed my classes that semester.

Then came my third arrest. That time, the police raided our agency's home. The agency closed down and the owners left the state. I bartered with my lawyer for sex and paid the court fee. My next arrest would no longer be a misdemeanor, and I knew I had to stop prostituting. I considered going back to school or getting a job. But I had that cocaine problem.

When Drew moved to Kansas, I moved with him. We freebased cocaine and he injected it. We stayed up for days on end, and when we ran out of cocaine and he got so paranoid that he started walking around the house with a loaded gun, I didn't like it anymore and I left him.

On the drive back to Omaha, the police pulled me over for driving twice the speed limit on the freeway. They arrested me for driving with an open container of beer. My parents told the judge about the cocaine habit and suggested rehab. I was court-ordered through a drug rehab. In rehab, I had an opportunity to really look at myself, and after that I got serious about my life. I started meditating again twice a day, stopped smoking cigarettes, began exercising for the first time, got a full-time job at a university, and took night classes in biology and computer science. I lived alone and supported myself. The night classes rekindled my interest in getting a degree, so I moved back in with my mother so I could attend school full-time. I made amends; I paid off my debts and spent a week in county jail for the third prostitution charge.

My mother went back to school to get a degree, and we took some classes together. I love studying with my mom. For two years, my mother and I studied together, meditated together, ate organic vegetarian meals together, and talked about our mutual interests. She graduated with a 4.0 GPA as a philosophy major, and I was proud of my smart mother who went after what she wanted.

I was mostly single in the years I lived at home and finished my studies. I had two boyfriends in those years. One of them was interested in earth homes, and I told him I once dated a man named Rick who knew a lot about them. I had forgot all about Rick and really had no interest in him, but that night, I called Rick's mother to get his number so I could ask him about the earth homes.

CHAPTER 5

MY 25 YEAR MARRIAGE

It had been four years since I talked to Rick. He told me he lived in Phoenix, Arizona, and was coming to Omaha soon to visit his parents. He suggested getting together. The next month when he was in town, he came over to my mom's house. When I opened the door and saw Rick, a warm feeling flooded my heart and stomach, and somewhere deep inside my core I felt an unusual deep loving feeling. Maybe there was something inside letting me know he was right for me.

He came in and greeted my mom, and then we went out. It felt like old times. We were happy together, and we talked about seeing each other again. He invited me to visit him in Phoenix over my spring break.

I landed in Phoenix a few weeks later, in an oasis of palm trees, mountains, sunshine, and love.

"Will you marry me," he asked one afternoon after we had sex.

"Yes!" I immediately replied.

He was everything I wanted in a man, and he was going to take me out of Omaha with its frigid winters, hot humid summers, and flat landscape. I was pleased he asked me spontaneously, right after sex. It seemed a tribute to my sexual prowess.

I looked around for a ring. He didn't have one. He didn't know he was going to propose.

Back in Omaha, I was no longer Schahrzad. I was a woman who was wanted by a man. I had a new responsibility and a new purpose.

Two months later he came to Omaha to visit me. We went to a jeweler and I selected a beautiful ruby ring with three small cut diamonds on each side. Our engagement felt official.

When my semester ended, I moved to Phoenix, Arizona to live with Rick. I was almost done with my B.S. in computer science, he was still in his first corporate job, and we were committed to building a meaningful life together. We thought about our jobs, student loans, retirement accounts, home improvement projects, whose turn it was to make dinner, taxes, the leaking roof on our fixer upper first house, the best prices for car insurance, whose junker car would be replaced first, and whether to go to graduate school. Wasn't that what we were supposed to be thinking about?

We didn't talk about intimacy or connection or spiritual life. I read my spiritual books and I meditated. I had practiced Transcendental Meditation for 1-2 hours a day since I was 12 years old. Meditating made me feel happy from deep inside, radiant, pure, and connected to the universe. Whenever I was regular in my practice, life flowed and went my way. He wasn't interested in spiritual books or meditation, so I wasn't sure if I should marry him. Sometimes we argued a lot and I thought of leaving. Each of us would say something meaner to the other. Sometimes I threw dishes at the floor to let him know how mad I was. The dishes broke. I didn't like my part in escalating the arguments, but I wasn't going to admit I was wrong. A few times I started packing boxes, but I didn't have a plan about where to go and I was broke. I decided since I was strong in my own meditation practice, it was okay if I did not share that with my partner.

We talked about growing our careers and having children. I got my B.S. in computer science and was hired to be a software tester for a raster-to-vector conversion software company. I made as much money as he did and we saved and prepared for our future.

We ran with the dog and we looked happy, but I was no longer that attracted to him. I didn't like his glasses or the way he dressed and some of his mannerisms had become annoying. Something was missing. We were not connected. We didn't talk about our feelings or things we didn't want to admit, we didn't make ourselves vulnerable, and we didn't have real intimacy.

We slept on opposite sides of the bed and our sex life was already boring. He didn't like to kiss, and we didn't have foreplay. I was proud I didn't like foreplay, because I thought foreplay was for weak people who couldn't get turned on without it. I loved sucking on his big cock that barely fit in my mouth. He didn't go down on me, and I was embarrassed to ask him to do it. I thought he should read my mind and know what I wanted, since he was my husband. I fantasized about other people licking my clit, usually women.

Our sex routine was predictable. He would wake up with an erection, lean over and put his penis in me, thrust for a couple minutes, and then it was done. I thought that was normal. I didn't know, or didn't remember, that men can last for 20-30 minutes if they wanted to. Often I wasn't turned on, so I kept KY Jelly in my bedroom dresser. I needed it almost every time. I had sex with him even when I wasn't turned on, because I wasn't going to be one of those women who didn't give her husband sex so that he had to cheat or get prostitutes.

He didn't like me being on top, so I lay on the bottom in the missionary position and looked at the ceiling while he thrusted. I was bored and didn't like it much, but I was horny at the same time and some of it felt good. And then he lay next to me with his eyes closed, reached over, and rubbed my clitoris until I came. Having an orgasm with him was taking longer and longer, as I was less turned on by him. Eventually it took too long and he didn't like giving me the handjobs anymore.

Our hot sex life had sizzled and I didn't know what to do about it. I figured it happened to everyone when the newness wore off.

I thought the problem in our relationship was in me, and I would have the same problem with anyone else. I knew I had flaws, after all. I gossiped often, especially about my family. I was insecure. I thought I needed certain material things to be 'good enough'. I didn't have those material things, so I felt less than other people. I felt less even when I was promoted to manager of my department. I realized I didn't like programming or the drudgery of testing, and although I felt trapped in my job, I lacked insight and confidence on reinventing my career. I went back to school at night for my MBA.

I decided to overlook the meditation part, the arguments, the lack of affection, the lower attraction, and the boring sex. I figured any other man I would marry would have flaws too. They might be different flaws, but there would be flaws. I wasn't sure what to do instead, and I loved him most of the time and he had everything I wanted in a man. I decided to stay and make it work. I focused on our mutual goals and the life we were building.

I was 26 years old when we married in the presence of our family and about 20 close friends. I wanted a bigger wedding, but we were broke and neither of us wanted to go into debt for an event that lasted only a few hours. What mattered was our life together. We didn't have money for a honeymoon, so we didn't go anywhere (until two years later when we had free tickets to Hawaii), but we had our fixer upper house and each other.

Rick and I still had those escalating arguments over mundane matters. Sometimes he got mad at me and slept in the guest room. We wanted to get along, so we went to counseling. We told our counselor about our one-upmanship in arguing, where each of us would say something meaner to the other.

The counselor looked at me. "Schahrzad, the next time you both argue, are you willing to just stop?"

I thought about it.

"No."

The counselor looked at Rick. "Rick, the next time you both argue, are you willing to stop?"

"Yes," he immediately answered.

And the next time we argued, he stopped. I was impressed! And then he did it again, and the next time I was willing to stop first.

Our arguing stopped but our closeness did not come back. When we talked, we didn't look each other in the eye. When I sought comfort, I didn't go to him; I went to my friends or family. At night after dinner, I drank red wine and talked on the phone to my married girlfriends, while he sat in bed and read. I didn't want to be in there with him. I knew something was missing, but I didn't care and didn't know how to change it.

We both wanted children, and soon we were a family. First came our daughter. Christine. I took a maternity leave and returned to work part-time with my breast pump. Soon after, my company closed several departments and laid me off. I wanted to stay home and be a full-time mom, and Rick said I could. I was deeply grateful to him. He was going to provide for our family, and our children would have a mom at home who could love and teach them like nobody else could. I was happy! Our son came 18 months later. Matt. We had two children in diapers, and I was tired and my interest in him waned. I was in love with my children, being a mom, and with having a family. I held babies all day and nursed and when the babies went to bed, I didn't want anyone touching me. I was also stressed from having two children so close together. I read parenting books, taught them, and played with them. When the kids slept, I studied for my MBA classes.

Rick was the dad I had hoped for. He changed diapers, held crying babies, packed up diaper bags, took the kids with him on errands, gave baths, told bedtime stories, tumbled and rough-housed, fed them, joked with them, hugged them, sang with them. Whenever I saw Rick with the kids, I thought to myself, *"this is my perfect life!"* I didn't want him sexually or for myself, and I didn't consider anything missing. We were a family.

When our son turned 2 years old, life became easier and my attention turned back to my husband and sex. I was horny again. I initiated sex more, but I just didn't enjoy it. I always worried about the kids waking up and needing me, or coming into our room, so I couldn't let go. I yearned for the sexual excitement and escapades of my earlier years, and I missed the sexual intensity he and I had when we first met.

He used to like making me come with his fingers. After we married, it felt like he did it as a chore, and he didn't do it for its own sake anymore but only after his orgasm, after he had lost his sexual tension. He lay next to me with his eyes closed and rubbed my clit with his fingers. I was so bored that half the time I couldn't come at all. Eventually I masturbated every time so I wouldn't impose on him, but it took much longer for me to climax when he was there. I had better orgasms on my own.

I became self-conscious of how long it took me to come, because he was so bored with it. I felt defective sexually, not responsive enough.

I had other sexual insecurities. I didn't like how my pussy looked. My inner labia were long, and the color was different from what I had seen in magazines. Maybe that's why he didn't want to go down on me, and if they were that ugly, I didn't want to make him go there.

I did not want sex with him anymore.

I was worried that I lost my sex drive, so I went back to the counselor to learn how to get it back.

"Do you masturbate?" he asked.

Of course I did! I masturbated almost every day. What did that have to do with anything?

"Yes!"

As soon as I answered, I understood. I *did* have a sex drive; however it did not involve him anymore. The counselor said we could recreate the feelings we once had. We just had to sit with our eyes closed and remember how it was when we met. I tried that when I got home. Then my daughter crawled up my leg and it was time to make dinner and I forgot. I thought of it a few more times, but I didn't really remember the feelings I had when we met. It was so long ago.

Sometimes I fantasized about men I knew, but I never considered actually doing anything in real life, because I was committed to being faithful in any relationship I had. I fantasized about oral sex with women. He knew I was bi and when I asked him if he minded me having sex with women again, he encouraged me to do it. I met some women through newspaper ads, and then I invited Zoe to visit. She and I went to Mexico for a weekend while Rick watched our toddlers. She made me come every time she went down on me, she was beautiful and sexy, and I loved making her come with my tongue.

After Zoe left, I tried to recreate a good sex life with him. I knew that I had a part in it, but I wasn't sure what. I read books on sex and asked him to go to Tantra and sex classes. He wasn't interested.

I blamed myself for not wanting him anymore. Our love went to other places, like our children, projects, friends, and pets. We looked at each other with disinterest. I wanted to change that, so I read books on self-improvement. I thought we could kick start a connection by doing intimate activities together and spending time alone. I wanted him to go with me to classes and read my books. I wanted him to go out with me, and have other couple friends. I asked him to go away with me for a night, a weekend, or even a week. He always said he would only go if we took the kids. I didn't know why he had to have the kids along on our trip, when the whole purpose was to have time alone together.

He had his own interests. He wanted to fix up our house, watch sports, workout, and play with our children. I was lonely and isolated, home all day with young children who didn't talk and had so many needs. We didn't know any teens for babysitting, our parents lived several states away, and I didn't want to leave my kids with just anyone, so I rarely got any adult time away from them. I made more friends with mothers through the preschool and mom's groups, but somehow it felt isolating because we just talked about our kids and not ourselves and our own needs.

In our free time, Rick and I ran with the kids, worked on our house, read the newspaper, and discussed current affairs. We gave each other gifts for holidays and attended our kids' soccer games. I handled the money, including our retirement account investments and stock purchases, and he never questioned me when I bought a new dress or something for the kids or the house. He wanted to live on acreage outside of town, whereas I wanted to live near a good school and other families. I let him have his way on the houses we bought and he made sure we had good schools. I didn't think I deserved to have it my way, because he worked so hard for us, and fixing up houses and having his own space were so important to him. We tried for our third child and we had a boy. Wilson.

I was a good mom, but not such a good wife. Rick and I did not hug or kiss in front of the kids. In fact, we did not hug or kiss at all. Emotionally, I didn't want to let anyone get too close and I didn't want to need people, because I believed in the spiritual principle of detachment. Maybe that was just a cover for avoiding intimacy. I knew I had built up some walls, but I didn't know how to let them down, and I really didn't want to. Rick probably had them too, because he picked me as a wife, and he never complained about our lack of closeness or asked for more intimacy.

I criticized him and many things about him, and I didn't like that in myself but I kept doing it. When I didn't like something about him, I told him and I expected him to change. I thought

I was right about everything. When I got mad at him, I wouldn't admit my part and I stayed mad at him and we didn't talk for three days. Then we just picked up where we left off and never talked about how to handle it better the next time.

"You're such a bitch to Rick," my brother often told me.

He was right. And then other times I was sweet and made him his favorite dinner.

When our kids were 2, 6, and 7 years old, Rick had a job offer in San Diego, and we moved. I enrolled our 2-year old child in Montessori preschool, as I had done with his older siblings. I loved that teaching method and had emulated the basic concepts at home for several years. The school did not have a part time program, so I enrolled him full time. For the first time I was home alone, without kids or school or a job. I was in a new city. I was lonely and bored. I researched stocks and handled our investments. It was 1999. I wondered why share prices escalated in companies with no profits, and why the majority of people could not see it was a bubble.

I yearned for more connection in my heart. Instead of connecting with my husband, or making new friends, I started an affair. I didn't cheat on him with a man. I cheated on him with a pill. I had read a Wall Street Journal article about buying hydrocodone online a few years earlier, but I was busy raising kids and it wasn't a good time to start taking pills. But there, feeling alone in San Diego, I wanted them. I went on the Internet and had a phone consultation with an out-of-state doctor. The doctor prescribed me a pill I hadn't heard about before, called norcos.

Norcos were not the strongest pain medication available, but they were a controlled substance and addictive. Norcos contained 325 mg acetaminophen and 10mg hydrocodone, twice the hydrocodone of Vicodin with less acetaminophen. I liked how the hydrocodone made me feel, warm inside in a way I hadn't felt ever before, yet still mentally fully alert. Initially I took them only before dinner, but within a few weeks I took them earlier in the day and eventually I took two when I got up in the morning.

The pills became my lover. I developed a tolerance and become addicted. Within a few months of regular use, I needed to take them every few hours to avoid feeling restless, flu-like, and physically exhausted. I needed them to function. I felt it was not good for me and I needed to stop.

I called Paula, my best friend from high school. Maybe telling someone would make it easy to forget him or her.

"I think I'm addicted," I admitted.

"You need to stop," she advised.

But I didn't. I kept taking them.

Our house in Phoenix finally sold, and I started looking for a house during the day while Rick and the kids were at work and school. I wanted a house in town, but Rick liked the freedom of acreage, and I thought since he worked so hard to provide for us and asked for so little, he should decide on the house. We bought an 1800 sq. ft. 3 bedroom fixer upper house on 5 acres outside of town. I was determined to not share a bedroom with him, because I wanted to avoid his sexual advances. I set up the bedrooms so one small bedroom was an office, one small bedroom was for Rick, and the master bedroom was for me and the kids. He readily agreed. Maybe he didn't want sex with me either? We didn't discuss it.

I had my children and my family life and I had my purpose. We had our family dinners on the patio, overlooking our acreage and all the mountains down to the south. We went to our kids' soccer games and took our kids on weekend runs in the preserves by our house. We took family trips and did family chores. We were a family, but Rick and I were no longer a couple.

Sometimes I got glimpses of the attraction I still had for him, buried under years of neglect. We scheduled a family portrait. We bickered all morning getting ready and making sure we wore matching whites. I couldn't stand him. At our photo session, we stood apart and put the kids between us. The photographer moved us next to each other, with our kids to the side. Rick put his arm around me, and I liked it and felt happy for the first time in a long time. And then the picture was done and so was our moment of affection. All I could see was his unattractive glasses, bulging waistline, and annoying mannerisms. I wished I was single and raising my children alone. I felt guilty for thinking that.

My mom came to visit. She knew me and could see I had changed.

"You need to talk to Schahrzad about those pills," she told Rick.

She told me about that conversation years later. She didn't talk to me about it and neither did Rick. I really thought he didn't like confrontation or maybe he didn't know what to do about it. So he pushed it all away and consciously he saw nothing. That was good for me. I kept taking the pills. He didn't say anything about the pills or the walls between us. We didn't think about counseling because neither of us cared.

The pills were not good for my body or inner beauty. They constipated me, and I took senna herbs daily. The senna gave me cramps and I knew they weren't good for my intestines. My eyes were puffy and often my toes or fingers were swollen. It was from the pills. Why did I eat organic food and run, yet fill my body with pills? I pushed aside the question. I looked in the mirror and saw I had lost my inner glow of joy, innocence, and purity. But I wanted those pills more than I wanted my inner joy back.

When we planned a family trip to German in 2001, I went cold turkey on the pills. I didn't want to be in Germany and see my family when I was on drugs. The first week of our trip I went through withdrawals. I had so little energy and was listless. I could barely get out of bed and had to drink large doses of coffee. My legs and entire body were restless, so I kept moving and walking. By the second week, I felt clear and happy. We came home and the kids went back to school. I didn't want to be on pills when I took Wilson to his first day in Kindergarten. I was proud walking him in, not being on pills. But the following day, I refilled my prescription. Why did I do that? I didn't know.

When our oldest kids were in middle school, our house burned in the largest wildfire in California history, the 2003 Cedar Fire. It was a giant adventure for our family, mostly because we embraced change and had good insurance. We rented a house in a desirable neighborhood in town we couldn't afford to buy in, and hired an architect to build our forever family home. We replaced everything that burned in the fire, and questioned our attachment to material objects.

Around that time, on a family ski trip, blood gushed out of my vagina. When we returned home, I went to the doctor. He said I had large fibroids on my uterus. I took medication that could shrink the fibroids, but over the next few months, the fibroids grew so large, I could no longer button my pants and the bleeding continued. I didn't want to remove my uterus, part of my womanhood, but it had to be done. I scheduled the surgery.

"I recommend removing your cervix and ovaries too, as a preventative measure against cervical and ovarian cancer."

Was he fucking serious? I didn't have any problems with my cervix or ovaries.

"Do you also recommend removing my gallbladder and spleen while you're in there, I mean why not take it all?"

"It's just a recommendation. It's your choice."

I chose to keep my ovaries so I could keep my female hormone production. I also did not want to bring on menopause and its associated negative effects and perhaps need hormone replacement therapy. As to the cervix, I had no idea why I needed a cervix at all. My neighbor, an OB/GYN, told me she kept her cervix when she had a hysterectomy. Maybe she knew something I didn't. The cervix would stay. I had a partial hysterectomy. After the surgery, I missed the feeling of my uterus tensing during orgasm, and my orgasms felt weaker, but a few months later my orgasms were strong again.

I worked with the architect on building our forever family home. It was a stapathya veda design and I had more fun because my daughter, Christine, helped me design the interior. The kids chose the colors for their bedroom and helped us assemble the built-in bookcase. Our house was done and we eagerly moved in. We had a beautiful master bedroom. I didn't want to be in there with Rick and face my absent sexual desire. The pills numbed me physically and killed my sex drive. I didn't feel aroused, and in fact, I realized I had not masturbated in years. The last time I masturbated, I couldn't orgasm. It made sense – the point of the pills was numbing my body, and they worked. I couldn't risk being found out. If Rick tried to get me to orgasm during sex and I couldn't, he could suspect pills and try to make me stop. But we moved into the master bedroom, and he didn't initiate sex with me, and I didn't stop taking the pills. By then, I was taking about 25 norcos a day.

Many times I wanted to stop with the pills. It was a huge embarrassment, to be dependent on a substance for my well being, to ask the pharmacist or doctor for early refills, and to take money out of our savings account to pay for my habit. But every time I stopped taking pills, after a few hours, I grew restless and listless and had no energy. The feeling grew worse and I knew it would take several days to complete the withdrawals. I didn't want to feel sick or listless. So I kept taking them.

The kids knew.

"Mom is addicted to pills," they said to Rick one night.

Rick did not say anything, and I quickly denied it. Why did they all believe me?

It was 2005 and I finally realized we were in a huge housing bubble. I started a website that explained why we were in a bubble. Our house was worth triple what we owed, even after the rebuild.

A few months after we moved into our new home, we sold it and cashed out the equity. We moved into a rental in town. Our plan was to buy a home again after the prices crashed.

My website became popular. Over one thousand visitors a day came to my website. I became a realtor at the urging of my friends, who said all those visitors would want a house to buy. My broker and I wrote research reports on our housing market, and used data and charts to explain why the escalating house prices were a bubble. I called myself The Straight Talk Realtor. National media called to interview me. I got outside my comfort zone and pushed myself into being better at sales. In my free time, I read nonstop about economics and watched all the national news shows. I became more interested in reading about mortgage backed securities and the housing market, than I was in having dinner with my family or talking with my kids about what was going on with them. I had the pills and meditation for my heart, the analytics for my head, and the healthy food and workouts for my body. I thought my life was really good, but I was disconnected from my feelings and true intimacy with anyone.

The kids were getting older and their friends became more important, so it seemed they didn't mind my absence, and we all drifted apart. The kids told me years later that they missed me during those years.

I kept taking the pills. I bought norcos online and when the online pharmacies shut down, I went doctor shopping. I kept a list of doctors and pharmacies to manage my purchases. That was becoming more difficult, because I had a prescription at every pharmacy chain in town, and it was hard to find new pharmacies, and doctors to prescribe the amount I wanted. By then, I was taking 30-40 pills a day.

The pills were easy to take while the kids were little and one day melted into the next. But when Matt was a senior, I couldn't stand it anymore. I needed to be fully present to take him to visit colleges and deal with his big step in life, something I had not done with my daughter. I couldn't do all that on pills.

I also wanted to be a part of this world again. I didn't like that glass wall around me and the world. Maybe I could live my life without those pills. Maybe that life would be better. But how could I stop? I heard an ad on the radio for a medication to help with withdrawals. It was called suboxone. I went to a doctor to get the withdrawal medication, and I took it for six months. My doctor ran lab work to check my liver, kidney, and thyroid function, and fortunately all my test results were in the normal range. I weaned myself off the laxatives. I did all this on my own, without telling my family or going to meetings.

Gradually, my body and my heart woke up. I felt more alive. Colors appeared brighter. My family appeared loveable. My clitoris started tingling (again). I started masturbating again – a lot. My heart felt warm. I started hugging people – a lot. TV shows and people were funnier, and I started to laugh, a deep laugh from deep in my belly.

"I love your laugh!" Rick often said.

Had I not laughed before?

Two months after I was off the pills, Rick and two of our kids went on a family reunion vacation with my side of the family. Our destination: a houseboat on Lake Powell. I was happy to be off the pills around my family for the first time in years. Our boat moved slowly through the beautiful serene canyons. I cooked and talked with my family.

"Where is Rick?" my dad often asked.

I went to look for him. Every time, I found him sitting alone on the top deck, in the sunshine, relaxed, content, and deep in thought. His face had softened as he relaxed, and he was handsome again, like when we first met. He was content, all alone.

"Hey, how are you doing?"

"Happy," he smiled at me.

He loved his solitude. I smiled and went back downstairs and cooked his favorite dinner: chilaquiles with mushrooms (with one clove of garlic).

One night I played on the shore, and I looked up and saw him sitting peacefully on a chair on the front of the houseboat. He looked so sexy in his baseball cap. I noticed his muscular body and strong shoulders. I wanted him again, for the first time in decades. I walked over.

"Can I sit in your lap?" I flirted with him.

"Yeah, sure," he smiled.

I sat on his lap and he wrapped his arms around me. I felt loved, protected, and turned on. I pressed into his strong chest and a moan escaped my lips. I couldn't remember the last time I moaned just from the way a man held me. I buried my face in his neck. I liked how he smelled sweet, with a hint of sweat. I turned my face to kiss him, and he kissed me back. His kiss melted my heart and my panties felt moist. I couldn't remember the last time we kissed. It had been well over a decade.

We kissed passionately like new lovers. I wanted to feel his naked body against mine and have him hold me tight. My pussy throbbed and ached to be filled with his cock. I was swept into a world of want and desire and lust that I had not felt in years.

"Let's go in the bedroom," I invited him.

The boat had one bedroom, and our kids were using it. We could easily take it.

"Let's go," he said.

He took me by the hand and led me into the bedroom.

"Kids, mom and I are using this room tonight," he announced.

We made love. It was passionate, lusty, and filled with love and desire. He was on top of me in missionary position, and I was lost in a cocoon of his strength and passion. Time stopped. Even though it only lasted a few minutes, I was emotionally completely fulfilled.

I woke up, turned on and excited to have more sex. I reached over and put my arms around Rick. I rubbed against him.

"No, I want to get my day going," he said, and got up.

I was disappointed and hurt. Didn't men want sex 24/7? He had sensed my lack of interest all those years and left me alone, but I was back. Wasn't he thrilled to be offered sex first thing in the morning? Maybe he would want to later that day.

That afternoon when I went on the top deck, he sat in the chair, looking out at the water and canyon walls.

"Hi Rick. It's so beautiful out here," I said.

"Hi," he turned around and smiled at me.

I stood behind his chair and wrapped my arms around him.

"Here, listen to this," he said softly.

He handed me his earphones. The song "Songbird" by Fleetwood Mac played softly in my ear. My heart felt warm as I hugged him from behind, looked out at the beautiful canyons, and listened to the sensuous music he handed me. I had romance again. Anything was possible in that new life without pills. He turned around and brought me in front of him.

"Come here, lift your skirt and ride me," he said.

He pulled me gently back towards him and lifted my skirt. I was surprised. That was not the Rick I knew. I was also worried one of our family members would come upstairs and find us fucking.

"What about the kids?"

He was calm and reassuring.

"Just sit on me. Quick. Nobody will know."

"What about my parents or the other family? They're downstairs."

It was broad daylight too.

"Come. Sit on me," he coaxed.

His hands were firm around my hips. I trusted him, and I trusted he would make it all okay if one of the nine people downstairs

48

in our houseboat walked up on that top deck and saw us. I sat on him and rode him. He felt good and after one minute he came and it was done.

We slept together that night outside on the front deck of that houseboat, and I liked being close to him. And early the next morning, while everyone slept, we made love out there in the open.

I was ecstatic. I believed a whole new world of sex, lust, and passion had just been opened to us. Best of all, I finally had the marriage I had always wanted! I was giddy with delight.

When we returned to San Diego, I wanted to make love to him and fuck him constantly. When I initiated sex, he told me 'no', so I had to wait for him to ask. I woke several hours before him, but I no longer got up. I lay in bed until he woke up, hoping he would want to have sex. He usually did not. When he did, I was swept away by passion and desire and got lost in him. And after two minutes it was done and he got up to shower.

One Saturday morning I lay in bed for several hours waiting for him to wake and maybe want sex with me. He finally moved and stretched. I hoped he would want me, but instead of reaching for me, he jumped out of bed. I couldn't bear it. I started to cry.

"Did you get out of bed to get away from me? I just wanted you to make love to me," I sobbed.

Rick was puzzled. I hadn't cared about when he got out of bed our entire marriage. Mostly I hadn't wanted him near me. He thought I had lost my sanity.

"Honey, I'm just going to play soccer. I'm not going into combat. I'll be home in a couple hours," and he hugged me and looked confused.

I had to tell him about the pills and that I wasn't numb anymore.

"I have to tell you something," I cringed.

"What is it?"

"Well, I was taking pills for ten years and three months ago I stopped and that's why I am having feelings again."

I looked down as I spoke. Then I waited. Rick had worked hard at a job he didn't like so much, to provide for our family. He was frugal and rarely spent money on himself. His first thought went to how much all those pills had cost.

"How much money did you spend?"

My heart sank. He had his wife back, and he just cared about the money. He said he knew I took pills but he did not know I was addicted. He was furious. He didn't let me touch him for days. For the next seven months, he slept on the sofa off and on. I was devastated. I was so vulnerable and needy after starting to feel again. Why was he on the sofa? I cried and sobbed almost every day, because I wanted him so badly and he didn't want me back.

My crying puzzled Rick and the kids. They had not seen me cry in years, if ever. I didn't try to hide my tears. I wanted to feel and be in my heart again, and show my kids the importance of feeling.

I felt overwhelmed and needed help handling my emotions. I convinced Rick to take time off work to go to marriage counseling. I told the counselor about the pills, my crying, and Rick on the sofa. I thought she would be sympathetic. Instead, she looked at him.

"How do you feel about your wife taking those pills all those years?"

Rick moved his foot back and forth and that's when I knew. He was furious. He told me after the session he felt deceived by me, and foolish for not seeing it. It was a deep betrayal, which I only really understood years later, as of this writing. It made sense that he was mad at me and wanted to sleep on the sofa. But why had he not told me he was mad? And could he ever let it go?

The counselor was sympathetic to his anger. Rick felt better for being understood and we grew closer after that appointment. I told him all the ways I longed to be closer.

"I want to have more sex with you."

"Honey, I need two to three days to recharge. And although you're so sexy and have such a beautiful body, you're kind of old hat and I don't get so turned on by you if we have sex everyday."

"I want us to be more affectionate during sex."

"Honey, sex is just physical," he explained.

"I'd like you to go down on me sometimes, and be with my while I masturbate, even if you're not in the mood."

"I don't want to do that. Sex just isn't that important. Let's go and get a coffee."

Rick loved me, but sex wasn't that important to him. He was being honest with himself and with me when he told me 'no' to sex many times each week. I felt so powerless, just waiting for him to decide if we would make love, aroused and wet, full of desire in my body and longing in my heart.

I was super mad at him though for not caring if I had an orgasm and for always coming first and so quickly, and then leaving me to finish by myself. It was unfair and I didn't know what to do about it, other than find a way to come faster. I got some sessions with a sex coach, and when he invited Rick on the call, Rick refused.

"Honey, just tell me what he said and what you learned. I'm not going to let another guy tell me how to have sex with my wife," Rick said.

I went to a sex therapist to learn how to come faster so he wouldn't be so bored with me. Rick went with me to the second appointment. I timed myself masturbating over and over, hoping to get my time down to less than 3 minutes. I was glad when I did. But other times it took much longer and I was disappointed. How could I get him back, when I was so much work in the bedroom?

I read books about improving relationships, marriages, and cognitive therapy. One marriage book suggested renewing passion in a marriage by transforming at least one partner. That changed partner brought in a new dynamic and novelty. I thought that could be the key to keeping passion in the relationship: if the partners keep changing from the inside, then they appear new each time they are together. I thought that might make Rick want me more, but I didn't know how to translate that into my own relationship because he thought there was nothing wrong.

He still sometimes slept on the sofa and our sex life was not satisfying. It was quickies and he came and got up and didn't care if I came or not. It actually seemed that he didn't want me to come and have pleasure. Why did his love for me stop outside the bedroom? Did he secretly hate me? Was he really not that into sex, or was he withholding from me? And how could I ever be happy in our marriage when I felt so emotionally unfulfilled in our sexual relationship?

He had never complained about our lack of intimacy in our marriage, so maybe that wasn't important to him, but it was important to me. I wasn't going to be married to a man who avoided sex with me and slept on the sofa. I didn't give up pills to cry over a man. I wanted to live a better life! I decided to leave him. I called a divorce mediator to find out if I could get enough alimony and child support payments from Rick so I could afford to leave him. It sounded like I could. I made an appointment for Rick and me with the divorce mediator. The attorney called Rick to verify the appointment.

Rick called me right away.

"Honey, I want you. I don't want a divorce. Let's talk tonight," he said.

And we talked and we got closer and I stayed.

Over the next three years, I wanted to make love to him, and fuck him constantly. I couldn't get enough of him. When we had sex, he moved me this way and that way into various positions. He always knew what to do. Oddly enough, the very position that had bored me so much earlier in our marriage became my favorite: the missionary position. I loved lying under him and being completely engulfed by him. His thick large penis with the big mushroom head gave me goose bumps when we had intercourse, especially in the rear entry positions. I loved the way his cock felt inside me in the coachman position, doggy style, and the reverse cowgirl. I was always soaking wet and puzzled why I ever needed KY Jelly when I was younger.

Sexually, I was different than when we met thirty years earlier. The positions were no longer the main thing. What made it hot was how I felt about him, and how he handled me in bed. When we made love, there was nothing but us. There was no space, no time, no other people, no thoughts; it was just him and me, moans, heavy breathing, sweat, and pleasure. No activity even came close to making me that happy: not my kids, my workouts, my career, friends, money, wine, clothes, travel, jewelry, or gifts...nothing gave me even a glimpse of the fullness I felt when I was connected so intimately with my man. What we had, money couldn't buy. That kind of hot passion I had only seen in movies, and I had it with him. All he had to do was touch me anywhere, and I was immediately turned on.

"I'm so turned on," I'd say to him.

"The wind turns you on," he'd tease me.

He was probably right. I had a high sex drive, but that didn't mean I wanted to have sex with other people. I didn't. I only wanted him.

There were other differences in me. Since I no longer had a uterus, I had no periods or cramping or pregnancy concerns to prevent me from having sex when I wanted it. I was free to be sexual at any time. I had no worries about toddlers walking in on us.

I also noticed something about my body. When I felt emotionally turned on, I felt tingly in my vagina. Then I wanted him inside me and it wasn't about an orgasm. I often felt satisfied emotionally after sex, with him or past boyfriends, even without an orgasm. When I felt physically turned on, I felt tingly in my clitoris and I wanted an orgasm.

The kids started teasing us about our newfound passion. The first 22 years of our marriage they had never seen us kiss. Then all of a sudden I couldn't keep my hands off Rick. The kids saw us in long hugs, laughing at each other's jokes, going places together, and kissing. But our kissing was not the passionate lusty kissing of movies. Rick did not enjoy kissing, so we kissed on the cheek. I loved to kiss, but I didn't kiss with Rick because he didn't like it. He would get annoyed and ask me to stop. Sometimes I forgot and I kissed his stomach on my way down to his penis for a blowjob. He would say, "Don't do that, it feels like fish lips". And it hurt my feelings a little but I knew my kisses were sweet and delicious and it was about him, not me.

And then something big happened. He no longer came home to the kids. He came home to me. When I went to the grocery store, he came along, just because he liked hanging out with me. We met for coffee after work and talked. We ate dinner together almost every night by candlelight. We took walks on the beach. He started to take an interest in our investments. When he snored, I thought of how nice it was that he lay next to me. Then after a while I noticed he rarely snored at all. Maybe he had snored all those years because something was missing and now he had it?

I wanted to make sure I stayed sober and off the pills. I thought I ought to go to 12 step meetings. I went to meetings at the alano club near my home in Poway. The people in the "rooms" were open. They shared honestly what was happening. I was impressed. Admitting our weaknesses and flaws made us closer. I felt like it was the old days of sitting around a campfire and being fucking honest. It was the only place I could think of, where people were completely honest. However, I disagreed with the powerless philosophy however. I wasn't powerless at all. I chose to take every pill I took. I also didn't see myself as different from other people. In fact, I finally was part of this world. Why did they say "we" are addicts and speak on my behalf? I also didn't like that questioning the 12 steps or the disease theory was discouraged. I didn't feel free. But I liked my sponsor and working the steps and the open sharing, so I stayed.

Rick had wanted me to get a job for years, because he didn't like being the sole provider. He only mentioned it a few times, but it was under the surface and I thought he resented me for being home and not contributing financially. He told me he wanted me to earn back the $100,000 I had spent on the pills. We made a list of our goals, and we needed more money. My real estate business was not profitable, and I really didn't care, but he wanted me to work, so I went to the temp agency and got an office job with a regular paycheck. I was glad he made me get a job, because that job gave me joy and freedom and power, and because I was bringing in money and no longer felt like a financial burden.

We moved to Oceanside, California to be closer to Rick's work. We rented a cute older home less than two miles from the beach. My job was just a ten-minute drive down the coast. We were happy together, with our beach life, a second income finally, and our dreams.

"I love your laughter," he said often.

"I love how you open me up emotionally," he said.

I was finally a good wife. I wanted to be better.

"What can I do to be a better wife?" I often asked.

"Cook more," he said.

I wanted his answer to be about sex and not cooking, because I didn't like cooking that much, but I cooked more anyway.

I talked about sex with my friends and almost everyone I met. An old-timer from Narcotics Anonymous, who had sex with many women before he got married, gave me a most valuable advice.

"You know what I don't like about sex with a woman? I don't like it if she has sex with me because she wants attention or she wants my approval or she wants to please me. I want a woman to have sex with me <u>because she loves sex!</u>" He emphasized those last words and smiled, as if he remembered fucking a woman who loved to be fucked.

Wow! Really! I wasn't slutty or immoral for liking sex? A man actually preferred that? An entire new world opened to me.

The next time Rick and I fucked, I remembered my friend's words. I allowed myself to like sex and not feel ashamed for it at all. The sex was better. I felt powerful, alive, not held back. And then I allowed myself more and more, to talk about sex with others. It seemed everyone I met liked a woman who liked sex, and who was open enough to admit it. Everyone, except my husband.

"Why do you always talk about sex?" he asked.

Why did I?

It was part excitement and curiosity about my sexuality and wanting to explore our sexual connection, but mostly it was because I was struggling with getting my sexual needs met, and I didn't know how. So I kept talking about it

I knew I was desirable and I felt loved by him, but my heart was breaking because I longed to show my love and express my feelings. I wanted to explore more of my feelings, and his feelings, and our passion and soulful connection together.

I didn't know how I could live with all that pain and longing. I had an image of wanting to be hit over the head with a frying pan and knocked out, just to get some relief from the excruciating pain in my heart. I asked my friends and searched the Internet for answers. I wasn't going to turn to drugs or alcohol. My meditation could not solve this either.

I sobbed for hours on the sofa until my belly hurt from sobbing. I felt selfish for that around my kids. It wasn't fair to them to see their mother crying and not being strong, but I couldn't hold in all that pain and longing. Maybe it was okay for them to see it.

"Mom, why are you crying?" one of the kids would ask.

"I want dad to spend more time with me and he won't," I sobbed through tears.

Then, a few minutes later, I had cried myself out and was back to doing whatever it was I did. Until I'd circle back to crying again, a few days later.

"Mom, are you crying over dad again?"

"Yes….I am," I would answer.

Most of the time, I hid in the bedroom crying in secret. Rick didn't like to see me cry, probably because he knew it was about him and he felt he should fix it, but he didn't know how or he didn't want to change anything, or maybe he just didn't want to look at himself. Other times I felt sorry for myself and wanted everyone to see it also. Maybe I was "wrong" for crying so much. Maybe I was too emotional or overreacting or not taking responsibility for my own emotions?

Outside the bedroom, I felt loved and free. Deeply loved. Totally accepted. Free to be how I wanted. He did what he said he would do, he provided for us, he was an alpha male, he was productive around the house and successful at work, he stood up to me. Maybe it wasn't all perfect, but I was completely satisfied with what we had outside the bedroom.

I was curious why he didn't want more closeness and intimacy. I didn't ask him to do something bad. I didn't ask him to take drugs or rob a bank or make himself 'smaller'; I asked him to make love to his wife, something that would make him 'bigger'. I didn't understand why he didn't want that too, so I asked a lot of questions. He answered me, and this is what he said.

"Sex is just physical," and then he gave me a long hug and held me all night.

"Sex is just not that important," and then his eyes lit up as he put on his shoes to go for a run or work out in his shop.

"The reason I don't go down on you is because I can only do that when I'm really turned on," he would say and then he'd wash the dishes and take out the trash.

"I don't know why I don't like to kiss you. I just don't," he softly. And then we sat together and drank our coffee.

"I just come fast, there's nothing I can do about it," he said.

"The reason I close my eyes during sex is so I can imagine it's someone else. I'm not saying this to hurt you, that's just how it is," he explained.

"I won't ever read your books on oral sex or any books on sex," he said and he picked up his western and read for an hour until he fell asleep.

Each time he said these things, my heart broke a little bit. And I cried to myself. I cried at work, I cried in the car, I cried with my friends. And that evening we met for coffee and talked and laughed and I was happy again.

I wanted to play romantic music when we made love, so I could feel more emotional with him. I asked for it once and he said no. And another time, and another no. And then I didn't ask again. I didn't have the courage to divulge my deepest most fragile feelings to someone who didn't want them.

"I love you," I whispered to him as I clutched him tight when we made love one night. I felt my heart open up and a deep intense pleasure deep in my vagina as I said it. My entire pussy opened up. I had never felt that before. I felt a definite connection between my heart and my body. I didn't need him to answer. I wanted to see what would happen to my heart and my body when I said it again, so I did.

"I love you."

"Why are you saying that?" he asked with almost contempt.

And he kept thrusting. I knew he didn't like me saying I loved him, because he believed in actions and not words, but I had thought he would like it in the bedroom. I was disappointed, but not enough to cry.

"I just wanted to say it," I told him.

I never said those words during sex to him again. I made myself a mental note that for him, sex really was just physical. I kept the mood going and we finished fucking, and I didn't say anything about it. But then I understood. I got it. He wanted to keep the emotion out of sex. I hadn't listened before when he told me sex was only physical. And my heart broke a little more that night.

Two days later, he woke up horny and he wanted me. I had just warmed up and longed for him, and in two minutes it was over and he jumped out of bed.

"I'm taking a shower," he said.

He left me there in that bed, with my pussy still wet, my clit throbbing, and my heart aching. I masturbated to relieve the physical pressure but I didn't know how to relieve the emotional pressure in my heart. Sometimes I would be sad and other times I was furious.

"NO MORE QUICKIES!" I wrote on our family whiteboard one morning. The kids and Rick didn't say a word about it.

I got up my courage and asked for something I wanted.

"I really like oral sex. Will you go down on me sometime?"

He agreed, out of love for me. He didn't like me to sit on his face or go down on me, but he did try. His tongue moved around in places that were not my favorite and all the instructions didn't help. I did not get an orgasm from his oral sex, and I couldn't remember the last time he had given me an orgasm in any way at all. To his credit, he kept trying.

I was not relaxed because he had an oral sex time limit and I thought we were approaching it. One day he licked my clit and it happened.

"Ok, it's been 20 minutes. My tongue is tired, and I'm going to stop now," he said.

It seemed fair. Why should he spend so long? But it also hurt me deeply. I loved going down on him. Why didn't he love doing that to me? Why didn't he want to please me? Why couldn't he make me come, and why didn't he want to? I wanted him to make me come at least once in a while. I felt flawed and unloved and bored. And my heart broke a little more.

And then three days later we had hot sex and I had a good orgasm with him, and I felt fulfilled and happy, and hoped it would stay good like that going forward.

I masturbated almost every day, and I had pleasurable orgasms. I was relaxed, I fantasized, and sometimes I used a vibrator and a dildo. I had used vibrators in the past, but stopped doing so because it seemed they desensitized me, gave me less intense orgasms, and required a dependence on a device for something so natural as my own orgasm.

I masturbated with my fingers, and used my slippery wetness so my fingers could glide. My own wetness made the best lubricant for rubbing my clitoris. I slid my fingers back to where it felt good, and I rubbed more and more. Sometimes I slid my fingers slightly to another position. As I got closer to climax, I sped up my rubbing and tensed my legs. Often I used my other hand to tickle or pinch my nipples, and that intensified my arousal. The whole time I fantasized about someone watching me. My orgasm built slowly and I never knew how long it would take for me to orgasm. Only about 10 - 20 seconds before I came, did I know it was imminent. My orgasms felt intense. My left toes would curl up and a wave of pleasure emanating from my clitoris spread out over my entire body. Sometimes I moaned softly, other times louder. Occasionally I cried for a few seconds afterward, and that was like a physical release kind of crying because I didn't have any feelings with it.

When I was with him, my orgasms were less intense. I thought it indicated something deeply missing between us. My orgasms with a partner ought to be better, at least sometimes. But they weren't, because I felt like a burden sexually, and I could sense his boredom, waiting for me to come.

I told him all the things I wanted to change and make better. We compromised on some issues, and that helped sometimes with the quality of our sex. But then the quantity declined even more because of his erectile dysfunction, which lowered his interest even more. I asked him to go to the doctor for hormone testing, but he said it didn't matter anyway because he would not ever take testosterone and sex was not that important to him anyway. I never thought of having sex with other men. I didn't want sex. I wanted intimacy with Rick.

How I could have a happy marriage when I felt so unloved and unfulfilled in the bedroom? I blamed myself for not being understanding, or for being too needy. I read in online forums and on the Internet and I learned it was common for partners to have mismatched sex drives. The higher drive person was left wanting and sad, just like I was. And often, it was the woman who had the higher drive. I read closely to learn what I could about how to deal with it and make it better. I never did find out.

To outsiders, we seemed to have the perfect marriage. But the reality was that all was not rosy. I cried a lot and my heart was breaking a little more almost every day. It was about sex and about emotional intimacy. I wanted him in a way he didn't want me. He liked sex, but just to satisfy his physical desires, and not as a way of mutual pleasure and connection. He showed his love for me in all the other places in our relationship, but not in sex.

I had a huge problem and he had no problem at all.

CHAPTER 6

OPENING OUR MARRIAGE

Rick was supportive of me going to 12 step meetings, however I was feeling less and less free at the meetings. Why were we talking about a useless habit years after it ended? It seemed like we were living in the past. Why did we label ourselves as addicts when we were sober? After 17 months of sobriety and working through 11 of the 12 steps, I stopped going. I drank a glass of red wine, and I felt free and powerful for being able to do what others said could not be done, and for expressing myself. Nothing was "released again". I didn't want a second drink, because I wanted to feel. I drank a glass of red wine at every dinner from the onward, and sometimes I had a second glass. One night, I even smoked some pot. I didn't like it. I spent the next nine months deprogramming myself by reading everything I could find on addiction as choice. I inquired within, and I asked myself what was wrong with me for taking on a drug habit for ten years. What was wrong with me? Why did I do it? I didn't blame some chemical or genetic disposition, I looked at my own motives. All that inquiry over leaving the "rooms" made me stronger.

Rick and I were enjoying our renewed connection. Our oldest two kids were away at college, and Wilson was usually at the gym or doing homework. Our life was good.

Onc night after dinner we were snuggled in bed.

"Honey, turn around, I'll massage your feet," he offered.

I happily turned around in bed. Rick gave excellent foot massages. As he rubbed my feet, I lay there and reflected how much I loved that man.

"Do you want to watch a movie?" I asked.

"That sounds good. What do you want to watch?"

"Let's watch some porn. How about the documentary on swinging?"

"Sure!"

I had been sexually curious and playful since I lost my virginity at age 16, and he had been a 'no' to almost everything I wanted to do, including going to sex shops, strip clubs, watching porn, or having threesomes.

I was thrilled he was opening up to watching porn. He liked the hardcore fucking videos. They did nothing for me. The movies which got my attention and turned me on were more sensual and realistic such as lovemaking between a man and woman. My biggest turn-ons though involved someone giving attention to a woman's clitoris, probably because I wanted someone, like my husband, to pay attention to, and love mine. I loved watching oral sex performed on a woman, girl on girl porn, or women masturbating. I also liked the educational shows about oral sex, pegging (a woman performing anal sex on a man with a dildo in a strap-on) and the lifestyle (formerly called "swinging").

I put on the lifestyle documentary I had watched a few days earlier. The video featured a married couple and the filmmaker who fucked the wife, while her husband watched. It was the hottest thing I had ever seen! My clit tingled when the husband instructed his wife how to ride the filmmaker's hard cock. She smiled at her husband, and did as he asked. I wanted my husband to get turned on watching me have sex with another man. I wanted to see him having sex with another woman. Perhaps being with other women would increase his sex drive and improve our sex life. I wasn't worried that he'd fall for another woman. I was sure he would never leave me.

We watched the entire movie. He seemed to like it, because he kept commenting on it. When the movie was over, I asked him if he wanted to have sex with other women.

"Yeah, I want to have sex with other women. Why wouldn't I?" he said.

I was thrilled!

"Yeah, I want to watch you do that too."

"How do we get involved in this?" he wondered.

"Let's go on some lifestyle sites and see what events we can find," I suggested.

We spent the rest of the evening discussing swinging and what that might be like for us. Then we fell asleep in each other's arms.

SWINGER PARTIES

The next day we joined a swinger site, not sure what to expect. Through the site we could access local events and meet other swingers online. That weekend, we attended our first swinger event. It was held at a club in midtown San Diego. Our group of about 10-15 people, mostly couples, was on the patio. A single woman, referred to as a "unicorn" in swinger language, was present. Unaccompanied men were not allowed at swinger functions. I was struck by how unattractive these people were and how little they seemed to care to welcome us. I couldn't picture myself having sex with any of them. The men were not good-looking like the man in the swinger video.

Only one couple came up and talked to us. They were in their late 40's. The wife was a voluptuous blonde, about 5'3", with large breasts. Her husband was about 6' and fit, but not handsome. After they introduced themselves, we asked them about STDs and the sex parties. Rick kept smiling at the woman, and I wondered if he wanted to fuck her. I imagined myself having sex with her husband, and the thought repulsed me. I didn't know if I should flirt with him anyway or not. I'd spent my lifetime avoiding flirtation with married men. Would she, or any of the other wives at the event, really want me to flirt or have sex with their husbands?

Our main concern with having sex outside our monogamous marriage was contracting an STD. We had already read about STDs on the Internet and we asked the friendly couple a lot of questions about STDs. The couple told us they had never heard of anyone contracting any STDs. As we went to more swinger events and sex parties later on, we kept asking about STDs, and we always got the same answer: the couple had never had any STDs and had never heard of anyone getting an STD. I think there was once exception and it was cured with antibiotics. We became a little more comfortable about having sex with other people.

Over the next few weeks, we attended more get-togethers and spent more time on the swinger site by uploading public and private pictures and viewing those of others. The photos people posted of themselves were erotic and arousing. We saw close-ups of labia, women in garters posing with their round asses sticking out, men posing shirtless with erect penises, and people engaged in sex acts. The sexy pictures sent us into sexual overdrive and kept us intensely titillated over the next 3 months. We exchanged messages with other swingers we wanted to meet. Our sex life became juiced by our heightened arousal.

We signed up to attend a play party. We paid the couple fee of $90, and then received instructions and an address by email. The party started at 7pm and went until the next morning. It took place at a large home in San Diego. The hostess had a smorgasbord of delicious food in her kitchen. Guests could bring their own alcohol. We brought a bottle of wine for Rick. I chose not to drink. I wanted to be fully present mentally, emotionally, and physically.

Gina, a friend of the hostess, showed us around. There was a room to put our purses and bags/change of clothes. There were many bedrooms, a large hot tub, a dance floor with a stripper pole, and a fucking swing.

Gina explained some of the rules. Single women could attend the party, but single men could not, because if single men were allowed, there would be too many with insufficient female matches. Women could walk around freely and watch others have sex, but men could watch only if accompanied by a woman, because presumably the man would stand in a dark corner and masturbate while he watched others fucking, and somehow they thought it was creepy. That made zero sense. I thought masturbation was a very vanilla sex activity, and if it wasn't welcome at a lifestyle party, then where?

The house was filled with couples. The women were beautiful and well dressed. The men were mostly overweight and unattractive. I still couldn't see myself having sex with any of the men.

I noticed two couples walk into the large bedroom. I waited a few minutes and followed them in. Several couples were on the two beds having intercourse and women were giving blowjobs. It didn't turn me on. One man who was getting a blowjob looked up at me and invited me to sit on the edge of the bed. He held my hand and tried to get me to join him and his female partner. I wasn't interested.

In fact, I wasn't impressed by anything I saw that night or any of the other nights we attended sex parties. The sex I saw was just intercourse or women going down on men. Rarely did I see a man going down on a woman. I did not see anal sex, gay sex, BDSM, masturbation, couples watching each other, or anything unusual. I was struck that these people were open to swinging, yet closed off to the wide variety of sexual experiences. Maybe I wasn't going to the really fun sex parties.

A novel item was the Sybian, a vibrator with a saddle-like seat and dildo attachments. A condom was placed on the attachment before a woman sat on it. Groups of people gathered around, as women took turns being stimulated to orgasm by the hostess, who operated the device. I was fascinated seeing women have orgasms in front of us.

Brianna, a beautiful voluptuous 35-year old woman, with medium sized perky breasts, and long thick curly brown hair, sat on the Sybian. I admired her beauty and bravery for sitting on that machine in front of us all. A man knelt behind her and played with her breasts and nipples while the hostess operated the controls. Brianna's breathing picked up. She closed her eyes and breathed harder and moaned louder and then she orgasmed right there in front of me. I was amazed and inspired. I wanted to have that kind of freedom to orgasm so easily and in public, so I stayed and waited for my turn.

But I wasn't as free as she was. I didn't want to remove my panties in front of all those people. I had to be relaxed and feel safe to climax, and for me that meant being in a bedroom or other private place with my partner. Public places didn't do it for me. It was dark though and I wanted to try the machine. I asked everyone who was watching, to leave. I put a condom on the dildo attachment, and sat on it. The hostess worked the switches. I felt the movements inside my vagina, the vibration on my clitoris. I was too self-conscious to relax so I asked her to stop the machine. I got up and got dressed, and milled around watching other people for the rest of that evening.

I was surprised how little sex was happening. The swingers were so slow to hookup. I figured anyone would have sex with anybody. However, that was not the case. Women would have sex with men they found attractive, so men had to flirt with and court women.

Rick and I liked the party enough that we attended several more. At the next play party, held at a hotel, Rick and I joined other couples in a hotel room. A man stood next to a woman who was asleep. The man motioned to Rick to come over and the two men talked. Rick came over and whispered in my ear.

"See that woman sleeping on the bed, and the man standing next to her? That's her husband, and she's not really asleep. He wants me to fuck her and come inside while she pretends to sleep. It's their fantasy," he said.

"What? He's not worried about her getting STDs?" I asked.

"No, he wants the cum in her so he can lick it afterward," Rick told me.

I found that intriguing. I loved hearing about people's unusual sexual fantasies. I later learned it was a common fantasy among bisexual men.

"Don't do it," I said to Rick.

I didn't want him having sex without a condom.

"No, no way, I won't," he said. We both watched that couple and found it interesting. Her husband talked to several men and then I saw one man was fucking her. Rick and I left before we ever saw what came next.

We attended another play party. I spotted a tall handsome man in his early 40's I'd noticed earlier. His name was Brian, and he was married to Brianna, the woman who had climaxed on the Sybian. I liked his confidence and his tall lean build. He reminded me of an athlete. He stood next to a bed where people, including his wife Brianna, were having sex.

"Can I give you a blow job?" I asked.

"You sure can," he smiled at me and pulled down his pants. I licked his balls and sucked on his cock. He kept telling me that I was so good at giving blowjobs. It was a compliment, and even more so when I found out later he was one of the biggest swingers around. I felt really satisfied with that, especially since I loved giving blowjobs and he had such a beautiful wife. Brianna lay on her back on the bed, her legs wide apart, fucked by several men, one at a time. She just lay there, moaning, while one after the other had intercourse with her. I heard her asking each man if he was wearing a condom. She was too drunk to sit up and look for herself. Her drunkenness was a turn off and I wondered if she really enjoyed herself. I kept sucking her husband's cock. He came in my mouth and when I looked at her, she was still being fucked on the bed next to us.

I found a young couple in their late 20's that I had met earlier in the kitchen. It was their first event they had said. They sat on the other bed and just watched everything. I walked over to them.

"Can I give your husband a blowjob?"

I wanted her permission. I was sure he would agree.

"Yes."

She seemed nervous. He pulled down his pants and sat down again next to his wife. I kneeled on the floor and sucked on his penis. I kept looking at her to make sure she was comfortable with it. Then he groaned and came in my mouth. I swallowed. I looked at her to make sure she was still okay. She looked a little mad, and she got up and walked away. I understood her jealousy. I left it up to them to figure out what to do about it.

I liked giving blowjobs. While I did it, I imagined how good it must feel for a man to have his cock licked, kissed, and sucked. Both men had totally loved it. I thought they were just saying that, but they weren't…they both said it was because I really enjoyed it and that's what made it so hot. They said a lot of women gave blowjobs as an obligation, and they were so amazed that I actually enjoyed it.

When I was done with the blowjobs, I went outside and into the backyard. Gina's boyfriend, Ralph, was in the hot tub, talking with another couple. I climbed in next to them and relaxed in the hot water.

"Rick and Gina are in a bedroom," Ralph told me.

I was excited for Rick. I found it interesting that Ralph and I talked so casually, while his girlfriend and my husband were in another room fucking. I felt powerful in my generosity. About half an hour later, Gina came into the hot tub and told me about her encounter with Rick. I felt so close to her for sharing that with me.

I was surprised I didn't feel jealous at all. I decided right then that Rick could have sex with all the women he wanted at the parties. Rick told me more details later and I still wasn't jealous. As for me, I really didn't want to fuck at the sex parties. I wasn't attracted to any of the men. In fact, I didn't want to kiss or have intercourse with any other man. I already had a man!

MY FRIEND'S HUSBAND

That fall, my best friend from high school died of ovarian cancer. Her husband Eliot called me minutes after it happened. His voice was tender and he spoke slowly, deliberately. Paula had died at their home in Denver, surrounded by him and their twin boys. As he told me how she had died, my heart was breaking. I had wanted to be with her at the end. She didn't ever tell me she was dying. She kept speaking of her progress through her chemo treatments, and then just a month before she passed, she stopped taking my calls. I didn't want to push myself on her. I didn't know what to say to a woman who was dying and didn't want to talk about her death. I just wanted to love her, to hold her, to be with her. I didn't get to do that. What I could do, though, was love her husband and her two boys. I could be there for them.

As Eliot spoke, I wanted to hold him close in a loving embrace. I had thought for years about how he was sexually neglected and perhaps shamed for his natural desires. He appeared vulnerable, perhaps in need of tenderness and love…and maybe even sex. I suddenly had the desire to give him a blowjob. I was surprised I didn't feel guilty for having those sexual thoughts about him as he spoke about my friend's death. I thought about her looking at us from wherever she was, and wanting me to give him the love that she didn't give him. It felt right.

I told Rick about Paula's death and my blowjob fantasy. Rick thought it was a bad idea because he had seen how Eliot had looked at me in the past. After the funeral, I approached Eliot with my fantasy.

"I have thought of giving you a blow job," I wrote.

I nervously waited for his email reply. Would he be mad at me or would he agree to it, or would he be shocked I would offer him sex while he was still mourning his wife's death?

"The fantasy is mutual," he replied.

I was instantly both relieved and aroused. We wondered whether Rick would approve of our idea. I was a married woman and I didn't cheat. Eliot and I agreed we needed Rick's blessing. That night when we laid together in bed, I asked Rick again about my fantasy of giving Eliot a blowjob. Rick was a fair man. He had sex with other women at sex parties. Rick's heart was also deeply sad for Eliot's loss. He wanted to give something to his friend who had lost a wife. That time, he said I could go to Colorado to have sex with Eliot.

Then my emails with Eliot gained steam and my arousal reached a level I did not ever recall feeling. My body was swollen with desire. My vagina was tingly and so wet, my panties were damp from all the moisture. I went to the bathroom and looked at my vulva. My outer labia were swollen and huge and my entire vulva was engorged. I had never seen that before and I was embarrassed because I thought it looked ugly.

There was another consideration for my husband. Rick couldn't make me orgasm anymore. It had been years since he had been able to make me come. He would try oral and manual clitoral stimulation and regardless of how much he tried or for how long, I couldn't come. He was curious if Eliot could make me come.

Rick sent Eliot an email: "My wife wants to fuck you. Have fun. She's a handful."

I was proud of my husband who was so generous with me, and trusted me to handle myself well. Eliot immediately called me to discuss a day I could fly to Denver. He booked my flight. He was just as turned on as I was. We continued writing each other steamy e-mails, keeping me aroused all day long at work and at home.

I packed some sexy clothes to wear for him. I wore a sexy dress for him, and he said he would wear a suit for me. I loved men in suits. On the plane, my pussy was still swollen and wet, and my panties were damp. I washed up in the airplane bathroom before we landed. I hoped my vagina smelled good and clean, and Eliot wouldn't notice the swollen lips.

Eliot picked me up at the airport in his new Land Rover. He looked dashing in his suit. I felt sexy and important that such a handsome successful man went to all that trouble to put on a suit for me. Eliot got out of the car to hug me, and gave me a warm smile.

"It's a good thing I didn't come in to get you. I'm hard as a rock," he said.

He opened my car door and I fell into his leather seat. I couldn't recall the last time a man opened a car door for me. I felt like a woman being courted and desired. He got in, leaned over and kissed me. His determined warm hard tongue pressed with wanting against my own. I was surprised. I did not expect this at all. I thought Eliot would give husband kisses, whatever those were. I didn't know anyone who French kissed like that. Besides, the last time I was French kissed was in college. I was nervous with anticipation. He drove straight to the hotel, and asked if I wanted a bottle of wine he'd brought along. I did not. I wanted to do this sober.

We checked in. He had paid the airfare, so I paid for the room. That way, we each paid half the expenses for our date. I wanted to show him I was there because I wanted him, not because he paid for my trip, and I didn't want the burden of thinking I owed him anything. At home, I had trouble asking for what I wanted in the bedroom, because Rick supported me financially and he resented it. I didn't feel like I could ask for something else in the bedroom and give Rick more to do for me that he didn't like. There with Eliot, I didn't want that burden. I could feel free and empowered sexually so I could experience whatever would happen, and ask for what I wanted, without obstacles or guilt.

We took our room key card and took the elevator upstairs. I felt like a woman having an affair. Both of us wore our wedding rings. I admired his strong body as I walked behind him. He was a few inches taller than Rick, about 6', and he cycled, skied, and did Crossfit. I couldn't wait to see him naked.

He opened the door to our room, let it fall close, grabbed me, and pulled me close. I let out a moan. Pressed up against his tall strong body, I felt protected and a whole new feeling came over me. I got lost in his manly strength. I went weak in the knees and fell back into his arms. His strong hands gripped me tight. He walked me backwards to the sofa and I collapsed on the cushions. He reached forward and continued kissing me. My body ached for his touch. My moaning was louder and he knew I was yearning for more. He lifted up my skirt and pulled my panties to the side.

I was felt eager and wondered how he thought my pussy looked. I had shaved my pubic hair except for the landing strip. Would he like it?

I was a little embarrassed about my enlarged swollen vulva lips. I thought it looked ugly. I was hoping he wouldn't mind. He didn't say anything. He just moved his head down between my thighs. His tongue touched my outer lips and I gasped. Nobody had been there in years. I loved that he didn't go right for my clit. He slid his tongue down and sucked and nibbled gently on my labia. I felt alive and powerful and pushed my hips toward his face. Then I sank back into the sofa. His tongue explored my inner lips and then my clitoris, as he circled and flicked it with his warm tongue. He moved his tongue off and on my clit as he slid side to side, and each time he made contact with my clit, a shot of pleasure shot through my entire body. He varied his technique, keeping me aroused and in suspense.

I looked at him, kneeled on the floor at my feet, his clothes still on, just wanting to give me pleasure. He seemed like he really liked doing it. It didn't seem like he was just doing me a favor. I had to know.

"Do you like doing that," I asked him. "You're really good at it!"

He looked up at me. "I love it! You taste so good."

I couldn't believe my ears. I had wanted my husband to say that for years! I was glad I had washed up first. I wondered if I would have tasted good if I hadn't washed up in the airplane bathroom. Rick asked me to wash up right before he went down on me, which used to make me so mad because I knew my pussy smelled clean and sweet. Maybe next time I'd not wash up right before. I let all those thoughts go, and sank back into the pleasure of my body and Eliot's warm breath on my clit. I allowed myself a few more minutes to enjoy the oral sex. It would take me at least 20 minutes of that to come, and I felt guilty having him spend so much time on me when I hadn't done anything for him. Besides, I was there to give him a gift.

I wanted to show him what I came for: the blowjob.

"Sit down," I invited.

Eliot got up and we hurriedly removed his shoes and pants. He wore Ralph Lauren plaid boxers. Hot! Rick always wore plain briefs and wouldn't wear any of the boxers or sexy underwear I bought for him.

We pulled off Eliot's boxers, and there awaited my big surprise. His penis was beautiful, hard as a rock, so erect it was almost touching his stomach. Surprisingly hard for a 52 year old man. I was proud I had turned him on so much. I hadn't seen a penis that erect in years, not even at the play parties. Rick's penis had been semi-flaccid every time the last few years. I couldn't recall a time he did not have erectile dysfunction. His soft penis had been a major disappointment in our sex life. Rick didn't seem to think it was a problem. He enjoyed sex anyway. He had finally agreed to take the Viagra and Cialis the doctor prescribed, however the medication did not make him fully hard. I sometimes could barely feel him inside of me. I was excited to see Eliot's erect stiff penis because I knew fucking him was going to feel extremely pleasurable.

Eliot sat on the sofa and I made myself even more aroused by licking his balls and asshole and sucking his cock. He moaned loudly and pulled me up. My husband did not crave me sexually, but that man did. His desire for me aroused me even more. I was ready to ride him.

We talked about using a condom and decided against it. Both of us had been in a monogamous marriage for over 20 years. We quickly walked over to the bed and I climbed up and lay on my back. He lay on top of me, held my body completely in his control, and slipped his hard cock inside me. I moved my hips up and down. Incredible pleasurable sensations filled me. I hadn't had such a good feeling in my pussy in years. My moaning was louder. I got on top and rode him slowly, letting the tip of his penis head just come inside my opening, and then I experimented with different moves. Eliot let me move as I liked. I buried my face in his neck and I rode him a little faster. I started to get out of breath so I sat up and looked at him.

"Ride me hard and put me away wet," I joked.

He laughed.

"I've got some ideas of my own," and we both laughed.

I liked that we could just be ourselves during sex. We could talk, fuck, and laugh. It didn't have to be so serious. We kissed and then I buried my head next to his shoulder again in the pillow, and just felt the sensations in my body as his cock stretched my cunt over and over and over. Then he made a series of quick thrusting pulses. I'd never experienced that movement and its intense pleasure before! I wanted it to last forever, but he stopped after a few seconds.

Then I started moving again. As we kept fucking like that, I became wetter and wetter. My body opened up more and I could take and wanted his penis deeper inside me. I felt a very sensitive pleasurable spot deep inside me, next to my cervix that I had never noticed. I pressed my hips down on him as hard as I could. My moaning was almost a wail.

"I feel like a wild animal," I said.

He laughed with delight in his deep voice.

That gave us a moment to catch our breath and I realized the patio door was wide open. I knew I was a loud moaner, so I asked Eliot to close the door. He got up and closed it. I watched him walk back to our bed. He was so strong, so sexy. He didn't keep fucking me. Instead, he sucked gently on my clitoris. I didn't recall anyone ever sucking on my clit or going down on me after intercourse. My heart swelled and tears welled up in my eyes for this man who tasted my feminine juices after being inside me. I felt so completely appreciated and valued. Eliot went down on me for a few minutes. I didn't think I deserved to have him down there so long.

"Come here," I beckoned.

When he rose up, I noticed he was rock hard. Going down on me had turned him on. It hadn't occurred to me that a man could be turned on going down on a woman. I thought only women got turned on doing that.

Eliot kissed me gently. I wasn't so interested in kissing him. I wanted his pleasurable rock hard penis thrusting deep inside to my cervix again. I felt a little selfish, to think of him in that moment as just a hard penis.

He moved on top of me in the missionary position, slipped inside me, and filled me with his cock. I went into a world of pleasure deep inside my body that I couldn't access on my own, as his cock spread and stretched my pussy. He went so deep. So good. He flipped me over again, so that I was on top. The pleasure kept building, as did my moans. I wondered if I could have an orgasm from the penetration. For years I had felt sexually inadequate because I did not climax from intercourse. I had finally accepted it as normal. Some of my friends climaxed from penetration. Maybe it could happen to me also. It was feeling so good. I almost laughed at the part of myself that didn't know my own body's sexual capabilities at the age of 51. I kept moving my hips. Then the pleasurable intensity subsided and the buildup to orgasm faded.

I slowed down and sat up. I looked at Eliot's handsome face, his strong arms and hands, and the wedding rings on our fingers. I marveled at the beauty of our moment and our encounter, and how fortunate I was that Rick allowed me that experience. I imagined Paula looking at us from heaven or wherever she was, and smiling at us.

I leaned down to kiss him. He kissed me back. I angled my hips forward so his cock head hit a sweet spot deep inside and then I made little pulses. Eliot and I got lost in our sexual rhythms, our heavy breathing, and my moaning. I didn't care if the entire hotel heard me moan. Our intensity increased as pleasure built for us both.

"I'm going to come," he said.

Did he want my approval?

"Go for it, baby!" I whispered.

He pumped faster and faster from the bottom, until he came with a loud long groan. I didn't know men made noises like that when they had an orgasm. I leaned over to kiss him again. I knew a man liked to retract after orgasm, so I was quiet for a little while. I gave him space to be.

We held each other without talking. I thought over my experience. The sex we had was more intimate, connected, and physically fulfilling than the sex I had with my husband. I was glad I wasn't having feelings or getting attached to Eliot. I wondered if Eliot would make me orgasm or if I would need to masturbate like I did at home.

He went down on me and after a few minutes I didn't think he could make me come, so I told him I wanted to masturbate.

Eliot lay next and kissed me, as I masturbated. His kiss softened into a gentle tug on my lip. I felt warmth in my heart and that turned me on even more. I didn't kiss him back because I was focusing all my attention on my rubbing fingers and my clit. I loved that he kept his lips on mine, and when I briefly opened my eyes, I noticed his eyes were open and he looked at me. His attentiveness and interest turned me on more. I got more and more tingly and then I came long and hard. He looked at me the entire time.

I wished that Rick would desire me like that, to be excited when I masturbated and came. I wondered if Eliot was so turned on with me, because I was new to him. Maybe he would not be that interested in a woman's orgasm either after 25 years together. Maybe I expected too much of Rick to still desire me.

As we lay in our afterglow, Eliot told me about sex with Paula. He told me how she liked it, about her multiple orgasms, how he only had sex with her to pleasure her and then rolled over, how he often pretended to be asleep when she came to bed looking for sex. He said her constant criticism of him left him feeling distant from her. I was impressed that he could still get hard and wanted to please her sexually anyway. This made me believe I was not expecting too much of Rick. We talked about many other things. Eliot was introspective, and I enjoyed my conversations with him. He liked to improve himself and he had many ideas and thoughts about people, relationships, and life. He made it clear our weekend was a special one-time event between friends. He didn't have feelings for me and he never told me I was beautiful or that he wanted to see me again. After about an hour of talking, he left to go home to his kids. He said he'd be back at 7am. I loved morning sex. I went to bed right away so I could be rested.

The next morning I got up early and went for a run. I was turned on and imagining more hot sex. I had brought my booty shorts, high heels, and a little T-shirt, and I planned to wear them that morning. I loved dressing up sexy, being playful and dancing for my man, and making him desire me even more. Rick didn't enjoy lingerie or sexy dances, unfortunately. After my run I showered, and put on my sexy seductress outfit.

Eliot knocked on my hotel door right after 7 am. He looked so handsome, his blond curly hair a stark contrast to his black Patagonia sweater and jeans. I gave him a hug and we kissed. His body felt strong and steady against mine.

"God, you look amazing," he said and eyed me up and down.

I felt sexy, alive, and desired in a way I could not recall.

"Thank you," I smiled up at him.

"Dance for me," he whispered.

"Come sit on the sofa," I said.

I put on Stevie Ray Vaughan music. It was sultry and sexy, perfect for dancing and fucking. I felt his gaze on me as I walked around in my high-heel sandals and booty shorts. I could see how much he wanted me.

"God, you're so sexy!" he said.

"Sway your hips for me just slightly, and then pull your shorts down just a little bit. Let me see you move like that."

I liked him telling me what turned him on and being his sex object. He sat on the sofa, leaned back, legs spread wide apart, ready for his performance. At first I felt a little shy, so I closed my eyes and felt myself as one with the music. I moved my body to the beat, very slowly. He sat back and admired me. Blues rock seemed the ultimate fucking music. *I want to fuck you slowly and deliciously to that* groove, I thought. I gyrated my hips slowly, while I looked at him. His eyes were fixated on my body. I pulled my shorts down over my hips ever so slightly and turned around and moved my ass in the way he told me it turned him on. I bent over like I had seen women do at strip clubs and pulled down my shorts. I turned around, and laughed. He smiled at me.

I walked over to him and straddled his leg. He held me tight while I ground on him, and in less than a minute our clothes were off and we were in the bed again fucking, making love, and just being two married people who had found pleasure, fun, lust, and sexual freedom for that one day. Then he drove me back to the airport.

On the flight home, I reflected on my wonderful weekend. I felt alive from our passionate sex that lasted for hours. I didn't have that with anyone, so I replayed in my mind the peak sex scenes from the weekend. I wanted that same good sex with my beloved husband. I wanted my husband to feel that same passion, interest, desire, and lust that Eliot had felt for me. I wanted my husband to kiss me passionately, to enjoy watching me strip, to moan hard for me when he came, to kiss me tenderly and to try new things in the bedroom. I no longer wanted the kind of sex we had. Back at home, I told Rick about my weekend.

"Honey, my weekend was amazing. Don't worry, I don't have feelings for Eliot," I told him.

"Great, that's good."

He didn't ask me anything. I don't think he really wanted to hear the details.

"I want with you what I had with Eliot. I want you to kiss me, to be hard for me, to look at me when we make love. I want to dance for you, to be desired by you, to have you lick my pussy, and to be hard."

He replied as he usually did. "Well, honey, sex is just not that important. I like what we have."

My heart sank. What could I do? I was so in love with this man, and yet so unhappy. Our sex life was frustrating. I couldn't express myself. I just couldn't bear being patient any longer. I had to call on my husband to be bigger, bolder, and to renew himself. I needed him to step it up. Then I just came out and said it.

"You're not a good lover. I'm bored with you sexually."

I left it up to him to figure out what to do about it. He left the room. He went into Christine's room, which doubled as the guest room while she was away at college, and he slammed the door. He didn't come out until the next morning. I understood. He needed space to digest the bombshell I had laid on him. I really didn't care what he did at that point. I loved him and I wanted him sexually more than anyone, but if all he had to offer was the kind of sex we had been having, I didn't want sex with him at all!

Over the next few days, the tension between us grew. My longing for merging passionately with a man had been awakened. My desire and longing to be back in that hotel room with Eliot, to get lost inside that man who held me with such passion, grew stronger. It wasn't about wanting to be with Eliot. I just wanted to feel the way I felt physically and emotionally when I was with him. What I really wanted was that same intense sexual intimacy with Rick.

I felt sad about what I wanted and did not have. Songs on the radio spoke to my longing. I was lost in world of blandness. Before my trip, I was happy and cried occasionally over Rick, but after my trip I was sad pretty much all the time and cried often. I felt completely powerless over my longing and sadness. Everything I usually did to improve my mood was not working: changing my thoughts and feelings, affirmations, a workout, talking with friends. I dealt with my bottomless sadness by pushing it away and talking with my best friends Mindy and Mary.

Rick saw my sadness and longing, and he mistakenly thought I wanted Eliot romantically. He became jealous, and pulled out our book on open relationships. He went straight to the chapter on jealousy.

Rick stepped it up. He became interested in being closer and improving our sex life. He put more effort into pleasing me. I felt happy once again. That Friday evening, we lay on the bed and talked for hours, sipping chamomile tea and feeling the fullness of our togetherness. I found the courage to tell Rick something I had never told him in all of the years of our marriage.

"Honey, did you know I was a call girl in college?"

I waited anxiously for his reply.

"I've known all along," he said while we were still in bed sipping on our tea. "It was in the newspaper when you were arrested."

What was a relief! I had been afraid our entire marriage of mentioning it, because I thought Rick would disrespect me if he knew. Such a big weight was lifted off my shoulders when I saw he didn't mind. I felt happy and free, except for the sex part. If I could just get him to fuck me more often, life would have been perfect!

Our improved sex life lasted only a few days. Rick's erectile dysfunction was getting worse and his interest in sex fizzled along with it. He didn't care about his declining desire. I wanted more hot sex, while he wanted less. I asked Rick if I could see Eliot again. I had never cheated on Rick and I wasn't about to start!

"You need to leave him alone for a while, let him get his life moving again and get a girlfriend. After he has a girlfriend, then you can go back."

But Eliot didn't get a girlfriend. He seemed happy being alone and at peace all alone in his home, after so many years of arguing and nagging in his marriage.

I didn't want to keep waiting. I wanted Eliot and the passionate sex he offered. If my husband wouldn't give it to me, I deserved to get it elsewhere. I didn't care of the consequences.

"Rick, I'm going to have sex with other men, including Eliot, and I don't care if you like it."

Rick had never restricted my freedom or tried to control me, but he argued against the visit to Eliot. I insisted on my rights. Eventually he said I could fuck whomever I wanted as long as he did not know about it.

I wanted to try having sex with other men to see if I would fall for them as I had for Eliot. I also wanted to have sex with women again. I hadn't been with a woman in years. I liked touching small breasts and licking clits and giving women orgasms. I thought for the first time about having sex with other couples.

SHE LIKED WATCHING ME FUCK HER HUSBAND

I went to a lifestyle party for women, so I could meet potential sex partners. One of the women hosted the party at her home. We each brought an appetizer and a bottle of wine. The women were ages mid 20's to early 50's, professional, and friendly. I looked around for women I found attractive, to either approach individually or for a couple's experience. I also hoped to meet women that Rick might like.

Linda, a well-dressed large-breasted woman in her early 50's, asked me to sit next to her on the couch. I did not find her attractive at all. Linda and her husband Roger were looking for a unicorn. She wanted to watch her husband fuck me, and since I was "fresh meat", she made sure to get first dibs on me. When I got home, I talked to Rick about my plans and asked for permission to hook up with them. The lifestyle term was "hall pass", meaning I had permission to 'play' alone.

The afternoon of our dinner date Linda sent me a text message. *"Be a good girl and wear something sexy for us"*. Their directions turned me on. I liked their flirtation with me, and that they took charge by telling me what to wear.

I met Linda and Roger at a restaurant in Encinitas. I wasn't attracted to either of them, but was hungry for new sexual experiences. At dinner, Linda sat close, and flirted provocatively. We talked about sexual experiences.

"It takes me a long time to come," I admitted.

"How long?" she asked.

"Probably 15-20 minutes, but it can be much faster or take even longer, depending on how turned on I am. How long does it take for you?"

"I didn't come fast until I met Roger. He gives me multiple orgasms, within minutes. He's so good in bed!"

She beamed at him. I wanted to find out if he could do that for me. They invited me to their house the following weekend.

"Take her shopping and buy her something sexy," Roger told his wife.

The next weekend I went over. Linda drove us to the sex boutique and I selected several outfits to try. Linda came in the dressing room with me and watched as I tried on the outfits. She bought two of the outfits for me. Back at their house, I changed into the bra/garter ensemble while she slipped into a short body stocking.

We did all that for her husband Roger. She was totally in love with him. I was just their toy, there for him to fuck, and for her to watch. They asked if I wanted to smoke pot with them. I didn't do drugs, so they smoked alone. (About two years later, I got a medical marijuana card and started smoking pot at bedtime.)

We went into their upstairs sex room. It was a small room with a queen size mattress, dim lighting, and red satin sheets. I undressed, and he immediately fingered me quickly and hard, trying to make me squirt.

"That doesn't feel good. It feels sharp and like I have to pee," I told him.

"Just relax, it's supposed to feel that way," he said.

"No, I just don't like it," I told him.

He stopped and they left to smoke more pot. When they came back, he said he could fuck me for hours. I really didn't want him fucking me at all, let alone for hours.

I stayed because I was hungry for knowledge of what my body could do, and curious about the imagined sexual prowess these swingers had, and what they could teach me. He tried to get hard but couldn't, so he went down on me. It didn't feel good, so I asked him to stop.

"I want Linda to go down on me," I said.

Linda took his place between my legs and licked me in the most pleasurable way. I was sure if she kept that up for 10-15 minutes, I would come. But then after a couple minutes she stopped. I didn't know if he asked her to stop, or if she really didn't like licking my pussy. Wasn't she bi? I was disappointed she stopped. I was horny and wanted to come, so I stroked my clit. While I masturbated, he kept saying "pussy", which turned me off and made it impossible for me to come. The word "pussy" meant vagina, and anything put in my vagina didn't get me off. If he'd talked about my clit instead, he probably would have had more success. I didn't like him enough to tell him that.

They left to smoke more pot. When they came back, he wanted to fuck me again. He asked me to get him hard. Why wasn't he hard already? I sucked his cock but I couldn't get him hard enough for intercourse. He stroked himself until he was partially erect, and then he fucked me doggy style while she watched and walked around us from various angles and took pictures. I found it amusing that she wasn't jealous at all and instead was taking pictures. Then they took another pot break.

After several hours and no orgasms for anyone, they suggested bringing out the sex toys. Linda went upstairs to get a basket of vibrators and dildos. They put a condom on each toy.

Roger said Linda and I ought to play together while he watched. She brought out a double-ended dildo and we used it together. She inserted the larger end inside her and the smaller end in me. She rocked rhythmically so we would each get vaginal penetration. It didn't feel good at all. She started moaning. Her moans sounded fake, as if she were moaning to try to turn me on. I wasn't turned on by it at all. In fact, I felt more pressured to have an orgasm making it even less likely. I noticed he stood at the doorway watching us. His gaze didn't turn me on either. I was disappointed that these sex experts couldn't get me to orgasm. By the time I left, it was 10 pm, we'd had sex for at least 4 of the 6 hours and none of us had climaxed. They would have their orgasms after I left, for they had their own story plotted out. As for me, I would have rather fucked my husband, and I was disappointed I hooked up with a couple and never got to do any oral sex with the woman. I made myself a mental note that from then on, I wouldn't have sex with couples if the woman was straight. To make sure she was bi, I would make out or have sex with the woman first, and if she was responsive and got turned on, then we would bring in the guy. I never saw them again.

HE GOT TURNED ON WATCHING ME MASTURBATE

That couples date had been a disappointment. I set up more dates with couples and single men. My goal was to find out if I got attached to other men as I had to Eliot, and to see if anyone could make me climax. So far, the answer to both questions was *no*. I kept looking.

I searched on the lifestyle website for attractive single men, and I met Larry, a single man in his late 30's. He and his ex girlfriend had been in the lifestyle for many years. We met for coffee one evening. I didn't feel attracted to him romantically or sexually. But I wanted to explore and he seemed sexually experienced. I asked him if I could come over, and he agreed.

At his home, he spoke matter-of-factly.

"How would you like to have sex? What do you want to do, what positions or how to start?" he asked.

I didn't know what to say at first. It felt like a business transaction. I thought he would kiss me and just start doing something impressive and take charge in some way.

"Well, I like intercourse and I like oral sex," I told him.

Larry nodded in agreement and walked closer and leaned over to kiss me. He stood far away from me and his lips were too soft and I didn't enjoy his kiss. I debated whether being there was even a good idea. I decided to stay to find out what could happen next.

We went upstairs, took off our own clothes and lay on his bed. It didn't seem romantic or sexy at all. I had imagined I would be turned on enough that we'd tear our clothes off each other. He had shaved his pubic hair, and it reminded me of a goat. Why would a man shave his pubic hair? I later found out it had become common sometime since the time I got married almost 25 years earlier.

Larry went down on me. His tongue was rough, and he used too much pressure. I thought of telling him to use a gentler touch, and I didn't because I was curious how the rougher touch would feel and if eventually it would feel better. I assumed other women liked it that way, so maybe I could like it also. I endured his oral sex for about ten minutes.

"Hey, why don't you get a condom?" I asked.

I had no idea if he was relieved he could stop or whether he liked it. He put on the condom and we fucked, but he didn't feel as good inside me as Eliot or Rick.

"How do you usually come? I want you to come first," he said.

"I masturbate to come," I told him.

His eyes lit up. I had been masturbating in front of men since I was in my late teens so I was quite comfortable doing so for him. I masturbated lying on my back with my head on the pillows, using my fingers to rub my clit, while he sat at the foot of the bed to get a good view. I liked that he was sitting with a clear view of my pussy. Being watched masturbating was my one and only masturbation fantasy. He looked turned on watching me. His eyes glanced across my entire body, from my face to my moving fingers on my clit. I thought he could be pretending to like it. In my reality, a man did not enjoy watching a woman masturbate, simply because my husband had not enjoyed watching me do that.

"Do you like watching women masturbate?" I asked.

"Yes. I love it! It's very sexy!" he exclaimed.

He sounded like he meant it. I believed him. I didn't know a man could be turned on watching me masturbate, because my husband Rick appeared bored with it. He would lay with eyes closed next to me when I masturbated. When I had asked him why he was not turned on by it, he said "Honey, I've known you for 30 years. You're old hat." He meant I was familiar to him. He didn't mean to hurt me. He was just being honest. Sexually, I just felt like an imposition, like I was just taking up his time and he was doing me a favor by being there. It would take me longer to come when he was there than when I was alone. I didn't feel loved or nurtured sexually when I felt like I was work. Here with Larry, we were just two people not even feeling any attraction for each other and yet he was turned on.

Larry's interest in my masturbation was turning me on, and I came in only ten minutes, a fraction of the time it usually took. Would Larry still be turned on watching the same woman masturbate year after year, and was I expecting too much of Rick? Most of all I wondered why at the age of 51, I was still asking these questions. I ought to know! And if I didn't know my body and men's responses to it, there must be many other women my age who didn't know theirs either. It seemed ironic that I was so sexual all my life, so educated, and lived in a highly open sexual age, yet knew so little about sexual interactions and my body.

I was ready to go home. However, it was only fair that he got an orgasm also. He said he wanted a blowjob. I gave great blowjobs and I figured he'd come in a few minutes and then I could finally leave. I started out slow, and then sucked more vigorously on his penis while I stuck my finger in his ass. He spread his legs so I could put my finger inside. After ten minutes, he still hadn't come. My jaw was sore and I wished it could all be over. I doubled down, used my hand more than my mouth, and kept going until he finally came. It dawned on me then that all the lifestyle men

I'd been with had trouble having an orgasm. I really wasn't sure why.

"Wow, that was great, especially with you licking my ass and sticking your finger in it," he told me.

Larry got bonus points from me for enjoying watching me masturbate and that he cared if I had an orgasm, so I considered seeing him for something else I wanted to explore.

"I've been interested in trying more anal," I told him.

"Yeah, that would be awesome, I love anal," he said.

"I think because you have that slender cock, it would go in easily and not hurt, so you'd be a good person to do that with.

I'd tried anal sex only three times: once when I was 20 years old with a boyfriend, and twice in the past year with my husband. I liked anal sex when it was done right, without hurting during entry.

Then I got dressed and left to go home. I wanted to tell Rick all about my encounter with Larry, but Rick wasn't really interested in the details. The only detail I told him was that Larry hadn't been able to make me come either.

Would I develop feelings for Larry as I had for Eliot? I did not. As the week wore on, and we emailed each other a couple times and became friends on Facebook, I decided I really didn't want to see him again. The possibility of trying anal sex with him wasn't appealing anymore and wouldn't be reason enough to go back.

I was also pretty sure I was done exploring men sexually for a while. My biggest sexual question was whether another person could give me an orgasm, and I already knew every man I had been with in the past 25 years (my husband and the men I had sex with during our swinging) could not.

Maybe a woman could make me come. I remembered how Zoe gave me an orgasm each of the half dozen times she went down on me. I remembered how much I loved her, and how much I loved to please a woman sexually.

I started to dream of having a girlfriend. I pictured a woman who was a friend and with whom I could explore sensuality and sexuality. I imagined going places with my girlfriend, holding hands, or just hanging out.

I would ensure my marital relationship stayed strong and I had two ideas of how to accomplish that. First, I could keep the girlfriend relationship mostly physical so I wouldn't develop feelings for her. I knew how to separate sex and love. My husband had taught me how. Just two years earlier, he had first told me that sex is only physical. At first I didn't believe he was serious and I was hurt. I made love to him, and my mind and feelings were just as important as my body. Then I saw that for him, sex was really only physical. It seemed people had a choice about putting emotion into sex. Swingers, certainly, made sex just physical. I thought I could have sex like that too.

Or, I could somehow deepen my connection with my husband while I formed a more intimate bond with her, so that my marriage had at least equal emotional attention and would stay strong. I would be sensual and intimate with her and not get attached, because I was in love with my husband.

I was sure an outsider would have wondered why I needed a girlfriend on the side if I was really in love with my husband. The truth was, as much as he turned me on and I couldn't get enough of him, I was sexually and emotionally deeply dissatisfied. I yearned for more closeness, romance, lovemaking, and sex that nourished my heart. I wanted to linger in bed in the morning with my lover and cuddle, make love to romantic music, walk together holding hands, and care about pleasing each other sexually and emotionally. I wanted to be with someone who cared about my pleasure and if I had an orgasm. I wanted all that without replacing my husband with another man.

I thought I could get all that sex and passion from a woman. Besides, I was sexually attracted to women. I loved giving women oral sex, and I thought I could do it for hours. I knew many women were not into oral sex, so I was hoping to find someone who really liked having it done. It had been 20 years since I last went down on a woman and I wanted to do it again so badly. I wanted to feel her clit on my tongue, I wanted to arouse her and make her orgasm, and I wanted her to do it to me.

I set about to find a woman for sex. First I looked for women on the lifestyle site. The few women who interested me did not want to meet me for sex, either because they were not attracted to me, but usually because they only wanted sex that also involved their husbands. The lifestyle seemed more catered to couple swapping and threesomes. I turned to online dating sites. Rick didn't mind at all. Maybe he was glad I was planning to meet some of my sexual needs elsewhere, and that would take the pressure off him.

MY SEXUAL RIGHTS

Rick and I kept attending swinger events. Rick's flirting skills improved and he attracted the attention of a beautiful 51-yr old divorcee, Nancy. Nancy and I had formed our own friendship at the sex parties, so I didn't feel jealous or left out. Rick told me he and Nancy sent each other sexy texts. He was getting more turned on by this texting, and he and I were having more sex. They set up a dinner date and invited me to join them. At dinner, I saw she reached her hand under the table and rubbed Rick's leg while she looked at him and smiled. That was a bold move I probably wouldn't have dared to make and it turned me on. I looked at Rick and he was smiling too. Then she leaned over and kissed him briefly. I loved sitting across the table from her, watching her flirt and want my husband. I hoped this would lead to them having a sex date. However, a few days afterward, their budding interest fizzled out, and they never saw each other again.

I thought I was done with men, but a few days later, my heart and body ached to see Eliot again. Rick didn't want me to, but I didn't care. My need to explore my sexuality and feelings were stronger than my interest in monogamy or his feelings. I was on a growth journey and I felt unstoppable. I was a woman, not someone's property. I had sexual rights. If my husband wasn't interested in my need for sexual connection, he ought to let me get those needs met elsewhere.

Of all the men I had sex with so far, I liked sex with Eliot the best because it was hot and also because he was a friend. Since we lived several states apart, we didn't see a way to easily get together. We decided maybe we could see each other the following month. I wanted to get Rick's permission, but was determined to go even without that.

"Honey, I really want to have sex with Eliot again and with other men," I told him one morning.

"No. You could fall for one of them," he replied.

"Well, we're going to swinger events and you're having sex with other women and I want to do that also. I'm going to. I don't care what you say!"

"Well, let me think about it," he finally said.

Rick had always given me my freedom. He didn't control people. I knew the only reason he had to think about it was because he was in love with me and didn't want to lose me. Rick's half permission to let me have sex with other men made me feel it was okay to keep emailing with Eliot. We wrote to each other about my marriage, sex, and his possible dating.

"I think I have a hall pass again," I wrote to Eliot.

Eliot said Rick might agree out of love for me, and not really want me to go. That was probably true. As long as he said yes, I really didn't care if he really meant it. I was getting fed up with not being able to express myself sexually with my partner. And yet I still loved him.

It was odd wanting two men at once. I had never felt that before. Maybe I had never given myself permission to want or feel that. I wanted both Eliot and Rick. I was reminded of the song 'Torn Between Two Lovers'. I wondered why the singer didn't realize she could love two men at once, like I did. I liked my friend Eliot for the closeness and hot sex, and I was in love with my husband Rick. Maybe I was polyamorous. I had seen a TV show about polyamory, being in love and relationship with more than one person at the same time. I had read a book on open relationships to explore that possibility and get tips on dealing with jealousy.

Perhaps my relationship with Eliot would blossom, and I would have him and Rick as lovers, or maybe someday he and I would be together. It didn't seem so far-fetched. I wasn't sure if seeing him again was a good idea, because I didn't want to get attached to him if he didn't feel the same way.

I called Eliot.

"By the way, after I came back from seeing you, I was so sad, I was crying for about a week. I don't know if I want to put myself through that again."

"Yes, we had a good time, but I'm busy now with work and the kids. Maybe I'll come out to San Diego in a few months."

It was clear he wasn't going to interfere in my marriage, and would limit our relationship in scope. I was glad to know where I stood.

Rick finally agreed to the hall pass, and I had permission to have sex with anyone at any time. Rick just wanted me home at night. I told my two closest friends everything that was happening, and how I felt. I needed to open up to someone and talk it all out. To everyone else, I hid the disappointments in my marriage.

I portrayed to the outside world that my life with Rick was happy, because I so much wanted it to be. I was also embarrassed to admit to others what an utter failure my sex life was. I

didn't want anyone pointing at me and mocking me for not having the same good sex that I thought everyone else was having.
So whenever our relationship was going really well, and I felt
good about him and us, I would post it on Facebook, and when
it wasn't going well, I said nothing to anyone. And sometimes
our sex sessions were very satisfying, especially when I was in
a very good strong mood and able to overlook all that I wasn't
getting.

PARK RANGER CATCHES ME WITH A WOMAN IN BACK OF MY TOYOTA SIENNA

I still fantasized about a girlfriend on the side, a woman to go out
with, and have sex with, someone to give me what he couldn't. I
opened an account on match.com.

I sent a message to an attractive blond haired 43-year old woman named Erica. She replied and said meeting for a hookup was
something new for her. She asked many questions about my history
with women, my relationship with my husband, if I had any children, how long I lived in San Diego, and what I was looking for. I
thought those were a lot of questions for a hookup, however I wanted to answer them. I wanted to talk to someone about my desire
for women. I wrote her back and told her *I love to please a woman
sexually*. She wrote back that I made her Wet, and that she loved
men but mostly she wanted their sisters or wives. Fucking hot!

She texted me a picture of her beautiful round plump breasts.
Her hand pushed down inside her pants, with the caption *This is
what I'm doing now*. I wanted my hand inside her pants. *I can help
you with that*, I messaged back. She wrote about the rhythm of our
hearts and rubbing clits together and it didn't matter how long it
took for anyone to come, and how she could come just looking in
my eyes. It sounded erotic and sensual and exactly what I wanted.
I thought she would be able to please me in a way a man could not,

because I wouldn't think she was rushing me. I would feel relaxed, knowing she was enjoying herself. We set up a coffee date for a few days later.

She was seated on a leather sofa at the back of the café. She greeted me with a beaming smile and a hug. I was stunned by her beauty. She had blond curly hair just past her shoulders. She wore a white blouse, a deep red scarf draped across her shoulders, and tight jeans. I sat down next to her. She faced me, and just smiled. I really liked her. She kept touching my arms as we talked. I liked her touch. She suggested we order our coffees, and we walked up together to order. I felt sexy and excited to be in public with a beautiful lesbian woman. We took our coffees back to the sofa and talked. She went to the bathroom and when she returned, she wanted to leave.

"Let's go for a drive," she suggested.

We walked out to my minivan and as soon as we got in the car, she leaned over to kiss me. I kissed her back. She was so soft and smelled so good! I wanted her alone with her clothes off in a bed.

"Let's get a hotel," I suggested.

"Oh, let's just drive," she insisted.

She gave me directions to a nearby park. It was close to dusk and the park was already closed, so we parked in the parking lot, which was still open. I pulled over to the edge of the lot and we started kissing again. I wished we had been in a hotel room.

"Let's get in the back seat!" Erica suggested.

"Sure!" I replied.

I wasn't sure what she had in mind and why we weren't at a hotel. We jumped to the rear most seat of my minivan. Our kisses grew stronger and we pressed our bodies close. She kissed my neck and lips. My panties were damp with excitement. I so much wanted to go down on her, to smell and taste her pussy, and feel her clit under my tongue. I thought as the lesbian woman she would take my clothes off first, but I unbuttoned her blouse first.

She wore a lacy black bra. I pulled up her bra and saw her round full breasts with pink nipples. I sucked gently on her nipples, and I moaned because I was so turned on doing it. She moaned too. I licked her nipples more, and together we removed her blouse and I unbuttoned her pants.

"I'm on my period," she said.

"I don't care," I told her.

I was too turned on. We slid off her pants. I was surprised, and very happy, that she let me. I myself would have been reluctant to let anyone go down on me during my period, because I would be concerned about the iron-like smell of blood. I kissed her on the lips, and on her breasts, and then worked my way down to between her legs.

Erica spread her legs and let me do as I wished with her body. Her pubic hair was shaved. I kissed her pubic mound and outer lips, and pressed my lips against her vulva and my tongue on her clitoris. So smelled so sweet, she was so soft. I couldn't tell she was on her period. She had probably washed up in the café restroom.

I licked her clit and sucked on her inner lips. I moved my tongue all around. She breathed hard and moved her hips up and down. Ahh! Licking her clit made mine throb. As I kept licking her clit, I felt it swell under my tongue.

And then she got hard…and harder…all the while I was getting aroused and wet and my own clit was hard too. I flicked my tongue sideways over the hard ridge of her clit. Her breathing got heavier. Her legs shook and trembled, she got wetter, and I could tell she was close to coming. Her moaning increased and grew louder; she breathed harder and moaned rhythmically as she heaved her hips. I licked her with determination to an orgasm as her moans filled the car. I stayed right on that same spot through her orgasm until she pulled away.

After she came, her kissed her sweet vulva lips and I looked up and saw her content happy smile. And then I sat next to her and we held each other. I didn't have romantic feelings for her, and I was sure she didn't have feelings for me either. I was horny and anxious for her to go down on me.

I took off my pants and fell back comfortably on the back seat. Erica knelt on the floor, and it started feeling good, but not spectacular. I closed my eyes and tried to get into it more, I couldn't. I looked down at Erica, with her thick mane of curly blond hair between my legs. Although her technique wasn't that great, looking at a woman between my legs turned me on. I leaned back and let myself enjoy the pleasure. Sometimes I opened my eyes and saw a woman and all that blond hair between my legs and it turned me on. I was stuck though in my arousal. It wasn't building, and I knew I couldn't come. I wasn't sure if there was something wrong with me or if she didn't have good technique. It was close to dark outside and cold in the car. I was very turned on and wanted nothing more than to come and relieve the pressure. I was wondering if I should just masturbate to finish myself off.

A flashlight shone in the car windows.

"You need to move your car, we are closing the park," a loud voice said.

We looked out the window, and saw a park ranger.

We looked at each other in part excitement, part worry. I hadn't been caught making out in a car since high school.

"Oh my gosh, are we going to get a ticket?" I cried out.

"Would the charge be indecent exposure in public?" Erica laughed.

"I can't believe he came over here!"

We ducked so he wouldn't see us naked. I wondered if he was turned on seeing two women naked making out in the back of a minivan. Maybe that would prevent him from giving us a ticket.

"Let's get dressed!" Erica was looking around for her clothes.

"Where's my underwear?" I asked.

I rummaged in the dark through piles of clothes on the floor. I was still so horny and disappointed that my oral session was interrupted.

I peered out the window. The ranger and flashlight had moved away from my car. His back was to us, and he probably waited for us to leave. It didn't look like he was writing up a ticket. We scrambled in the dark to find our clothes and get dressed. Then we drove off. The ranger stood there until we were gone. All I had on my mind was wanting an orgasm.

"I'm so horny. I just want to come!" I told her.

"I know," she said. "Just drive around and let's find another place to park."

We drove around and pulled into the far end of a parking lot at a community park. We got in the back seat. Erica leaned back against the side of the car, and I got on top of her, and leaned back. I pulled down my pants and masturbated as she held me. I was aroused yet my masturbation wasn't building into an orgasm. I couldn't see her, kiss her, or touch her, and when I opened my eyes I was looking straight ahead at a parking lot. I closed my eyes and started fantasizing. Then I remembered we were in a parking lot and worried someone might find us there. Any outside thoughts interfered with my buildup to climax. It took me a long time to come. It felt like work. After I did, we lay there like that for a few minutes. Then I drove her back to her car.

Driving home, I wondered why this woman hadn't been able to make me come, why I could make her come, and why it took me so long to have an orgasm. Was it her technique? Was I really that difficult to get off? Maybe I wasn't turned on by women after all, or maybe only by some women?

When I got home, I was excited to tell Rick all about my crazy adventure and the park ranger.

"Honey, I'm home!" I yelled out to Rick when I got back.

"Did you have a good time?" he asked.

"Yeah! But the park ranger caught us!" I told him.

"Seriously? " Rick was laughing.

"Yeah, and I went down on her even though she had her period and I got her off really good," I told him.

"What? You went down on her when she had her period?" Rick was shocked.

"Yeah, I couldn't even tell. She tasted sweet and it really turned me on going down on her. But she couldn't make me come!" I told him.

"Hmmm…maybe you need to try again. Honey, you need to go to a hotel room and spend the whole day with her making out, have some coffee, then make out some more," Rick said.

I was really happy that Rick shared in my enthusiasm and that I had married a man who was secure in himself and supported whatever made me happy.

Erica e-mailed me the next day to say what she liked about our encounter. She said it was hot, that I was lusty and went for what I wanted, and that I was about to discover the rich world of lesbian sex and relationships. However, I didn't have that same sense of awe and getting lost in a woman that she seemed to describe. I was definitely interested in seeing her again and having more oral sex, new sexual experiences, and maybe some tenderness and sensuality between us that I hadn't had with Rick.

After some back-and-forth planning and some cancelled dates on her part, I met Erica at a hotel. She was watching porn on her laptop when I arrived. I had suggested the site, which featured high-definition close-ups of women masturbating to orgasm. Their clits and pussies pulsed, and they moaned and grimaced when they came. I could tell it was real, and so could Erica. She was extremely turned on. She closed up her laptop and I sat down on the bed.

I wasn't feeling as turned on by Erica anymore, because she had been so back-and-forth about when and where to meet, and she seemed pre-occupied with her new job situation and not really present with me. I didn't feel a connection with her. The only reason I stayed in that hotel room with her was my curiosity about being with a woman and what else I could experience. I gave her an orgasm going down on her, just as I had done in the car a few days earlier.

She went down on me. It felt good but not amazing. After about 15 minutes she stopped.

"It's taking you too long to come," she said.

I felt very hurt. Her words fed my sexual insecurity that I was not sexually responsive. I didn't want to let my feelings break the mood.

"Really? I have a thing about that, because my husband tells me I take too long."

"Well, that's your issue and that's on you," she said. And she came up to lie next to me.

I was really surprised, because I thought of women as giving and thought they loved giving oral. I didn't expect her to have a time limit. I was also hurt, but decided she just didn't have a great capacity for giving and she wasn't very good at oral, which were all her problems, so I pushed my hurt away.

"Here, I'll just masturbate," I suggested.

And I masturbated while she held me. There was nothing romantic or sexy about the way we did it. After we were finished with sex, we went out to dinner. We talked about our fantasies. She wanted to talk about men and penises.

"I love men. My best friends are men. But a penis has as much use for me as turmeric. I don't like turmeric," she explained. "I asked one of my friends to jack off in front of me once, and it didn't turn me on at all. When he ejaculated, I thought it was gross," she continued.

Then she told me she wanted a man to watch her fuck a woman. She and her previous girlfriend had talked this over often and had almost done it once.

I thought about whether I wanted a man watching me with a woman and if that would turn me on. I knew I didn't want Rick watching me with Erica or with any woman, because I was tender with women and I didn't want my husband to see that part of me. He liked his sex quick and he didn't do it tender and slow, so I felt weak and embarrassed around him to show that part of me.

After dinner, I drove her back to the hotel. She didn't ask me to spend the night, and I didn't want to. So my search for a girl-friend was still on.

WE COUPLE SWAP

We went to our last swinger party on New Year's Eve 2012. A couple I'd never seen caught my attention. Tim, a handsome, dark-haired man in his early 40's, strode across the dance floor followed by Krista, a slender red-head in her early 30's, who wore a long dress and choker necklace. She exuded sexual energy in every step of her swaying hips and dreamy eyes. They walked up to the big bedroom. I waited a few minutes, and then followed them in to watch. Over a dozen naked bodies were fucking on the bed. Tim held an attractive older woman, probably in her early 60's, on his lap. He bounced her up and down slowly on his penis, as they gazed in each other's eyes. I was surprised that a young man could connect so intensely with a woman so much older. Their eye contact during intercourse made me wet and aroused. Krista was in the middle of the bed, surrounded by naked bodies, and moaned loudly while riding a cock. She seemed like she was in the middle of an orgasm. Tim didn't seem to mind that she was having so much pleasure with another man's cock.

I watched a few minutes and returned to the main room. I sat on the sofa and watched people on the dance floor and stripper pole. A little later, Tim came downstairs and sat next to me.

"I really enjoyed watching you with that older woman. You made such an intense connection with her," I told him.

"Yes, she was quite erotic."

"Is your girlfriend bi?"

"Ask her."

Just then, Krista came downstairs and sat between us on the sofa.

"Are you bi?" I asked her.

She looked me straight in the eyes. "Yes, I am."

She looked so beautiful sitting there. She told me they were from Virginia, and traveling through the country.

"We just went online to find out what to do for New Year's Eve, and we found this event, so here we are. We're only in town for three days," she told me.

I leaned forward to kiss her. Her lips felt soft, and kissing her made me wet. I pushed my body into hers and kissed her harder. She responded likewise. She breathed heavier and moaned softly, and she leaned forward into me. She was definitely bi. I looked up to see if Tim minded, or if he expected to be included. He was just watching the dancers. Rick came and sat on the other side of me.

"Can we go in a room?" I asked Krista.

"Sure," she said in a soft voice, as she looked me in the eyes.

She turned to her boyfriend. "Tim, we're going in a room. You guys can come later if you want."

Tim nodded in agreement. Krista took me by the hand and led me across the dance floor, through the kitchen, and down the hallway to an empty bedroom with a massage table. We kissed each other and took off our clothes. She was stunning. She had white skin and small breasts and a lean body. I liked her confidence and that she didn't need her man to be there, and that she just went off with me. I liked her more than any of the women I'd been with so far. She lay down on the massage table, and I kneeled on the floor, licking her pussy. She smelled sweet. Her vulva was beautiful, and her vaginal opening was barely noticeable. It was small and tight, just like those of other women who had not given birth. But she had given birth. I found out later she gave birth by C-section. I was curious to someday see a pussy of a woman who gave vaginal birth and how her vagina and pussy looked, because I thought mine was ugly after giving birth. My vaginal opening was stretched open a little. No man had complained about it, but I was insecure about it.

I had barely been licking her, when the men, came in. I was still sure I wouldn't be removing my panties for Tim. I wasn't that attracted to him.

"I don't want to kiss you or have you fuck me, but I'll give you a blow job," I told Tim.

"Sure, that's fine," he said.

I liked that he was just going with the flow. Rick put on a condom so he could have intercourse with Krista.

"Stay standing," I told Tim.

I knelt on the ground and gave him a blowjob. A minute into it, he looked down at me and said, "Hey, let's watch them!"

I was thrilled!

"Yeah, I'd love to," I said.

Finally! A couple that knew couple swapping was hotter if we could watch our partners give and receive pleasure!

I watched Krista lay on her back on that massage table, writhing and moving, as Rick stood at the edge of the table and penetrated her deeply. She looked at him longingly with those faraway eyes, moaning, writhing, moaning louder, and apparently having many orgasms from it. I had never seen anyone look so beautiful or move so lustily during intercourse! They noticed we were watching. I went back to sucking Tim's cock. I felt a warm rush of liquid in the back of my throat. I looked up at him as he finished coming. Krista was smiling at her boyfriend, so she and Rick took a break. I was curious about all her moaning she had done while Rick fucked her.

"Do you have orgasms from intercourse?" I asked.

"Yes!"

I was envious and at the same time hoped she could give me some tips on how I could do that. If I could have vaginal orgasms I could climax during intercourse, an activity that I could do with my man, and not have to rely on masturbation or oral sex, which seemed boring and tedious for a man to do or observe.

"How do you move like that during intercourse, how do you know how to move?"

"I just do what feels good. I just let go, and feel my body, and I move the way it feels good," she explained.

"Well, don't you have to move in a way the guy likes too? Rick doesn't like me on top, because it doesn't feel good, so I move the way he likes it." I told her.

"Oh don't do that. Don't worry about what the guy likes. Just move how you like. Be selfish."

Wow. I had never thought of that. I didn't have to move the way a man liked. I could do what I wanted. I couldn't wait to try that out. I wondered what intercourse would feel like, if I just moved how I wanted!

"How did you learn to look at people like that? Your eyes and your gaze are so sexy and seductive!" I told her.

"Oh, Tim taught me that," she said laughing. "He taught me the importance of eye contact and luring my lover in."

Krista turned to Rick. "Do you want a blowjob?"

"Yes!" He replied eagerly.

She took my husband's cock deep in her throat, all the way down. She sucked him and sucked him, and Rick's head was bent back in ecstasy. Finally he let out a loud roar as he came in her mouth.

"Oh my god, that was the best blowjob of my life!" he yelled out.

My heart dropped into my stomach. I was furious and extremely jealous! I couldn't believe he had said it. Even if it were true, which it apparently was, did he have to say it like that in front of me? I'd never be able to compete. I had tried deep throating in my youth and had gagged on the penises. I didn't want to do anything sexually that was painful or uncomfortable or made me gag. I'd written off deep throating as something I'd never have to do because Rick loved my blowjobs. My reality was shattered. To give him the best blowjobs, I would need to deep throat going forward. I didn't want to learn to deep throat.

Mostly, I was jealous and hurt. I fought back tears, and could barely talk to anyone, as I got dressed. I didn't want the others to know I was jealous. We had to walk through the large living room to get to the front door. I braced myself. All eyes were on the four of us, as the swingers gauged how good our encounter in the room had been. I fought hard to keep back my disappointment and tears. I wanted to pretend it had been a good time.

In the car, I let Rick have it.

"How could you be so insensitive? I am sooo jealous!" I yelled.

"Oh honey, I'm so sorry, I'll make it up to you," he said. "Listen, when we get home, I'll go down on you until you come."

That was a nice offer and it settled me down. By the time we got home it was about 3 a.m. and Rick kept his word. He went down on me, for 45 minutes. However, he couldn't make me come. In fact, I couldn't remember the last time he had made me come.

Despite my jealousy over the blowjob, we had connected very well with Tim and Krista, and we all wanted to have more sex. Krista mesmerized Rick. Over he next three days, Rick and I met up again with Tim and Krista. Then they continued their cross-country vacation. I stayed friends with them afterward.

In mid-January, Rick told me he was done swinging. He said he didn't like the person he had become. I understood what he meant. The constant search for new sexual encounters and the titillating pictures on the lifestyle site left us constantly horny and looking for something outside ourselves. We deleted our profile on the lifestyle site. But my sexual energy, desire, and hunger for more experiences were as big as ever.

I began to question both my own and society's rules and expectations regarding sex. How free were we sexually as a society? I had so many questions.

Women seemed to hold back from sex due to social pressure, not due to a lower desire than men. It had been a challenge for me and Rick to find women for sex, yet women were just as horny as men. Prior to meeting swingers, I believed men preferred women who had 'saved' themselves, women who were 'good girls' and who did not sleep around with multiple partners. Were women just ashamed to own their sexual power, or why were they less likely to hookup with people they didn't know?

I questioned monogamy. Why did most people believe they could love only one person? I had feelings for all my lovers, and yet I stayed in love with my husband. My husband wasn't jealous of me going out, as long as I slept in his bed at night. He felt secure in our relationship. Why didn't more couples open up their marriage? Could a relationship sustain an open marriage long term?

I questioned lesbians and their sexual know-how. The best girl-girl sex I had in my life was with bisexual women, not lesbians.

I was still in love with Rick. On the two days a week he worked from home, I went into work late so he and I could talk at home or walk on the beach. We had a favorite spot at the end of Wisconsin Avenue in south Oceanside, a section of beach with large rocks. I liked to climb down and sit on the rocks. We both laughed when I was splashed by the incoming tide.

I started playing piano again. We had our family dinners with Wilson. When Rick came home late from work, I waited so I could eat with him. I just loved being with him and how he made me laugh.

Our sexual relationship, however often left me in tears. Rick still gave me frequent '*no's* for sex. In fact, for his birthday gift, I told him he we would not have sex that day, and he was happy with the gift. We had sex with intercourse about 2-3 times a week, however the quality was declining rapidly. Rick's ED was getting worse so his erections were softer and I could barely feel his penis. He no longer woke up with erections, and on some mornings he couldn't get hard at all, regardless of what he or I tried. I wanted more connection, but I was getting less. Even when we did have intercourse, for me it was always over too fast.

I asked Eliot, my friend in Denver, if he still wanted to get together, and what he was thinking in terms of logistics. Eliot waited three months from our first encounter, and then flew out to San Diego for the weekend. I was concerned about developing more longings, or even feelings, for him. Although he was attentive and passionate, and our sex was beautiful and hot, I did not get attached. Sex wasn't just about orgasms, but mine had become a source of curiosity. I had wondered if he could make me come the second time, but he couldn't. I masturbated to come. I wondered if any man could make me come. I drove him to the airport, and when he got out of the car, I wasn't sad at all. But then, over the next few days, my memories of his hard cock grew stronger and I dreamed of riding him and our next rendezvous. Damn. What happened in the space of a few days that made me want someone more?

One evening, my friend Mary and I had plans to attend a meeting for meditators at the Transcendental Meditation (TM) Center in Encinitas. I was glad to finally have a friend who also meditated. Just as I was leaving the house, Mary called.

"Hey, Schahrzad, let's forget about the TM Center and go to the polyamory potluck meetup group instead!"

Mary laughed. She sounded playful.

"Sure, let's go!" I said.

The event was held at Kamala Devi McClure's house in Pacific Beach. Kamala Devi was a nationally known polyamory spokesperson I had seen on a cable TV show about polyamory. The small living room was filled with about 30 people. She instructed us to do some group exercises involving eye gazing, which I found very uncomfortable. A man sat across from me, and we sat and looked each other in the eye. I wanted to smile or run away, but I stayed and did it.

Kamala Devi's primary partner was the father of her young son. They both had a variety of other men and women in close relationships. She stood up and talked to us.

"We have 11 lovers in our pod, and at our next meeting, we will discuss adding another person. Everyone practices poly differently, but one of our best practices is to only add lovers that are enhancing to the previously existing ones."

She and her lovers all practiced yoga, meditation, self-growth, and authentic communication, so their lifestyle had a much more alluring charm than just the random hookups I had seen with the swingers. Mary and I were totally intrigued by it.

I had questions for Kamala Devi. She lay on the sofa with a woman in a non-sexual embrace.

"Kamala Devi, can I ask you a question," I asked.

"Yes," she smiled at me.

"Rick thinks I will love him less when I have other lovers. Is that true?" I asked.

"That's a limiting belief," she said matter-of-factly.

"Wow, I love that. But he gets jealous. What can he do?" I asked her.

"Give attention to your existing partner in proportion to the attention you are giving your new partner," she advised.

"I have another question. I had sex with my high school friend's husband after she died."

I wondered what she would say.

She smiled. "That makes sense. And what a beautiful way to honor the memory of your friend!"

CHAPTER 7

"DO PEOPLE EVER LEAVE A MARRIAGE AFTER 25 YEARS?"

I was crying over Rick more frequently. I was almost in despair. Why didn't he want me? Fortunately, I had my monthly dinner with Mindy that week. I told her everything. Usually we were both happy, and sometimes one of us was sad over a guy. That evening, we were both crying over a man. Between sobs, I laughed at our situation.

"Gosh, we have such bad timing, to both be crying over men at the same time and not able to comfort each other," I said between sobs.

"Yeah," she almost broke into a smile and went back to sobbing.

As we sat and talked, a thought popped in my head.

"Do people ever leave a marriage after 25 years?"

I couldn't believe the words came out of my mouth.

"Yes, they do.

I gave her words some consideration.

"Well, how would I support myself if I lived on my own?" I asked.

I had a job, but I didn't work enough hours to pay my own rent and support myself.

"Your life will be different, but you will still have a life," she answered. "Maybe you will live in an apartment instead of a house. Maybe you will live in a cheaper part of town."

That didn't sound appealing at all, and I didn't give it any further thought.

"I'M SO TIRED OF BEING TOLD 'NO'"

A few days later, I was getting coffee with a friend at the Starbucks in my old neighborhood. I ran into my former neighbor Greg. I had been friendly with his wife Rachel, and had not seen either of them in years. Greg looked upset.

"Are you okay?" I asked.

He looked at me. It seemed he debated whether to tell me anything. My friend went to use her phone.

"I'm so tired of being told '*no*'," he said. His face looked tense and he shook his head side to side.

"She keeps refusing to have sex with me!"

His eyes were downcast. He looked so sad and vulnerable. So other people had sexually unhappy marriages too? Why was he telling me that? I barely knew him.

"I'm so sorry," I said.

"And when we do have sex, she constantly asks if I'm done yet or says '*hurry up, hurry up*'. You know, that's what it must be like to get a hooker."

He looked at me. My heart broke for him. I thought back to my session with the marriage counselor, at a time I thought I lost my sex drive.

"Does she masturbate?" I asked.

"I don't know," he replied.

"What? You don't know if she masturbates?"

"No, I don't know. I don't see her do it," he replied.

"Well, does she like women? Is she gay?" I asked

"No, I don't think so."

"Gosh, I'm so sorry Greg.   Rick tells me '*no*' all the time and I'm tired of it too."

"She has no emotion during sex. She just lies there telling me to hurry up. Damn, she won't even let me go down on her. I just want to please her so much. And she doesn't go down on me at all, not ever."

"Is she Catholic?"

"No, she grew up in the conservative South though. And when we do have sex, she leaves her clothes on. I'm just tired of the constant rejection."

"Wow, I'm so sorry. Why do you put up with it?"

"Have you seen my wife? She's gorgeous!"

His mouth broke into a smile. He was obviously smitten.

How could be so in love with her, when she was so cold to him, telling him to hurry up while he was making love to her? Was he was a selfish lover? If so, why didn't she tell him? Maybe she didn't know how to change it? Maybe she was how I had been many years before, when I said nothing? Surely a counselor could help.

"Have you guys gone to marriage counseling?"

"She won't go."

"Oh, that sucks. Rick tells me no all the time. I lay there in bed wanting him, and he tells me no. He won't kiss me, he won't go down on me, and he gets off quick and leaves me lying there. I cry over him a lot." I told Greg everything.

"I'm really sorry," he empathized.

From that day on, his words kept ringing in my head every day: "I'm so tired of being told 'no'". I didn't know anyone else shared the same pain I did: in love with my spouse who kept telling me no to sex, and just being fed up with it.

"I am so tired of being told *no*. I'm so tired of being told *no*. I'm so tired of being told *no*."

Besides being tired of being told no, I was also getting more tired of many aspects of my sex life: Rick's worsening erectile dysfunction and his quickies, getting my orgasms only from masturbating, coming last every time, and no kissing. I questioned my sexual attraction to men. I'd had sex with several men besides Rick, and none of the men had given me an orgasm with their hands, mouth, or penis. What if I just didn't like men in some deep down way?

I dedicated more time to finding a girlfriend on match.com. I spruced up my profile. I had a sassy face shot and a tag line "Need some girl-girl time". My profile started with: *Ferociously bi and, please don't hold this against me you beautiful lesbian women, I am also married....*

I was only interested in lesbian women, and I knew some lesbians thought bi people just couldn't make up their mind. I felt really encouraged after getting a message from a 42-year old lesbian who liked my openness and said *bi chicks are hot.* I liked her acceptance and view of bi women. She gave me too much credit. I wasn't turned on by women in the same way as I was by men. Few women turned me on, and being with a woman was mostly about sex and possibly friendship.

I FINALLY GET GOOD ORAL, AND IT'S NOT FROM MY HUSBAND

I looked through the profiles and was immediately attracted to Sarah, a fit attractive 51-year old professional woman. She looked a little masculine, and had thin lips, and both were a big turn on. We met for lunch. She was nervous about meeting me, and her hands were shaky. She was also nervous because she found some coworkers seated nearby, and she didn't want to be seen on a date with a woman. Lesbians still hid their identity in 2014? I asked about her last relationship.

"I was married for 20 years to a woman," she told me. "I had artificial insemination and gave birth to two girls and a boy, and my wife adopted them."

I had never known a lesbian couple and loved getting a glimpse inside her life.

"Why did it end?" I asked.

"My wife lost interest in sex. We slept in separate rooms the last six years of our relationship. "

"Wow. My husband and I also slept in separate rooms for about that long too. Why did you stay so long?"

"For the children. But I have a high sex drive and I'm always horny, so I finally decided enough is enough and I left her two years ago."

"Wow, that's the same reason I left my marriage too! Good for you!"

"I haven't had sex since I left her," she told me. Her voice was still shaky.

All in all, she hadn't had any sex in eight years, and she was really turned on, so I could see why she was so nervous.

"What? Why not?" I was shocked.

"I didn't want to sleep around, and I was also self conscious about the weight I gained from the pregnancies. I've been working out and eating better, and now I'm fit and confident, and ready to get out there and date, and voila, you're my first date." She smiled at me.

"Well, you look great!" I told her. She did.

She invited me over, and we went straight to her bedroom and started kissing. I could feel myself very wet. Her breathing deepened as we kissed.

"I want you to go down on me," I almost begged her.

I pressed my hips closer to her body.

"I can't wait to taste you," she said.

She looked at me and I noticed her pupils were dilated. I wondered how wet she was and if she could make me come. We undressed. Her lips brushed my neck, then my nipples and she slowly made her way down my body. By then I was really wet and my clit was throbbing.

I shuddered when her tongue brushed my thighs. I wanted her tongue on my clit, but she didn't go straight there. She licked and sucked on my outer and inner lips, which showed me she definitely liked pussy.

Her tongue hit my clit and I gasped. She innately had the gentle touch that brought me to orgasm. She licked my clit so gently, just the way I liked. As her tongue circled my clit, I could feel the pleasure and intensity kept increasing, more and more, and my moans grew louder. The more I moaned, the more excited she got. She moaned and panted so hard, that I looked up, and I saw she was sweaty and her hair was stuck to her forehead. I wasn't used to seeing women turned on and aroused like that, but I realized right then that my partner's arousal was a key for me being able to come.

As soon as I saw how turned on she was, I relaxed mentally and my orgasm started building from deep inside me. I heard my breathing get deeper and heavier, and then I could feel an orgasm was imminent. Sarah flicked her tongue lightly on my clit, just teasing the orgasm out of me. It felt like my clit swelled up to reach her tongue, and then I exploded into a deep long intense orgasm that lasted for almost 30 seconds.

"Oh my God, thank you so much!! That's the first time anyone has made me come in about 20 years!"

She smiled. I felt giddy inside from my new experience and I was thankful to her for putting in all that effort to do it. I looked at Sarah. Her hair was matted to her sweaty forehead. I had been a lot of work or she was very excited or both.

"Wow, that was amazing, I can't believe you made me come going down on me."

I didn't recall if Rick ever gave me an orgasm from oral sex. I remembered one boyfriend in college made me come from oral sex, but I didn't recall if anyone else ever did.

I couldn't wait to give her the same pleasure.

"Lie down."

She lay on her back. I went straight to her pussy and I saw how wet she was. Soaking wet. I was good at oral. I made every woman I was ever with come from it. Going down on her wasn't as much of a turn-on after I had already come, but I did it for the fairness and the challenge. I used a gentle touch on all women. I always heard different women like different things, but I never had anyone complain about my gentle touch and all women came from it. As Sarah's breathing became deeper and steady, rhythmic, I licked my tongue mostly on the ridge of her clit, and stayed in one spot. I knew she liked it because her breathing got heavier. She was so sexy as she got turned on. Her legs shook, and I knew she was close to coming. And then she came and moaned loud and pulled away from my mouth.

I lay on top of her and kissed her on the forehead.

"What we did was so beautiful! We each just gave each other an experience that got us all lit up. More women should have casual sex!" I told her.

Why could she make me come but others could not? Was I sexually more turned on by a woman, and why? Could a man ever get me to orgasm? Was I unusually good at oral sex, because every time I performed oral sex on a woman, she had an orgasm?

I was so thrilled about my oral sex orgasm, I had a second date with her. She invited me over. As she made our coffee, we talked about our dating.

"I met someone. I can't see you after today." She blushed and smiled. I could tell she really liked that woman. Why did she have me over then?

She continued. "She and I haven't progressed to kissing yet, but I'm horny, so I'm definitely wanting sex with you today."

That time we had sex in her living room, and it felt like it was just physical. I wasn't emotionally or mentally attracted to her, and the sex seemed boring because we just took turns going down on each other. I didn't care that we wouldn't see each other again.

I called Sarah one year later, and she said she was still with that woman and they were totally in love.

FELL MADLY FOR JENNA

I went back online. That's when I met Jenna. I got a message when she marked me as a 'favorite'. When I saw her profile picture, I felt a warm rush in my body and my heart skipped a beat. *Damn, she's fucking hot!*

She was the type of lesbian that turned me on immensely, but was rare to find: beautiful, sporty, androgynous, slender, 5'10", with dark hair. She wore a baseball cap backwards. She was 49 years old and lived in Los Angeles.

I was immediately smitten and sent her a message.

Hi Jenna, you're so hot. I can't wait to meet you.

She replied the next day.

I'm just looking for something casual. I will be in San Diego soon and stay at a hotel downtown. I will let you know.

It was cold and rainy the day she finally came to San Diego, about two weeks later. She combined our date with visiting some friends who lived here. She texted me when she arrived, told me I could park in the garage across from her hotel, and suggested two restaurants for dinner. I liked that she took charge and knew of good places to eat, even though she was from out of town. I could just relax into the date.

"Are you staying the night?" the parking attendant asked when I pulled into the garage.

"If I get lucky," I replied and laughed.

His eyes grew wide. I liked getting reactions from people just by saying what was actually on my mind.

I texted Jenna '*here*', and walked across the street to the hotel.

When I entered the lobby, a slim brunette walked briskly towards me. It was she. My heart raced. I was stunned by her beauty and strong determined walk. Her strong shoulders, energetic walk, and stylish clothes were huge turn-ons. She had it all. She wore a heavy black leather jacket, jeans, and walking shoes. Her brown shiny hair fell just past her shoulders. She definitely looked like a lesbian. As we approached each other she smiled and said, "Hi. Let's go."

I kept looking at her as we walked. *God, she's so fucking beautiful and sexy!* She opened the door for me, and guided me on our walk a few blocks to the restaurant. She put her hand on my back to move me past oncoming pedestrians. I liked her energetic gait and how she guided me.

We talked as we walked through the cold blustery evening. At the restaurant, she walked up to the hostess and announced her name. I stood back and watched her take charge. I felt safe and cared for. When I went out with Rick, I made the restaurant reservations and walked up to the hostess. Having someone take charge like Jenna did was a turn on. I got excited thinking that the people around us imagined what might be between us sexually.

She teased me about my online screen name as we followed the hostess to our table.

"Megan, huh?"

I smiled. At the table, she pulled out her phone and put on a pair of stylish reading glasses. I watched her across the table, mesmerized by her beauty and style. She looked like a hot executive as she messaged someone on her phone and read the menu. She was a woman who looked like a woman, yet acted like a man. The waitress came to get our drink order. I ordered red wine, and Jenna ordered scotch. A beautiful woman ordering scotch was the sexiest thing ever! A sense of awe overtook me. *She's sexy as fuck, a woman who acts like a man!* I looked at her with the same wonder and admiration I had previously felt for handsome successful businessmen. I wondered how she would be in bed. Would she love going down on me? How would she kiss?

"My girlfriend left me," she said, and looked right at me.

Just like that. She just admitted it. They had been together for 14 years, and a few months earlier, the woman had just left. Jenna told me she was devastated by the breakup. I couldn't see it in her face. She hid her emotions well.

"Wow, I'm sorry." I didn't know what to say.

"I did everything for her," she told me, and looked right at me. She must have sensed I was wondering if she'd do everything for me too, so she laid that to rest.

"I'll never do that again."

"How is it being single?" I asked.

"It was very difficult at first, and now I'm happy again. I'm very busy and I don't want a relationship."

I admired her for being so happy as a single woman. I loved being in my relationship with Rick. Would I be so happy if I were single?

"I love to watch porn of women masturbating. I'd love to sit across from you in a chair and have you watch me do that," I told her.

She took a drink of her scotch.

"I don't watch porn."

I took that as she didn't watch porn and she didn't want to watch me masturbate, and then I didn't want to tell her more fantasies.

She told me about her math degree and her work in commercial real estate. She loved the L.A. Lakers basketball team, had 'pretty good seats" and went to most of the games. I imagined going to a basketball game with her. The idea turned me on. I had never been to a sports game because I really wasn't into sports. I would definitely go with her! We ordered our meals, and enjoyed our food as we continued talking easily.

The waitress brought the check and put it in front of Jenna. Usually a waitress puts the check in the middle. Jenna had an air of authority and the waitress treated her as the person in charge. Jenna paid our bill. It turned me on that she was like the man, and I couldn't wait to get back to the hotel room.

We quickly walked back to the hotel through the cold and drizzling rain. In the room, I walked over the window to look out at the downtown lights. Jenna walked over to me, and leaned over for a kiss. I kissed her back. Her kiss was ordinary. It didn't turn me on, so I was a little disappointed, but I was curious about what would happen next. Somehow we kept kissing and fumbled off our clothes and eventually we ended up in that large soft bed that took up most of the small room.

She sat on the bed, and took off all her Indian rudraksha beads on her wrists and a long strand of deep blue lapis lazuli beads around her neck. I had not noticed them before. My heart beat a few harder beats, I felt hot, and my head felt light. I was familiar with meditation and Indian prayer beads, and had rarely seen anyone wearing them outside a meditation retreat. I had never been with a lover who was interested in meditation. I imagined myself wearing Indian beads and meditating with her. She placed all her beads on the nightstand, then came closer and kissed me again. We fumbled out of our clothes, got under the sheets and lay next to each other, hungrily kissing.

"Do you like strap-ons?" she asked.

Her question took my by surprise. Why would we need a strap-on? If I wanted penetration, I'd be with a man! I hadn't thought about using a strap-on with a woman. Wouldn't women want clitoral stimulation? If they wanted vaginal penetration, wouldn't they get a man? I didn't know what a strap-on or vaginal penetration could do for me.

"No, I don't want a strap-on. Penises are overrated."

The words just came out of my mouth. I surprised myself with those words. Did I really not like penises? I liked men, but penises didn't give me orgasms and they didn't stay hard long enough and they moved too fast and they didn't always feel good and many penises were out for themselves and their own pleasure and they had let me down. I wanted a different kind of sex: pleasure we gave each other to our clitoris. There was no need for any penises or penetration.

"I didn't expect that from you," she said in an upbeat voice. She seemed pleased. "I brought some strap-ons, but we won't use them."

She motioned toward her overnight bag in the closet. Then she kissed me again. She pressed her hand on my pubic mound, while she massaged my labia with her fingers. The whole time, she looked me in the eyes. It felt good! As she massaged my labia, she watched me as if I were her little toy. Her face was right up against mine, her eyes open, looking right at me. I was a little uncomfortable kissing someone with eyes open, but I was willing to experiment. I looked at her beautiful face, with its smooth skin, her brown eyes, her hair thrown softly around her face. She didn't have any wrinkles, which was surprising for her age of 49. I wondered if she had a procedure done. Whatever it was, it worked. She was gorgeous!

I leaned closer to kiss her. Her lips were tender and gentle, yet I could feel her strength in them. I kissed her deeply and took in all of her strength, and I got lost. My tongue merged with hers and I didn't want to stop kissing. I nibbled on her soft lips that became one with mine. Where did my lips end, and hers start? I didn't recall ever having felt so satisfied just with kissing.

She responded to my passion with fervor. I didn't know I liked kissing so much! I had never kissed like that, nor did I know how much kissing aroused me physically and emotionally. A new door was opened. I experienced the pleasure of kissing for the first time in years, with someone who liked it too. My body felt warm and my heart was full and happy.

We kept rolling around in that bed, and we couldn't stop kissing. She lay on me and rubbed her clit on my pubic bone. She was getting more and more turned on, rubbing harder and harder. My pubic bone felt sore and I wanted to move away, but I liked her and didn't want to make her stop what was giving her so much pleasure. She ground harder. Damn, she was strong! I was a little scared for a few seconds. I almost thought I had a man in that bed. I remembered she lifted weights and trained for marathons. Her grinding was making my pubic bone hurt a lot. I almost wanted to cry. I wanted to tell her, but I did not want to kill the mood. I decided we'd have a talk later about what we each liked, and for now I'd just endure it. Mostly, I was curious how this would go, and what she would do next. She stopped the grinding and lay down next to me.

She put two fingers in me, deep inside. She moved them in, out, slowly and sensuously, then a little deeper with each thrust. I was extremely wet. My whimper turned into a moan. She stretched her fingers apart in a v shape, in and out slowly, until I picked up a tempo of my own and pushed up my hips to get all of her inside me, as deeply as I could.

"Deeper, go deeper, deep, deep," I begged. "More, more more…."

I kissed her hard and pushed my tongue deep in her mouth with the same vigor she used to stick her fingers up my cunt. My moans were loud, I felt like an animal, I wanted to be fucked so deeply and have it never end. It felt good, or maybe even better, than a penis. I had never been finger fucked so well in my entire life!

Finger-fucking me turned her on also. She lifted me up and turned me on my stomach and fucked me doggy style, then she moved me facing her, all the while kissing and/or finger fucking me. She was strong and I felt a little scared by how she basically tossed me around on that bed, but I just let her do it. I was barely aware of her. I just felt my body and I got lost in myself. I caught my breath and I looked at her, at her beautiful brown eyes, intently on me, as she fucked me harder and deeper.

Jenna slid her fingers in my pussy and held them in place. I wrapped my legs around her. With her other arm, she reached behind my back and lifted me up. I was afraid I would fall backwards, so when I was halfway up I leaned back on my hands. She wanted me to let go so she could pull me all the way up. I hesitated. She held me tightly and firmly and gently looked me in the eyes.

"I've got you," she said.

I've got you.

"I don't know, I'm afraid to let go," I said.

"I've got you," she repeated.

The words *I've got you* rang into my heart. Those words were about her providing me with the security to let myself be vulnerable, not knowing what came next and just letting go and trusting. Mentally it excited me.

I let go and surrendered to her and trusted her to hold me. I let go of my hands and she pulled me all the way up so I straddled her. I looked her right in the eyes and wrapped my arms around her back. Her fingers inside me felt so pleasurable I didn't know why I ever needed a penis. I moved my hips up and down on her fingers. I felt like I was in a far away land, the pleasure was so intense. I leaned backwards and looked down. I saw her two fingers inside me were spread wide apart, and I moved my hips to let her fingers slip in and out. I rode her, sometimes looking at her, just getting more and more turned on. My moaning was turning her on madly, so she said, "that does it", and she lifted me up, carried me over to the wet bar, sat me down, and finger-fucked me in earnest. I was in a faraway mental zone, lost in pleasure, barely aware of my surroundings.

I just let her fuck me, just fuck me with pure pleasure. My back bumped against some glasses, I think, because I heard clanking. The clanking glasses took her out of her zone, because she slowed down a bit and carried me back to the bed.

I wanted to taste her and run my tongue all along and around her clitoris. I wanted to slide my tongue inside her and just feel her vulva all over with my tongue and mouth.

"Can I go down on you?" I asked.

"Yes."

She had long curly brown pubic hair, lots of it. It was sexy as hell. She tasted sweet. I licked her clit in many different ways, and at the end, I focused on the ridge, which was getting harder, and the knob, which was harder still, until she had an orgasm. Then I moved up and lay on her while we kissed.

"Will you go down on me?" I asked.

At first she hesitated.

"I don't know where you've been," she said.

But then she did it. I expected to be taken to new heights. A lesbian woman who had been in relationships ought to be a master at oral sex. She started to lick around my labia in places that didn't feel so good and she used too much pressure. She was horrible at oral sex! It didn't feel good at all, and after about two minutes she stopped and rolled on her back and looked at the ceiling.

"My neck hurts," she said.

That sounded final. She didn't replace her tongue with her fingers. She just lay there. What kind of lesbian was she? I wondered how she thought I, or any woman she was with, would come if she was going to stop after two minutes. The penetration wasn't doing it, and she couldn't do oral long enough. How would I have an orgasm with this woman? Back to the same old standby that bored me so much: taking responsibility for my own orgasm. There had to be a better way, but I wasn't sure what it was.

I reverted back to what I knew: masturbating. It's not what I wanted, but I tried to make the best of the situation. I lay next to her, and she watched me the entire time I masturbated. At times we kissed, other times I'd stop and close my eyes. I couldn't get turned on enough to come fast, and my arousal was not building. She lay there next to me and watched me, but that didn't arouse me. If she'd moved down to my hips and watched my fingers or said something hot or done something, it would have helped. She seemed really set on doing what she wanted, so I didn't feel comfortable asking her to move or do what I wanted. She had already indicated she would not watch porn with me. I closed my eyes and fantasized about someone watching me. I felt my orgasm building, so I opened my eyes to look at her just as I was coming. She was looking at me too.

We kissed for a long time and held each other. Her sweet kisses pulled me into a faraway land. I couldn't stop looking at her, and kissing her. The sex wasn't perfect, but I thought we could talk about it and improve on the parts I didn't like. I thought about whether she and I would start dating, and whether she could be the girlfriend on the side I wanted.

"I like being in a relationship," I said.

"All women like being in a relationship."

"But you don't."

She didn't answer.

We started kissing again and I was horny and wanted to have sex again, yet at the same time I was satiated and sleepy and simply too tired.

I looked at the clock. It was 2 a.m. I had to get home. Rick had told me I could have sex with other people as long as I came home to sleep. I always came home. But at that moment, I didn't care what Rick wanted. I wanted Jenna. I wanted to let that sleepy feeling overcome me while I was wrapped in her arms. Would she want me to stay?

"I'm supposed to go home to sleep, but I don't care what my husband thinks. I'm tired and I want to sleep with you."

"You can sleep here. You can use my toothbrush," she offered.

I was happy she wanted me to stay. I left in my contacts, and I fell asleep in the warm bed with the soft sheets and white down comforter, holding Jenna, the beautiful lesbian who fucked me like a guy. Throughout the night and every time I woke up, I snuggled up next to Jenna and kissed her. She kissed me back. I didn't worry about waking her. I wanted to kiss her and I felt welcome to do so. I thought ahead of how the next morning would go. Maybe we'd go walk around the harbor? That's what Rick would have wanted to do. He would have wanted to get up and go out and explore, and I would have been left in that bed feeling alone and wanting him. I dreaded the morning, thinking she would want to get up and walk around the harbor, and I wouldn't be able to kiss her anymore. I drifted back to sleep.

I woke at sunrise and saw her stretch her arms above her head.

"Do you want to get up?" I asked.

"And do what?" She kept lying there, all beautiful and relaxed.

My heart felt warm and my mind raced with all the possibilities. She was going to stay in that bed with me! Maybe we could cuddle and have more sex. I wanted to go lick her pussy again and started to move down on her body.

I thought she would offer to wash up before I went down on her. She didn't. I was a little worried she might smell or taste badly and that I wouldn't like her anymore if she did. I licked my tongue all around her vulva. She tasted as sweet as she had the night before! I inhaled. She smelled sweet too. Why did Rick ask me to wash up in the morning before going down on me? Jenna was proof that women's pussies were sweet and beautiful, and not some nasty dirty thing that needed to be constantly scrubbed and washed.

She came quickly. After she came, she fingered me for a short time and then she stopped probably because she wasn't turned on anymore and we both knew the fingering wouldn't make me come. She didn't offer to do anything to make me come.

"I'll masturbate," I said.

She didn't say anything. She lay next to me, and she watched me as she had done the night before. I was disappointed that our sex was so predictable again. But then she kissed me, and I was happy. We held each other for a little while, and got dressed.

"I'll go downstairs and get coffee. It will taste better than making it in the room," she said.

"Wow, thanks. Just don't get too close to people in the elevator, unless you want to turn them on. Your hands smell like my pussy," I said, laughing.

She smiled and left to get our coffees. When she returned, she had a grin on her face.

"I remembered what you told me about my fingers smelling like pussy. I had just got on the elevator, when a couple came in with their two children. So I stood in the very corner of the elevator so they wouldn't get the smell of pussy." And she laughed.

We drank our coffee and talked. She held the cup by its body instead of with the handle, and for some reason that just seemed so lesbian and therefore turned me on. I decided I would try that at home.

"I better go," I told Jenna.

She insisted on walking me to my car.

When I got home, I was ready to defend my sleepover to Rick.

"It's okay you spent the night with her," he said.

I was relieved. Apparently, a woman didn't threaten him.

I texted Jenna when I got home. I suggested seeing each other in two weeks. She texted back to say she had a nice evening with me, and was glad everything worked out. She didn't say anything about seeing me.

I was miserable that night, lying in bed with Rick. It was the first time in years I did not want him. What I wanted was kissing and connection, a kind he had never provided. I thought about Jenna. How could I ever be in love with him again, when he wouldn't kiss me at all?

Over the next week, I replayed in my mind the highlights of my date with Jenna. I wanted to be with her again. I wanted to talk with her about spiritual things, go to a sport game, have sex and experiment sexually, and I didn't want to wait two weeks.

I texted her and asked to see her again. For two days, I didn't hear back from her. I kept checking my phone. Nothing. Then, I received a text from her. My heart raced. I thought she might want to see me again. I would have got in the car right then to drive to her house. But her text just said she had enjoyed my company and hoped I had a great week.

Oh. *Enjoyed your company, have a great week.* My chest felt heavy. She didn't say anything about me coming up there, or scheduling another trip to San Diego to see me. Why wouldn't she suggest seeing me again? She had enjoyed herself very much. I was puzzled. Perhaps she didn't know how much I liked or, or maybe she was afraid to be hurt again, and if so, then I could show her I was serious and she might trust me and let herself go. I battled the urge to text again or heaven forbid, call her. I didn't want to turn into some kind of stalker or desperate lovelorn woman. I knew I had to keep myself together. But I didn't *feel* together at all.

I kept going about my life as usual, working, meditating, grocery shopping, exercising, and dating. But I was less interested in Rick. I thought about Eliot's hard cock and riding him. I thought about Jenna's kisses and holding her close. Both of them had opened a new door and made me realize what was missing in my marriage.

A week later, I texted Jenna a naked picture. My heart jumped when I saw she replied. She wrote that she had just come home from the gym and my picture made her all hot. She said she needed a cold shower. She did not mention seeing me again.

A week later I sent Jenna another text to let her know how I felt. I hoped that would make her interested in seeing me again. My children responded to love, so if they weren't interested in doing something, I could get them to change their minds if I just kept inviting them and showing them love. I figured this worked for dating also. (It took me another year to learn that wasn't so.) I thought if she knew how much I wanted her, her heart would open and she'd want to see me again.

Jenna didn't reply. I longed for her more and more, for tenderness, being fucked deeply for a long time, and getting lost in kisses. I longed for how she made me think, and our conversations. And she ignored me. I fell into an embarrassing pit of longing and sadness.

How could I cry and be so sad over a woman I met only once? I struggled to make sense of my attachment and longing. Maybe I transferred my longing for connection with Rick, onto her. Was it because I admired her and wanted to be like her? Or was she just someone with whom I happened to have strong chemistry? Was it her kisses, which opened a new place in my heart?

I felt miserable and cried often. It seemed everything made me want her. I was still dating other women, but I really just wanted to be with her. Sometimes when a man chased a woman, he got her. Maybe I could get this woman too. I persisted. I sent her more texts. I wrote how I thought about her during the night, and *remembered how sweet it was to reach over and hold and kiss you.* Jenna didn't reply to that or other texts.

I kept looking for lesbians ages 40-52 online. I hoped to meet someone as enchanting as Jenna, who was equally interested in me. For women, I set my search radius to 200 miles, because usually I couldn't find attractive women in San Diego County. Physical attractiveness was important to me, and it seemed the most beautiful lesbians usually lived in Los Angeles. The lesbian population in San Diego was small, so there were few women to pick from. The number of lesbians on match.com in the 40-50 year old age range, in the zip code with a high gay population (North Park neighborhood), was ridiculously small. I counted the number of results:

Straight women	1,896
Lesbian women	64
Straight men	over 2,000
Gay men	264

But the biggest problem was that most lesbians in that age range were unattractive and overweight. They didn't seem to care about appearance; however single women in that same age group who were interested in men were very attractive. Gay men also kept up their fitness and appearance. It seemed that anyone wanting to attract women could let their appearance go, while anyone trying to gain a man's attention had to work to stay attractive.

Many of the women who responded online did not want to meet a married woman. I heard back from a Mexican Jewish girl who sweetly declined, and wrote she was looking for a good Jewish girl. A woman with the email handle named after a flower wrote me saying she didn't understand why I was still married if I obviously enjoyed sex with women. I heard back from a woman named Mary who seemed intrigued by both my bisexuality and my married status. *Might be kind of exciting*, she wrote.

I relaxed some of my criteria and arranged some coffee dates. On dates, I had a harder time relating to lesbians because our lifestyles were so different. Often they had not been married, and since there were no children they often had a series of shorter-term relationships. None of the women I met so far had children.

I met a few of the women for dates, including Mary. She was a beautiful 44-year-old lesbian, yet I felt no attraction for her. Over dinner, all I wanted to talk about were Rick and Jenna and my broken heart. It really wasn't fair to her. I was not dating material in the state I was in. I decided to stop meeting new women until I was not sad anymore.

I was still talking with Eliot, mostly about my marriage and dating. I also wanted his hard cock. He said I could come back to Denver for a weekend visit. I told Rick what I was doing and booked a flight.

Then, a text message came from Jenna. She said my persistence had paid off, and she could come see me the next weekend. I was ecstatic she wanted to see me again, but that weekend

I would be in Denver with Eliot. We set a date for two weeks away. I chuckled at my multiple lovers. I was married woman, setting up consecutive weekend rendezvous with a man and a woman. Which one would excite me more?

RENDEZVOUS IN DENVER

When I boarded the plane a few days later for Denver, I wished I could be with Jenna instead. During most of the flight, my thoughts lingered on Jenna and memories of our first and only time together. I longed to learn more about her androgynous lesbian lifestyle, hear her stories, and get lost in her soft skin and passionate lips, her fingers deep inside me.

I rented a car at the airport and drove to a hip new restaurant in town to meet Eliot for lunch. He arrived in his Land Rover just as I pulled in. He looked so handsome in his brown cashmere sweater. Over lunch, he kept me entertained with stories. I paid half the expenses, just as I had done before. I liked paying my own way, so I didn't feel like I owed anyone anything, especially in the bedroom. I also wanted him to know I was there because of him, not because he could pay for me or had more money.

After lunch we drove to the hotel. As soon as we walked into the room, he grabbed and kissed me. I started moaning right away. I was already lubricated. I wanted to fall into his strong body and get lost in his cock. He tore off my clothes and sat me down on the sofa, spread my legs wide, and licked my vulva and clit. It felt so good. I ran my hands through his hair and across his smoothly shaven face. He flicked his tongue lightly across my clit. I watched him pleasing me.

"Wow, that feels amazing!" I said.

He looked up. My pussy juices glistened on his lips.

"You taste delicious," he said.

He went back to enjoying my pussy. After a few minutes, I pulled him up and kissed him. We took off his clothes, and he sat down. I licked his scrotum and sucked his penis. I was glad he did not shave his pubic hair. He had a beautiful penis. I looked up at his strong body and hands. He still wore his wedding ring, and I wore mine. We were married friends, in our familiar roles. Except that we were having hot sex with each other.

I was really horny and just wanted to ride his cock. We didn't use a condom. He lay down on the bed and I took his cock inside me. Oh my god. Fuck. He was so hard! He felt soooo good! I moaned with each thrust and then he was all the way in. I moved up and down on his hard cock in the way it felt good to me. My moaning was louder. I didn't care if he liked it or not. It just came out of me. Shallow strokes, mid strokes, deep strokes, slower, faster....I used use his cock to make myself feel good. I remembered what Krista had told me that night at the swinger party, *don't worry about what the guy likes. Just move how you like.* I tried different angles and moved how I liked and figured he would just have to endure it although he wasn't complaining. I smiled at my humor. Fuck, if Rick could be that hard my life would be perfect! I wouldn't even be in Denver at all.

I just kept fucking him. I wanted him deep inside. He was thrusting from the bottom and sweating, and I was out of breath from pumping. And then I buried my face in his neck, wrapped my arms tightly around his upper back, and ground and swiveled my hips to feel his hard cock stroke me. I angled my hips in various angles to see what I liked and make it feel better. I bore down hard on his pelvis, taking him as deep inside me as I could. What was that delicious spot deep inside my pussy and why had I not discovered it before?

Rick stayed rock hard. I was impressed. I'd been riding him for at least ten minutes and he was still rock hard. I sat up and looked in his eyes and it turned me on. He was so handsome, so hard, so charming. Why didn't I have feelings for him? What was it about connections between people and this mysterious element of chemistry and attraction? I was glad I didn't have feelings.

I wanted to see his cock move in and out of my pussy. I shifted my weight from my left knee to my left foot, so both of us had a good view of my pussy and the base of his cock inside. I pumped up and down off my left leg and we both watched his cock slide in and out of my pussy. My long inner labia lips brushed his glistening cock with each thrust. I wondered if he could feel my lips wrapped around his cock. I didn't ask. It looked sexy as fuck though. I watched and pumped until my legs got tired, and then I lay on his chest.

He turned me over and entered me from behind, doggy style, my ass high up in the air. He thrust in me deliberately and slowly, not just for himself but also to give me pleasure. I was soaking wet. I was moaning so hard, I was sure the adjacent room guests could hear. I didn't care. I liked that I was free and making sounds out of my own pleasure. He flipped me over onto the missionary position, and fucked me while I was safely under his body.

In between his most pleasurable thrusts, Jenna would pop into my head. I wished I were with her instead. Then his pleasurable cock would bring me back to the moment. I liked the missionary position with him. That was the customary position that Rick and I preferred and I hadn't often done with other men

Eliot stopped thrusting, and went down on me. I liked that he liked doing it. I couldn't come from it though. My fantasizing didn't help, and then I felt guilty for closing my eyes and ignoring my lover. Eliot went down on me a long time, but I couldn't come. I told him I would masturbate to finish, and he played with my nipples while I rubbed my clit. The whole time he looked at me, and he sometimes kissed me. After my orgasm, we fucked more until he came.

We lay together afterward and talked. I was really curious about Eliot's sex life with my friend Paula, from his view. He had told me before the trip that I could ask him anything I wanted about his relationship with Paula. I loved her so much and I wanted to be part of their closeness and intimacy in a way I had not been let in before.

"I came home from work to the boys, not to her. She was usually still at work. When I heard the garage door open and I knew she was coming home, my stomach would sink. She always had something to criticize. I wanted to leave many years ago, but I stayed for the boys. "

"Why didn't you go to counseling?" I asked.

"I asked her about it a few times, but she smirked at me whenever I suggested it," he told me matter-of-factly.

I was curious about what happened behind closed doors in other couples' homes. Paula and I had not talked about their sex life, mostly because when I was younger I wasn't talking about sex. After we were both married I didn't want to talk about my boring sex life, and later when Rick and I were having sex and I wanted to talk about it, Paula would change the subject. All I knew was they didn't have sex often but she thought he was good in bed, and otherwise I really didn't know much about her sexually. I remembered wondering if I would find him good in bed too.

"Did you guys ever have sex?" I asked.

"Rarely. She rarely wanted sex. I resented her from all the years of criticism, so I just did not want her sexually anymore. When she came to bed and I knew she wanted sex, I usually pretended to be asleep."

"Really? Wow, why didn't you just say no to her like Rick does?" I wondered.

"I didn't want to deal with it. Then other times I would get her off and then roll over and go to sleep," he told me.

I was amazed what a good man he was, to get her off even though he didn't feel like it. He was the opposite of Rick. But maybe that was no better, since he did something he did not want to do. I definitely understood about the criticism and I knew my disdain for my husband over many years had separated us. I had also been around Eliot and Paula enough to see her criticize Eliot a lot, and she often complained about him for no reason.

"When he comes home from work, he just wants to go for a run, or watch the news. He should help me with the cooking or help the kids with their homework," she often complained.

"You're a stay at home mom, and your kids are in high school," I said.

She looked at me blankly. I understood. I had criticized my husband most of my marriage, while I was nice to everyone else. I knew other women who did not appreciate their loving husband who supported the family. I didn't have the answer on how love, passion, and wedding bliss turned into criticism, resentment, and avoiding each other in the bedroom.

"She did tell me you were awesome in bed," I said.

"Yeah, I knew how to get her off really well."

He told me a few intimate details of their sex life, and how they met and fell in love in their junior year in college. It made me feel so much closer to him, and to her. He seemed to enjoy recounting some of their happy times together.

"Do you want to go to dinner?" he asked.

I did. We dressed up and he took me to a nice restaurant. It felt like a real date, not just a fuck date. We ordered a cheese plate with eccentric honeys and mustard, and red wine. Then he drove me back to the hotel and went home. I didn't mind him leaving. I didn't feel that intense loss I felt after I parted from Jenna. Why was I attached to one, and not the other?

It was the last time Eliot and I hooked up. Our relationship returned to being platonic, which was mostly his choice. I was grateful. He lived far away, I was married, he had no interest in a relationship, and my attachment level was low. It didn't make sense to make anything more of it.

What I learned from Eliot was my love of fucking and hard cocks, and I saw for the first time clearly, what I didn't have in my marriage. It was okay if I never saw him again. He gave me a great gift.

After my weekend with Eliot, I didn't feel so sad over him. I still had my date with Jenna the following weekend. I was curious what it would be like to have sex with her, after having been with a man. Eliot's cock had felt so good. Would I still like sex with her?

KISSING HER

She stayed downtown at the same hotel. I texted her I arrived and waited for her at the elevator. I couldn't go up without a room key. I was nervous. An elevator came down. The doors opened, and she came out and just stood there.

My heart melted. She was so strong and beautiful. She wore yellow Abercrombie pants. Her shoulder-length curly hair rested on a stylish gray sweater. She stood at the elevator door and looked at me intently. She waited for me to come to her. It was such a confident move, and it turned me on.

I walked over to her and we got in the elevator and rode up.

"How was your day?" she asked.

"It was great. I had a really good run this morning. "

I didn't know what else to say.

She had a brisk gait. I liked her energy.

She opened the door to her room. Inside, I put down my belongings. I had brought some overnight items that time: toothbrush, contact solution, oil to give her a massage.

I sat in the chair. She lay on the bed, and propped her head on pillows.

"What sign are you?" she asked.

She cared about my sign. Did she want to consider whether we would make a good match for dating?

"Libra."

She didn't tell me if it meant anything.

"I have to get up early tomorrow to meet my friends for brunch."

Was she suggesting there would be no sleepover? I hoped she didn't mean it. I was sure she'd change her mind once we were snuggled up in bed together.

"I want to keep seeing you," I told her.

"But you're married," she said, and looked right at me to gauge my response. I wondered if she waited for me to say I wasn't planning to stay married. But I really was in love with Rick.

"My husband doesn't mind if I keep seeing you."

I wanted him, and I wanted her. I wanted them both. I contemplated if I would leave my husband for her. No, I wouldn't leave one person for another. That's what emotional people do. At most, I would leave him and move out and start dating her, see where it went. We talked about exercise, meditation, and relationships.

"What is the most important ingredient in a relationship?" she asked.

I thought for a long time. I liked that she made me think and that she asked for my opinion.

"A willingness to get along," I finally said.

"Respect," she said matter-of-factly. "I've thought about it a lot, and it's respect".

"Hmmm...I'll have to think about that."

I joined her on the bed and we kissed.

"Let's just get under the covers," I suggested.

We took off our clothes and snuggled under the warm down covers. We wrapped our arms around each other and kissed. I got lost in her again.

"What do you like about men?" she asked.

I liked her probing questions. I had not liked penises on our first date, but after all the good sex with Eliot, I liked penises. But I liked fingering just as much. What did I like about a man?

"I like their strength."

Yes, that was it. I liked their physical strength, their mental strength, and their emotional strength. I liked that they were more logical and less emotional, I liked the security and protection they provided. I liked the stories they told. I liked that they liked to go out into the world and be outdoors, start businesses, take risks, provide. Then I realized, Jenna had all that. She had enough male energy to be all that and it made me want her even more. She was man and woman, all in one.

We went back to kissing.

"I just love kissing you. You're like a drug," she said, rolling me around in bed.

She had never done drugs. She just hungered for my sweetness. The kissing left us wanting more and more. But besides kissing, the rest of the sex was mediocre. She came from being turned on by what she did to me, and what I did to her. It was one-sided. I wasn't going to come from what I did to her, and she wasn't giving me enough clitoral stimulation. I masturbated to come. After sex, we lingered in endless kisses, and I felt warm inside. I looked down at her beautiful face.

"You're such a beautiful lesbian, so obviously beautiful lesbian," I said to her lovingly, looking in her eyes.

Jenna covered her eyes with her hands and started to cry.

"What? People can tell I'm lesbian?" she sobbed.

"Yes, of course. You're beautiful!" I told her.

It had not occurred to me that she hid her lesbian identify. She was so obviously lesbian, that she had to see it too. Our society was still prejudiced against homosexuals? Really? Jenna wiped her tears away and we hugged and got lost in another kiss.

I still hoped I could spend the night. I had brought my toothbrush and contact solution, and was ready to brush my teeth and snuggle up to her.

"I have to get up early," she announced, signaling it was time for me to leave.

"I brought my overnight things in case you wanted me to stay," I said, still hoping she would ask me to stay.

"No, I have to get up early tomorrow." She stared at me intently, waiting for my reaction.

It was final. My chest felt heavy and my eyes teared up. She saw. "Are you okay?" she asked.

I wasn't sure. I got dressed, grabbed my purse, and slowly walked to the door. She kept looking me in the eyes as she walked me to the door. I turned around to face her.

"Yeah, I'm okay," I said through moist eyes.

"I'll walk you to your car," and she grabbed her jacket.

I fought back tears as we walked through the lobby, across the street to the parking garage, and up to my car. Why had she asked me to leave, when she had said kissing me was like a drug? At my car, she gave me a quick kiss and walked away. I watched her. My heart was breaking.

"Don't forget about me," I yelled out.

She stopped and turned around to look at me.

"How could I?" she said in a longing sensuous voice.

I messaged her a few days later and told her of my longing. I asked her about her plans to see me again. I wanted to know how she felt. She texted me back and said she didn't want a relationship.

I was devastated. I thought of telling her I just wanted sex and not a relationship but that wouldn't have been true. I didn't want her as a fuck buddy. I wanted her as a girlfriend. I wanted to snuggle with her and go to sports games.

I asked my friends for advice on how to feel happy again and forget about Jenna. Would pursuing her pay off? Or was pursuit like stalking? I had not dated in so long, I really didn't know dating rules. In my friendships I made over my life, it seemed our interest in each other was mutual. Was there something wrong with me to be interested in someone who was not interested in me? Was she not right for me? I decided to express my feelings and pursue her for a while.

"I'm going to send her flowers," I told my good friend Mary.

"Leave her alone," she said.

"But I want to express my longing and desire. I want to show feelings, not repress them. It's okay if she doesn't respond."

I sent flowers to her office. She didn't respond. A few weeks later, I called her. She didn't answer, so I left a voice mail message and told her I wanted to see her again. She didn't respond. I wondered if she liked me also, but resisted her desire because she did not want a relationship. If I pursued her, perhaps she would relent. But mostly I wanted to express my passion. I wanted to feel, to love, to connect, and to let someone know I was interested. If I didn't do that, wouldn't I be shutting down part of myself?

Jenna blocked me on Facebook and probably on her phone, and I never talked to her again.

I learned two important lessons from Jenna. First, I didn't want to be afraid of relationships, afraid to feel, and push people I liked away from me. I wanted to stay open. The other lesson was how much I loved kissing.

CHAPTER 8

ENOUGH IS ENOUGH

Rick and I ate dinner together by candlelight and were in bed at 9 p.m. as usual. Rick lay on his back reading a book. I wanted to be close to him. I snuggled up against him, and reached over to rub his stomach. That always turned me on. I started grinding a little against him. It just felt good to be close like that, just a little turned on. I wished he would want to make love to me, but I already knew he wouldn't since we had sex the day before and he liked to wait two to three days between our lovemaking.

"Not tonight. I don't want sex tonight."

He almost sounded mad. He was probably annoyed with me, for wanting sex again.

I had heard 'no' so many times. That night, I heard his *'no'* in a different way. It penetrated to my core, the area where I loved and protected myself. I felt a surge of confidence, boldness, and conviction. New thoughts popped in my head.

I have to take care of myself and move away from the longing and the pain. Get over to my side of the bed.

I turned away from him, and lay on my side of the bed.

I need to just stay here, protect myself from being turned on with nowhere to go.

I grabbed my pillow tightly under my head. That seemed a fine solution. And then it hit me.

I need to just stay here <u>permanently</u>.

For me to love and protect myself and avoid hearing 'no' again, I had to permanently stay on my side of the bed, and not ever try to get sex from him at all.

But then…. why even be in this bed?

The bed held no answers. It held only pain. I remembered my friend Greg, and his wife who always told him 'no'. His words rushed into my head. *"I'm so tired of being told no."* Damn it, I was fucking tired of being told "no"!!! I grabbed my pillow.

"I'm sleeping in the guest room."

I got up, stormed out of the bedroom, and slammed the door. Our daughter was still away at college in Iowa. I went into her bedroom and lay in her soft comfortable queen size bed. I fell asleep right away. He didn't come after me.

I woke up early the next morning to a bright beautiful bedroom. Sunlight beamed through the beach curtains and filled my room with light. I felt peaceful. I didn't miss him. I didn't want him. I was surprised! What happened? Was I really done with him? How long would I stay in this room? Would he come after me? What would the kids say? I didn't know.

I opened the windows and the ocean breeze blew the curtains around. I looked around that cheerful room, with the white bed, bright green desk, white nightstand, and oak wood floor. The walls were lined with pink bookshelves and memory boxes filled with colorful perfume bottles and glittering jewelry with large beads. The bedroom I shared with Rick was dark, with its dark carpet, dark bed, and rattan shades on the window, which blocked the light.

That morning I moved to my own rhythm. I did what I wanted and had stopped doing for Rick. I played my familiar Indian chanting music. I got up at 5:30 am, when I woke up, instead of laying in bed waiting for Rick to wake up.

When I came out of my room, I ran into Wilson. He looked puzzled.

"Mom, what are you doing?"

"I got mad at dad and I slept in Christine's room."

"O-kayyyy."

He looked at me for an explanation.

I didn't have an explanation.

"I'm tired of crying over dad," is all I could come up with.

I kept moving to my own rhythm, a rhythm I created. That night I was alone in my bedroom, alone in my bed. I noticed I didn't want him anymore. For the first time since that summer vacation three years before, I didn't want him. I wanted to be far away from him. What was I going to do next? I could stay in that bedroom for a few months, maybe a year, and just co-exist with him in that house. I loved that house. And I was financially dependent on him; I couldn't support myself on my job alone. My son was still at home and I didn't want to break up our family. I could stay in that bedroom. I just needed to find a new way to spend my evenings.

I turned to red wine and Netflix. I drank 2-3 glasses of wine every night and watched The L Word, a Showtime series featuring lesbian relationships, which had played all seasons. We didn't have cable TV, so I had never seen it. I was turned on watching all the hot sex scenes between lesbians. I didn't feel good about all that wine and movie watching, but I thought it was okay temporarily, to take my mind off leaving Rick.

The mood in our house was about the same, except for the awkwardness of Rick and me tiptoeing around each other and not interacting. I called our two other kids the next day to let them know I had left their father. None of them were surprised.

First I called my daughter in Iowa.

"Christine, I'm staying in your room for now, so if you come home from college to visit we'll have to figure something out."

"That's fine, Mom."

Then I called Matt, who was in college at UCSD.

"Matt, I'm sleeping in Christine's room now. Dad and I broke up."

"Okay, Mom."

That's all he said, so I didn't really know how he felt.

" Wilson, we'll be sharing the bathroom now, so you can help me keep it clean."

"That's women's work," he joked.

And then we both cracked up laughing. He didn't really believe it was women's work. He and his siblings had been cleaning since I put child-sized brooms and mops into their hands as toddlers. In fact, Wilson had a part-time janitorial job. Did he revert to joking as way to deal with what had happened? Time would tell.

After two days in Christine's bedroom, I wanted to stay. It was cheerful; I could listen to my meditation music, get up when I wanted without disturbing anyone, and do my long meditations again. She would need her bedroom when she came home to visit from college, but I would deal with that when it happened. I moved my bathroom supplies, clothes, alarm clock, and personal belonging into my daughter's room and the bathroom I shared with Wilson. I didn't tell anyone about it, because I didn't know what had really happened and what to say.

My commitment to myself had always come first. My attachment to Rick no longer fit in with my commitment to life, growth, freedom, power, and self-expression. I felt free. I hadn't realized how trapped I had been before, with a lover who did not let me fully express myself emotionally and sexually and who didn't see a problem with that.

A week passed. I was still sad over Jenna but I was no longer sad over Rick. My desire for Rick had gradually eroded by too many disappointments over too many years. I didn't want him anymore. But I still wanted Jenna. I remembered laying naked, skin on skin, lost in her kisses. I was needy and vulnerable, and that probably made it harder to let go once I got attached. I probably was smitten with a fantasy of her, but that logic didn't affect my deep longing for her.

What was happening with my marriage? How did it change so suddenly? Was it over? Why would Rick just let me go and not try to get me back, and why didn't he want more intimacy with me? Did he have resentments against me? I went online and found articles on passive aggressive behavior and withholding. Maybe he had all those resentments against me, built up over the years. I had been a bad wife for much of our marriage. I had cut him off sexually, criticized him for years, and not worked when he wanted me to. Maybe he hadn't let all that go and he couldn't let it go.

"Mom, maybe Dad will be happier with a new woman that he doesn't have all those resentments against," my daughter suggested.

She never said what resentments she had in mind and I did not ask. But if he had resentments, why had he loved spending time with me? Did he love me but had resentments underneath the surface that only showed up in the bedroom?

Maybe he had low testosterone? But he still had a sex drive. I asked him to get his testosterone checked.

Maybe he was gay, and that's why he didn't like kissing me? But I saw he was attracted to women.

It was a little awkward living together in the same house. I avoided Rick because I knew he was sad over me leaving and I didn't want to give him false hope. I also wanted to create some space between us so each of us could reflect alone on what had happened, and let it all sink in. Mostly, I didn't want to talk to him. I didn't see the point of repeatedly telling him why I had left.

Since Wilson and I had adjacent bedrooms and shared a bathroom, we saw each other more and became closer. The past years, I had spent less time with the children, first because of the pill addiction and then because I spent more time with Rick, and I had felt guilty about it. I had a chance to reconnect with my youngest son. Wilson asked me more often to tuck him in at night.

"Mom, Dad wonders why you don't talk to him," he asked one morning.

Seriously? I was frustrated that Rick had no clue why I left or why I didn't talk to him. So I sent him an email and explained why I left. Rick replied the next day and he told me that he loved me very much. He was willing to try testosterone and marriage counseling. He didn't like kissing me that much, and he thought he had just lost the sexual attraction to me over our years together.

I was happy he wanted to try testosterone and marriage counseling, however I wasn't waiting for him to change. I had already left him and if he did those things and then I became attracted to him again, I would be open to that.

I started telling people about our separation. First, I told my friends. Then I told my mother, sister, and brother, and co-workers. I didn't tell my dad about my separation, because I didn't think he would understand. He liked Rick and he believed in family and marriage.

My sister and I were very close, and I could tell her anything. In many ways, we were alike. I had been there for her when she divorced years earlier.

"It's okay, I'm glad you're happy now," she said.

My brother and I were also close. He told me that the main problem of my marriage did not reside so much in Rick being a bad husband but rather in me having changed. Rick was still the man I had married 25 years earlier. He had not changed that much, but the real problem was that I had. I was glad my brother didn't criticize me for being a bad wife. I thought he would tell me I was selfish for leaving.

I talked with my family and friends, and as far as I could tell, Rick didn't talk to anyone. I felt sad for him. I knew he was feeling sad the way I had felt sad over him once, but it was his path in life to grow through it and figure it all out. I couldn't take the growth or pain from him.

I was in the guestroom, but I wasn't thinking seriously about divorce. I wasn't going to make a snap decision. Maybe he and I would reconcile, despite our lackluster intimate connection. Or would I end up leaving him for good?

CHAPTER 9

SEPARATED

A month passed. I wanted to remember the day we separated. I looked at the calendar and I couldn't believe it. The night I moved into my daughter's room was the first day of spring, March 21, 2012. It was also Persian New Year. It signaled new beginnings. It seemed symbolic. It felt like I had done the right thing. I had started a new life.

I didn't want Rick back, but I missed our affection and laughs. I missed the cuddling at night, the foot rubs, and the hugs. I lay alone in that bed at night and cried myself to sleep.

I looked for coping strategies. I tried new activities: rock climbing, Crossfit, the TM center, and of course lots of walks and talking to friends and dating. The kids were surprised and impressed with my new activities, especially rock climbing.

I became extra aware of what made me feel better, and what made me feel worse. I needed to do more of what improved my mood. I noticed listening to sultry music made me even sadder. I found it hard to listen to music I had once enjoyed because it just made me cry.

I wondered what was the right thing to do. Would something magical happen that would bring Rick and me back together? Or would I stay in that bedroom away from him? I was open to either possibility.

I thought about Jenna and her kisses. I was embarrassed to cry over a woman I met only once. I felt weak for not being in control of my feelings. I didn't recognize myself. I was not a person who cried over other people. I used all the tools I knew to cheer myself up: working out, meditation, talking and being with family and friends, and choosing my thoughts and simply thinking of something upbeat.

Every minute dragged on in endless misery. I frantically tried to think of happy things, like cherry blossoms. Sometimes I loved reliving my time with her, because the memories were so enchanting. Other times, I wanted to push away the sadness of the longing.

I thought of escape in a bottle or pills. No, I didn't want to get drunk, or numb my feelings. Escape would only set me backward. I wanted to come out of my breakups a better person, not a worse person. I wanted to be pruned by life, to be made richer and deeper. I left Rick's bed to be more and feel more, and numbing myself would just be a setback to all I had endured and worked for.

I escaped in more Netflix. I read a book on breakups. I met my friends and talked through my feelings. I took walks in nature. I went to Crossfit. I meditated. Yet I still cried. I cried at home, I cried at work, I cried in the car listening to music. I decided to not listen to any more sultry music.

Sex was still forefront on my mind. I was horny 24/7. I did not want another relationship. I wanted sex. I thought about having sex with men and dismissed the idea. Men and sex usually involved feelings, romance, and relationships. I didn't think it would be healthy to get emotionally and romantically involved with a man so soon. I believed that after a relationship ends, it was healthy to take time to oneself for a few months or years, before starting another relationship. I was sure a man wouldn't want to date me anyway, still married and living at home with my husband. I couldn't imagine bringing a man over for dinner. I was too sad anyway to go on dates. What would I talk about? My marriage? I definitely didn't feel ready to date men. Some day I would date men again, but not then.

I was still curious about women, especially lesbians. Earlier in my marriage I had met a few lesbians I was attracted to, but none would date me because I was married. Without the husband, I could have more opportunities to date lesbians.

I turned off my man radar and started looking at women differently. I doubled down on my efforts to meet women. I updated my online dating profiles with better photos. I joined lesbian meetup groups. I set up a search for women ages 45-59 who were lesbian or bisexual. I still had a heightened fear of STDs, which I assumed were passed by men, and I felt safe dating lesbians. I wanted to avoid bisexual women, because I thought they were more likely to have an STD since they would be having sex with men.

I scheduled about one date a week, and that was all I needed to feel satisfied. But maybe I wasn't ready to date. I was talking to the women I met about my separation and Rick. My friends said they never talked about their exes on dates. I considered whether it would be healthier to take a complete break from dating until I had topics to discuss other than my marriage, separation, or husband. However, the dates were enjoyable to me so I gave myself permission to continue.

SHE SAID SHE FELT USED

I met Andrea online. She was a 42-year-old lesbian who worked as a paralegal. I liked her and we made a dinner date. I waited for her outside the restaurant. She pulled up on her motorcycle. She wore a black leather jacket, jeans, and boots. She was dressed like a man. Fucking hot! She loved drinking wine, so we ordered a bottle with dinner. I liked being sober to have sex, and I had to drive, so I had only half a glass of wine. I was very attracted to her. We talked over dinner about sex and relationships, and then she invited me over.

Back at her place, we sat on her sofa next to each other and kissed. Her kisses aroused me, and my whimpers turned to moans. I reached my hand in her shirt to play with her nipples. That turned me on even more, but not her. She stopped me.

"I don't like my nipples touched. I like my entire breast touched," and she showed me by rubbing her hand in circles on her breasts. That was a mood killer because she had told me to stop doing something that really turned me on.

Rubbing her breasts in a circle the way she wanted was complicated and work. I was still curious though about what sex with her would be like.

I straddled her on the sofa, kissed her, and rubbed her breasts, paying attention to do it the way she liked. We got really turned on and went to her bedroom. We took off her clothes and then I went down on her. Her clit was large, and fun to lick. I sucked and licked her clit, and she got more turned on, but after about 20 minutes she had still not come. She didn't say if my technique needed to be adjusted. She didn't say anything at all. I considered she could be mentally stuck, as I often was, and I realized I relaxed knowing my partner was into it and not going to stop, no matter what.

A friend had told me she had her best orgasm ever when a man who was going down on her grabbed her legs tight at the end, like he meant it. I decided to try this on Andrea.

I leaned into her pussy. I grabbed her legs tighter like I meant it. That turned me on more, and I started grinding on the bed and softly moaning. She responded. Her body felt warmer, her vulva and clit felt slightly more swollen, her breathing got a little heavier. I was thrilled with my discovery. I had figured out how to get into a woman's mind, to get her to relax, so she could build her orgasm. If someone did that to me, maybe I could come from oral sex too? I kept licking her, holding her tight. As she got more aroused, I went for the button part of her clit and just licked it nonstop until she came. I stayed and held her legs a little longer, then lay on top of her and kissed her.

I didn't have feelings for her, so I didn't want to kiss too long. I just wanted to have an orgasm. I got off her and lay on my back. She moved down to between my legs and put her mouth right up on my vulva and licked me all over. I wanted her to make me come, so I focused on the sensations in my body and gave her directions: softer, get into a rhythm and stay with it, softer, just stay in the same spot. But she kept moving and it didn't feel good and I was just wearing her out without moving the action forward. I went to my old standby: masturbation. I just wanted to come.

"Here, come up here and play with my nipples and I'll masturbate," I offered.

As soon as I came, I wanted to leave. I didn't feel a connection with her, and there was nothing to talk about. I forced myself to stay and cuddle and talk.

"Every time I have sex with a woman, we start a relationship," she said.

What the fuck? Really?

"You don't have to. You can just have sex for its own sake, for your pleasure," I told her.

She seemed to like that idea.

She told me that next time, she would use her strap-on. I couldn't wait. So when she invited me back a few weeks later, I was excited. About the strap-on, not about her.

It was a hot day. We drank ice tea on her balcony and we talked about strap-ons and her previous relationship. Her house, like many in San Diego, did not have air conditioning, so she had opened all the windows. It was so hot, so even after we took off our clothes, I was still sweating. I really didn't feel like having sex when I was hot, but I was curious and horny.

"We really need to be quiet during sex," Andrea told me when we were in her bed. Once, her neighbors told her they had heard her and her girlfriend having sex and she was embarrassed about that. I didn't think she could be serious. Asking me not to moan was like asking me to not get wet. It was just part of my sexual expression. Plus it turned me on to do it. We lay in bed and started kissing. I waited for her to mention the strap-on. I didn't want to push her outside her comfort zone.

"Do you want to use a dildo?" she asked.

"Yeah, sure!"

I was excited to try it. Finally. I couldn't wait.

"I'm not going to use my harness. We'll just use these dildos by hand," she said.

Bummer. Why was she holding back? I came back specifically to try the strap-on and she had changed her mind. Boring. Well, I could make the best of trying the dildos.

She got up, opened a nightstand, and pulled out three small dildos of various sizes and some lube. I was surprised how short and narrow the dildos were, and curious what she would do with them. She picked out a very short narrow dildo for me to use on her. I put a little lube on it and penetrated her slowly. Her vagina was extremely tight, since she wasn't used to being penetrated. She moved her head back and moaned. I went in and out very slowly, gently.

I kissed her and then I pulled out the dildo and went down on her. As her moaning increased, I put the dildo back in and moved it in and out while I licked her to an orgasm. She was very quiet when she came. She almost didn't make a sound.

"That was really good," she said after coming. I felt proud that I had given her that. Then she went down on me. It felt good and I started moaning.

"Shhh..the neighbors will hear," she whispered.

Being told not to moan was a huge turn-off. I wanted someone who encouraged me to make more noise, not less, someone who called on me to express myself more, not less. She was going down on me, but my arousal was not building no matter what I fantasized. Her technique just wasn't that good. I masturbated.

After I came, I really just wanted to leave. I felt like a guy. I finally understood why a man left after sex. We had given each other pleasure and because sex was all I wanted from her, when the sex was over, there was nothing keeping me there. Without the sexual tension or an emotional connection, she was not useful or interesting.

She texted me a few months later and said she felt used. It was an interesting view. I gave her a good time and orgasms. How was that using her?

I never saw her again.

LUSTING FOR A MAN

I was still curious about what it would be like to have a relationship with a woman, but I was bored having sex with women. We just took turns going down on each other and there was too much feminine energy.

I missed the power and strength of a man. I liked how I got lost in a man during sex and in conversation, and I hadn't got lost in any of the women besides Jenna, and the sex with her was not good at all. I wanted a cock. Up until my mid 40's, I did not enjoy penetration that much. During our open marriage, with Eliot and Jenna, I discovered my love of penetration and long deep fucking. I loved being finger fucked or having a very hard cock inside me, even though it didn't make me come. Women were not the answer to my sexual hunger. I had turned to women because I thought they could make me come, but it turned out most could not.

I was curious what it would feel like to have sex with a man again. When I got more turned on with women, it was mostly because I believed a man was not turned on by my pussy or body. Rick seemed to just like my body for him to get off, not because he was turned on by touching or pleasuring me. Yet I preferred men sexually, romantically, and emotionally, and for companionship, and therefore I knew that long term it would be a man I would choose for a relationship. But how could I be in a relationship with a man if a man couldn't make me come?

I did not know if sexually a man or a woman could satisfy me more. I definitely had a lot more exploring to do with both women and men to find out what would satisfy me sexually.

I wanted to find a lusty tall strong man with a hard cock who could dominate me, fuck me with abandon, open me to new ideas and ways of having sex, and who actually got turned on by my moaning. I wanted hot sex. I needed a man.

I used my online dating account I had set up to search for women, to look at men's profiles. My type of man was professional, fit, at least 5'10" but preferably a bit over 6', confident and sensitive, who liked the outdoors, and who could make me laugh. I looked for men within 25 miles of me. I started online conversations with several interesting attractive men, ages 55-59, with careers in engineering and sales. I set up coffee dates. Some of the men cancelled our coffee date before we ever met.

I showed up dressed in my professional work attire. I wasn't going to wear anything sexy for a man I had never met! The men had to earn the right to for me to dress sexy, plus I wanted to be with a man who valued my intellect and my personality, not just my body.

I met Tom, a 49 year old, successful, tall, handsome, single dad, for coffee. His charm and flirtation excited me, but I lost interest when he suggested that we go out and get drunk for our next date. I didn't want to get drunk and I didn't want to date men who thought getting drunk was fun.

PUTTING ON A SHOW

About three weeks after the separation, Rick and I took the boys on a previously planned one-week vacation to visit Christine in college in Iowa, and our parents in Nebraska. The trip was tense for me because I was resentful of Rick for having let me down emotionally and sexually, and I didn't like being on the trip with him. He was not mad at me. He was sweet to me as he had always been. How could he be so sweet to me, when I was the one who left him? Why was I so mad, when I had already left? Why did I long for Jenna's kisses when it was obviously over? I didn't like any of that in myself.

Rick and I pretended in front of our families that everything was fine. I was glad to see my parents. I told my stepmom about my separation, but I did not tell my dad. It was hard for me to speak with my dad because he only listened to me if I spoke in Farsi, and I spoke Farsi at a beginner level. I had avoided meaningful conversations with him over the years due to that language barrier. Instead of learning Farsi better so we could be closer, I made him wrong for not speaking with me in English. But mostly I didn't tell him because I thought he wouldn't understand leaving an otherwise good marriage over sex or emotional connections. I wanted to only tell people who I was sure would be supportive. Rick didn't tell his parents about the separation either.

We had a family dinner at his brother's house. Rick looked very handsome that night and I was horny, a dangerous combination. When he went downstairs in the basement, I followed him and rubbed on him; he grabbed me and we giggled. We were both turned on.

I wanted him that night, so we slept together for the first time since the separation. We fucked on the floor, so our parents couldn't hear the squeaking mattress. Our sex was hot and lusty. We spent the night together cuddled in bed, and he was tender and loving. I felt close to him again. I thought we could possibly get along again or get back together. I wasn't sure. I still planned to go to counseling because a one-time hot hookup with my husband did not mean everything was going to be permanently better. When we got back home, he said he'd never take testosterone and sex wasn't important to him, but he still wanted to go to counseling.

MARRIAGE COUNSELING

We made an appointment for counseling. The intake counselor, a friendly middle-aged licensed social worker, was tasked with evaluating us and devising a treatment plan. Another therapist would provide our actual counseling sessions.

"Why are you here?" she asked.

"I'm tired of being told 'no' to sex," I told her. I was sure she would side with me.

She looked at Rick.

"Sex just isn't that important to me," he said.

I was sure she would give him exercises to do, or tell him he ought to try to please me even when he wasn't in the mood, or to get him to be more in touch with his feelings.

Instead, she looked at me.

"Sex isn't everything! You have a long marriage here and a man who loves you, and you would throw that all away for sex? Who will take care of you in your old age?"

I was furious! How did she dare she tell me what to do, when I came to her trying to figure it all out? Besides, I was married to an old man already. He had wrinkles, age spots, skin cancer, and erectile dysfunction, yet I loved him and yearned for more connection and closeness. I wasn't running from age, at least not consciously and at least not then. It seemed she was projecting her own beliefs onto me and not being a professional or even like any of the women I knew who all loved sex. I knew she had no ground to stand on.

"Is this your opinion or is this based on research?" I asked.

She looked surprised. She looked at me and didn't say a word. Rick didn't say anything either. Maybe he was happy she sided with him.

"A relationship is more than just sex. Sex is just not that important in relation to all the other parts," she told me.

I knew she was giving her personal opinion and not being professional. I wasn't going to let her bully me like that.

"Is this your opinion or the official viewpoint of this California HMO?" I asked her.

The therapist didn't answer and changed the subject. We talked a few more minutes and then she wrapped up the session.

"Let me make sure I understand why you are here today. Let me repeat back what you both said."

She turned to me.

"So Schahrzad, sex is so important to you, that you left him because of it?"

I nodded in agreement.

She turned to Rick.

"Rick, sex is just not that important to you. You were happy with how things were and you don't want to make a change to get her back?"

"Yes," he said.

The therapist didn't give us exercises or ask us to compromise. She recommended individual counseling.

Rick and I went back to the front desk and made our appointments for individual counseling. I was digesting what she had said. Her recommendation for individual counseling was my first view into the idea that marriages did not need to be saved. The individual mattered too. The receptionist said one of the other counselor s had an opening in 15 minutes. I told the woman behind the desk that the therapist we had just seen was prejudiced and projected her personal beliefs into our session, and I wanted a different person. I was pleased an opening was available right then.

My assigned therapist was a woman in her 60's. She walked me back to her office and we sat on opposite sides of a low coffee table.

"What brings you here?" she asked.

"My husband keeps telling me no to sex, and if there's no sex, we're just friends, so I'm done."

I waited for her reaction.

"I understand that. A vital sex life makes a vital relationship."

I felt understood, so I told her about Jenna, my sadness, and my inability to express myself with Rick.

"I don't know whether to stay with him or leave. I really could go either way. I want to know what's the right thing to do."

She seemed impressed by how well I was handling everything and told me it was normal to be unsure of what to do, and to be sad. I felt better. She suggested that I schedule another appointment with her three weeks later.

After seeing the counselors I felt stronger. I took a stand for my sexual freedom with the first therapist, and I was validated for doing so by the second therapist.

I didn't want Rick anymore, but I was open to staying with him if that was the right thing for my life. I was not attached to him or to a certain outcome. I was committed to my personal growth. I had to decide through the counseling if it was better to compromise on the emotional, spiritual, and sexual connection I wanted with my partner for the sake of staying married, or whether it was more important for me to honor my needs and move on without him. I planned to stay in Christine's bedroom until the answers became clear.

"HAVE YOU EVER HAD THAT WITH HIM?"

I went to my second counseling appointment. The counselor and I talked about how my life was going. I told her I was still crying over Jenna, and filled her in on work and my new activities.

"What do your kids think about your separation?"

Her question surprised me. I didn't believe people should stay married for any reason other than it was the right thing for them. Kids needed love, but they didn't need both parents.

"The kids are supportive," I told her.

Wilson and I were closer since I had moved into his sister's bedroom. My older kids were at college so I didn't see them regularly. They seemed to understand. But the truth was that I wasn't sure how they felt. I could not see inside their hearts and minds.

"What do you want in a relationship?"

"I want my man to make love to me. I want him to want me. I don't care about jewelry or money or travel or gifts. I want to feel sexually valued and loved, I want to be kissed and desired, I want to be playful and close and talk about our feelings and make love."

"Have you ever had that with him?"

I felt an ache in my heart. The room went blank for a split second, and I teared up.

"No."

It was a profound realization. For the first time I realized that I wanted something from him that he had never given me and probably never would. I wanted him to be different than the man I had married.

In that moment, I gave myself permission to leave. I was no longer a woman giving up on a marriage. It wasn't about right or wrong. It was about what I wanted in a relationship.

With only half the session done, I looked for things to fix in my life. I wanted to take full advantage of the counseling and improving myself. I brought up something about my mom. She just smiled at me.

"Don't go looking for problems. You are doing amazingly well! We don't need more sessions, but if you ever want to talk, please call and make an appointment."

"A SHIP IN HARBOR IS SAFE, BUT THAT IS NOT WHAT SHIPS ARE BUILT FOR"

Quote by John A. Shedd

I didn't want to play it safe. I wanted to play fully, so I could keep growing and changing and becoming more, as I had done my whole life, and be with someone who wanted the same. I wanted to feel more, get more into my heart, and be vulnerable. I couldn't do that with him. It was obvious I had to leave. My marriage had to end.

I would just stay in Christine's room for a year or so. I wanted to stay in my cute beach house, and I didn't think I could afford my own place. Wouldn't it be better to stay, and see if we could reconcile? I was surprised when my friends brought up the subject of me moving out.

"It's too hard for Rick to have you living there when he's still in love with you. You ought to move out," my 51-year old married friend said.

She had known us both since our kids were toddlers. What? She didn't think we should reconcile?

"I don't think I can afford to move out. We have debts and I don't make enough money," I said.

"Well, find a way to make it happen," she insisted.

I invited my 25-yr old yoga teacher friend for dinner, and sought her advice.

"You ought to move out. Don't worry about the money. After I moved into a place I couldn't really afford, my yoga studio needed me to teach more classes and I made the money I needed. Your money will appear too," she said.

I felt inspired. She called on me to be bigger and greater, and make something happen. I decided I could do it!

I thought about our children. They took our separation and my dating in stride. I couldn't believe that was actually true, so I kept looking for signs they were hiding their feelings. I couldn't find any signs.

Christine was in Iowa and busy with her own life. She wasn't paying much attention to us, except when we talked on the phone. She had been in a 3-year relationship and understood the ups and downs of relationships, why I was unhappy, and why I wanted to leave.

Matt had moved out a few months before, and I didn't see him much, because he went to school full-time and worked 25 hours a week. I brought up the separation each time I saw him and asked him how he felt. He said he didn't care. I thought he cared a little bit, because he looked down when he said it. I liked that he was sensitive and cared about relationships. Maybe I read more into it.

Wilson blossomed during the separation. He studied hard for his next chemistry test and received the highest score in his class. Wilson was setting personal bests at every track meet. His track coach gave him the first compliment ever, and told Wilson he was not the same kid he was last year. Maybe he worked harder to be good to make up for what he thought was wrong at home, or maybe he just liked the extra attention I gave him. He had always been the most sensitive and easy to read of my children and he seemed genuinely happy.

I thought the biggest reason the kids took our separation so well was because Rick and I wanted to get along and we didn't argue. We didn't fight over money or who would take what, or talk negatively about each other to the kids. Both of us encouraged our children to stay in touch with the other parent.

I asked my kids what they thought about me moving into my own place. Each of my children told me I should move out and move on. Even they saw my marriage was over.

My friends were right. I had to move out. I needed to find a 2-bedroom rental near Wilson's school, so he would have a short commute to school. But first, I had to separate our money.

CAN I AFFORD TO LEAVE HIM?

I had to decide what I would take or leave and then see how Rick responded. Financially, Rick had supported me our entire marriage. He let me stay home to raise our children. He didn't owe me anything financially. I wasn't going to ask him for alimony or child support. Besides, I was independent and strong and didn't need anyone to support me. My new life would be my own creation, not a holdover of my life with him.

I didn't want to be one of those women whose lifestyle was dependent on a man she no longer wanted in her bed. I was entitled though to half of what we had purchased and saved in our marriage. I had invested the money he earned, so I thought the retirement accounts and savings belonged equally to both of us. Besides, the law agreed. California was a community property state, meaning that property acquired during marriage belonged equally to both spouses.

I still did not want to see or talk to him, so I emailed him that I would move out and file for divorce, and wanted to discuss splitting our finances. He asked when I was available to talk. I had handled all the money in our marriage. His paycheck had gone into my checking account since before we were married. I brought Rick up to speed. I emailed him instructions on paying all the bills, auto deposit, and changing our checking accounts.

Rick made me a very generous offer. He said he would take money out of our retirement account, money he had mostly made, and pay off our credit card debt with its high monthly payments, so we could each afford to live on our own. He also let me know he was hurt and crying, and couldn't sleep, and couldn't imagine dating. I felt a little sad for him, but I knew he would get over it within a few months.

I still wanted Jenna. I wanted to share my excitement over my new life and let her know I was available. I sent her a long email to let her know I was leaving Rick. Maybe she would want to date me if I had my own place. She didn't reply.

CHAPTER 10

MY OWN PLACE

I had almost given up on women, when I met Malory, a beautiful 49-year-old attorney from Los Angeles. Her profile said she wanted a relationship. She had two toddlers. The kids were a turn-off for dating a woman, because I didn't want a lesbian as a life partner or even as a live-in girlfriend. Young kids needed time and attention and would be in the way of sex and going out. But she was so beautiful, so I contacted her. We talked on the phone. On our first call, she asked me about STDs.

Malory had lost gay male friends to AIDS in the 80's, so she was super sensitive about catching an STD, especially AIDs. She asked me to get STD tested before we met up, even though I had just been tested three months prior and was negative for everything. I went to my HMO to get the full range of STD tests, and emailed her the results:

> *Attached are my test results. They are negative for Hep A/B, HIV, syphilis, gonorrhea, and chlamydia. I had my HPV test during my pap exam four months ago and it was negative also.*

She thanked me for getting tested and told me that I was passionate and how much she appreciated my energy.

On our next call, she said she had spent hours finding just the right place for our first meeting.

"I spent all afternoon driving around to find a nice restaurant for our brunch date, and I found a 5 star restaurant with an incredible menu."

That was overkill. I always picked a local Starbucks for my first meeting, because with coffee it was easy to leave if we didn't click. Nonetheless, since she wanted to invite me on a nice brunch date, I agreed to go.

Meanwhile, I was looking on craigslist.com for 2-bedroom guesthouses for rent near Rick's house. I invited Wilson to look at places with me. I sent him emails of craigslist ads I found. Wilson looked at one guesthouse with me and then lost interest.

After days of looking, I couldn't find a guesthouse that I liked, so I asked "the universe" to send me the perfect apartment. "The universe" was that inner stillness and silence that was in me and in everything, the unbounded oneness underlying creation. That was the place I went inside my meditation. When I wasn't sure what to do, I talked to the universe by making a request. Sometimes it seemed to work. That day, someone gave me the idea to look at an apartment rental website. I changed my search to local apartments and immediately I found many nice complexes not far from Rick's house. I made appointments to visit three complexes. I didn't like the first two complexes, and fell in love with the third. An upper floor double master was available the following week. I felt like I was aligned with the universe. Everything was falling into place. That made me feel like what I was doing, was right. I came home, excited, and told Wilson.

"Wilson, I found a beautiful apartment! It's a double master on the second floor, which means you have your own bathroom in your bedroom. The complex is full of trees, and it's only 15 minutes away. Do you want to see it next week?"

"Mom, you better take it before it's gone. Good units go fast!"

I drove right back and put down my deposit. I hoped a good running trail was nearby. I drove around the neighborhood and found a park with dirt trails and native vegetation about ½ mile away. I walked the trails and smiled at my good fortune. I loved running outdoors on hilly dirt trails, and had missed the trails and canyons abundant in Poway when we moved to Oceanside. Finally I had my trails back! It was as if the universe had sent me the perfect apartment, and it was confirmed I was doing the right thing.

I went home and started packing. I packed sheets and towels, my clothes, and a few dishes. I planned to take my daughter's bedroom set, half our Persian rugs, and our baby grand piano. I left everything else for Rick. I didn't have a sofa or dining room table. I could buy that later.

Rick saw the boxes stacked up in the living room and he looked sad. How could he be so sad while I was so happy? He wasn't laughing anymore or making jokes. He had deep circles under his eyes. He told me he wasn't sleeping well. But he did not ask me to stay.

Matt called and said he would come over for Mother's Day. I asked Rick if he and the kids wanted to come over for dinner. Rick said he would make dinner. How could he be so nice to me, when I was the one who left?

I felt high….high on my freedom. The sun shone brighter. People appeared more beautiful. I was free. I splurged on some new clothes to wear that spring, as well as a couple outfits to wear for my dating life.

I moved on a Friday, while Rick was at work. I hired the same movers who had moved our family the last three times. The morning of my move, I texted Christine in Iowa.

Movers are almost here.

Mom, I'm so proud of you. You have so much courage.

I created a home I wanted, not a replica of what I had. I liked bare minimalism and I wasn't attached to things, so I didn't hang up my pictures, I didn't get plants or a pet, and I purposely avoided buying anything for the apartment. I pictured the apartment as a temporary home. I figured eventually I would move in with a man who had a place, or we would get a place together. I didn't dream of buying my own place one day. I still didn't think I could ever afford it.

SHE FINGER FUCKED ME BETWEEN HER KIDS' CAR SEATS

On the first day of my freedom in my new apartment, I had two boring dates with lovely women whose conversation bored me to tears.

The next day, I drove to meet Malory for Sunday brunch at a beautiful resort in Santa Monica. She was already seated at a table outside. I first noticed her shiny curly brown hair. Her full breasts and a black lacy bra peeked out underneath her brown low cut shirt. She wore jeans and cowboy boots. She was sexy as hell! I walked over.

"Hi. Are you Malory?"

She beamed a smile and her beautiful eyes sparkled. She stood up to hug me.

"Yes. Schahrzad?"

"Wow, you're gorgeous. I love your top!"

She was drinking champagne and orange juice. We helped ourselves from the delicious buffet. So many crab legs! Yum. While we ate, she sat close to me and leaned over to talk, and then she put her hand on mine. I was uncomfortable with her move. Handholding was something between two people who knew each other and wanted closeness. Was I resisting intimacy or was she taking liberties? I was new to dating. I left my hand under hers, to challenge myself and get the experience. The waitress put the bill in front of Malory and she paid.

"Let's walk around," she suggested after she paid our bill.

We walked through the hotel, and she took my hand. Again? I didn't like her doing that but I let her. We stopped in the restroom.

I noticed an awkward moment as we both went into stalls and I was about to hear my date urinate. I figured I just had to get over it if I was going to date women.

Just as we walked out, she turned around and kissed me. Her lips were soft. She pressed forward and put her arms around me. I liked kissing her. She turned me on. She was getting turned on also, because she kissed me harder and grabbed me tighter.

"Come, let's take a walk," and she took me by the hand.

"Where to?" I asked.

She smiled. "Hmm…I don't know yet, let's just go.'

We walked around at the resort and she took my hand. I let her do it again, even though I did not like it. I did not like being so gutless, so after a couple minutes I pulled my hand away. She was beautiful and sexy and I wanted to fuck. Why did I want to fuck and not hold hands?

"Can we get a hotel?" I asked, hoping we could hook up.

"My babysitter leaves in three hours," she said.

Did that rule out fucking that day? Wasn't she horny too? She didn't offer for us to go to a hotel.

"Let's get my car," she said.

The valet brought her large pickup truck, and we went for a drive. While she drove, she again put her hand on mine. I was uncomfortable with all the handholding. Why did she keep doing it, and why did I let her? I was gutless. I could leave my husband, but I couldn't tell this woman to stop holding my hand. Weird.

Malory drove to an office parking lot and parked next to an apartment building. Sweet, she wanted to make out at least. I wanted to be in a hotel so we could be comfortable having sex. Sex in a car was uncomfortable and reminded me of being in high school, with guys who couldn't take me into a real bed.

"Let's get a hotel," I suggested again.

"I need to be home in two hours because my babysitter is leaving," she said.

She motioned to the back seat. I turned around and saw two car seats.

"Here, let's get in the back."

I preferred a hotel, however I wanted sex more than I wanted to avoid having sex in the car. So I got in the back and she followed behind. I took off my shoes and straddled out of my pants. I sat in the narrow space between the car seats and she laid on top of me, her chest pressed against mine, her breath in my ear, in broad daylight in a parking lot in Los Angeles. I laughed to myself at our lust and spontaneity.

And then, between two car seats, toddler books and animal cracker boxes, she finger-fucked me. She fucked me deep...well.... long. She knew places inside me that I didn't know existed. I moaned louder and moved my hips to her rhythm.

"Feels so good," she whispered in my ear.

How did she know? I got lost in her, lost in her touch and her fingers, and the pleasure deep inside my body. I was wet and moaning loudly. She got so turned on by my wetness and moans, she took off her pants.

"Do you like strap-ons?" she asked.

"I've never had one used on me, but I'd like to try it."

"Yeah, you'd like that, next time I'll fuck you with that."

And then she laid on me and finger-fucked me slow and deep, and kissed me tenderly. Then she whispered softly into my ear.

"I feel you. When we're apart and I tell you that I feel you, this is what I mean."

And she moved her fingers inside me. I made a mental note of how I felt, so I could remember it when I needed to.

Then she went down on me. My clit swelled in anticipation. I shuddered the second her warm tongue made contact. She hit me in the right spot. I struggled to spread my legs wide apart so she could really get closer, but the car seats were in the way. She flicked and circled her tongue around my clitoris until I was so close to coming, but she didn't have enough room in that backseat to really get between my legs the way we both wanted, so I masturbated to finish to orgasm.

I went down on her and she came within five minutes. Afterward, as she drove me back to my car, she put her hand on mine. That time, I pulled away.

"YOUR CANDOR IS REFRESHING"

I met a few men in their early 50's for coffee, but I just wasn't attracted to them. And then came Rudy. According to his online profile, he liked cycling, live music, travel, and his business ventures.

We set up a coffee date for 1pm on a Tuesday. He was already seated and sipping his latte when I arrived. He looked as handsome as in his profile pictures. He stood up and shook my hand. I liked what I saw. Rudy was about 6' tall, lean and fit, with a flat stomach, which was very impressive for his age of 52 years. His hair was grayish, and he had a nice tan and dimples. I was glad he didn't come in for a hug, as men often did. I didn't like to hug men I just met. I preferred a handshake.

Rudy started by telling me all about himself, mostly his success at work, his successful college age boys, and his many accomplishments. He then apologized for going on and on, and asked me about myself, and specifically what I was looking for.

"I'm dating lesbians, however the sex so far is boring and I want a man to fuck on the side."

He was intrigued. I didn't mean women were boring. It was just that I preferred men.

"I'm not used to women being so open. Your candor is refreshing."

"Thank you," I said. "I like to ask for what I want."

I had frequently seen him online as "active", and I wondered if he was a player.

"Are you a womanizer?"

"No, not at all. I have been in a few relationships since my separation two years ago. Each relationship lasted about five months."

"So you're not divorced?"

"No, my ex wife is a bitch and is dragging this out. She thinks I have more money than I do, and even her lawyer can't stand her," he explained.

Aside from talking poorly of his ex, Rudy seemed like a great potential sex partner. I needed to get to know him more to decide if I wanted to choose him for a sex partner. I wasn't attracted to him because I couldn't get a sense of what he was about, but he was handsome and seemed like a good possibility. I wanted to do something that set him in a relaxed environment so I could see his real self. We set a date to run the next weekend. Then I left to meet Ed, my 3 pm coffee date in Encinitas.

HIS HIGH LIBIDO

"I have a very high libido," Ed told me over coffee. He was a fit 54-year-old computer consultant, with wavy brown hair and a charming smile. I told him that nobody could make me come anymore, and I had my orgasms by masturbating. He assured me he was very good at oral sex. I liked hearing from a man that he enjoyed pleasing a woman. It turned me on. I wasn't sure if he was my type though. He had not been STD tested in almost a year, so he agreed to get tested before we had sex and email me his test results. We decided to make a date after he had his results.

That weekend, my son Wilson moved in. We went shopping together and bought him a bed, drafting desk, linens, and a TV for his x-box. He didn't want to hang any pictures. Rick and I didn't have any court orders, not even for Wilson's visitation. We agreed that Wilson would alternate one week with each of us, and it was up to Wilson to make that happen. Wilson knew I dated both men and women, and he didn't mind it, as long as I did not invite any sex partners over on his weeks in my apartment. He proudly told his friends about his 'lesbian mom', which was certainly not true, but was his way of telling his friends I was cool.

"I LOVE EATING PUSSY"

Rudy, the man who found my candor refreshing, met me at the trailhead for our run. He was mostly a cyclist, in great shape, but not so used to running, especially running hills. He kept up with me quite well for the entire hour. We talked while we cooled down afterward. He told me about his contributions to his clients, business partners, and children, and giving back to the world. He sounded like a great guy. I became more interested in him.

"You want to go for coffee?" I asked.

"Sure."

We relaxed over coffee and talked in detail about sex, and what each of us liked. He leaned in and was intensely interested in me, which, combined with my interest in him, made him more attractive. He liked giving pleasure to a woman and making her come.

"I love eating pussy," he said.

That got my interest. A man who loved eating pussy. A man who appreciated and loved that part of a woman, that I felt had been neglected for so long. I wanted to spread my legs for him and have him lick my clit all over and see if he could make me come.

We set up a date for him to come over another time. We didn't hook up right then, because we were both sweaty from our run, and I considered that date an interview date.

FILED FOR DIVORCE

It was my 25th wedding anniversary. It was a good day to file for divorce.

I put on my grandmother's diamond necklace. When my mom gave it to me, she had said, "only wear this on special occasions." Filing for my divorce was a special occasion: it was a one-time event (I hoped), and it was a day of great pride as I took a stand for my freedom. I filed the paperwork as if I were applying for a mortgage. I didn't feel sad.

I paid to have Rick served. He would have 30 days to respond. If we moved through the process without any conflicts, our divorce could be final in six months.

FINALLY! – MORNING SEX

I sent Rudy a text message about my divorce filing and asked him if he could come over early the next day to hook up. My favorite time of day for fucking was early morning. Waking up to a hard cock was a huge turn on, and it had been years since I'd had that luxury. Fortunately, Rudy also liked morning sex.

At 7 a.m., I was showered, in sexy lingerie, and horny, waiting for him. I heard a knock at my door. I opened it, and there was Rudy, with his gray hair, chiseled face, and manly cologne. He was the first date in my apartment. He came in, and we immediately kissed and got out of our clothes. There was nothing romantic about it. We were both just horny. I wanted his cock and he wanted my pussy. It was just physical between us, but not in a hot, I-need-you-right-now kind of way. We just wanted sex, that's all.

He took off his pants in my dining room. He wore tight red spandex briefs, which I found unusual. He looked like a gigolo or someone about to do a strip tease. I had never seen a man wear such briefs. We had already talked about STDs and safe sex, and I had purchased a large box of Trojan condoms with this date in mind.

I pulled down his briefs, and his erect penis popped out. He was so hard, his cock almost touched his stomach.

"Come, let's go in the bedroom," I invited him.

He followed me in and lay down on my bed. I licked his ass and balls, licked his hard cock, sucked and licked his head, and just played around with my tongue, mouth, and hands on his cock enough to get myself more turned on. Then I just wanted to fuck him. I didn't care if he wanted more oral. I got a condom out of my nightstand, put it on him, got on top, and slid his erect penis inside me. I shivered. Damn, he felt fucking amazing! I was moaning louder and louder. Rudy's dick fit me just right. I had never felt a penis that good. He was extremely hard and stiff, and he was slightly larger than average, with a nice girth.

"God, you feel so good, you're so hard!" I told him.

"That's because you turn me on. You make me so hard."

I kept riding him. He thrust his hips rapidly up and down in short quick strokes, a move which sent shivers up my spine. Fuck! Felt so good! With each stroke, I felt pleasure deep in me. My moans turned into a scream of sorts and then I caught my breath.

"Oh my god, oh my god, oh my god, oh my god," I whimpered.

I didn't want his deep thrusting to ever end, but he was getting too aroused and so after a few seconds he stopped. I rode him some more and he liked it a lot. I felt his cock get wider inside me and I could tell he was about to come.

"I'm coming," he said and let out a loud long moan. I kissed him forcefully and deeply while he came, just pushed my tongue deep in his mouth as his cock throbbed inside of me. And then I lay on top of him. His cock got soft and slipped out of me. He took off his condom and I took it from him. I put it on my night-stand to throw away later.

I asked him if he would lie next to me while I masturbated. It was going to be the same way I always came with Rick, that same boring way. I thought maybe he could make me come. He didn't offer to use his hands or tongue on me, and I didn't want to ask. I couldn't relax unless a man did something he really wanted to do, and I just thought he wouldn't want to do either, and if he did, he would say so. Maybe he got turned on watching me masturbate. I didn't ask.

Rudy held me and watched me eagerly while I masturbated, which was the opposite of what Rick had always done. I was getting more turned on by his enthusiasm, and I came much faster than I had with Rick. I kissed him while I came. So hot. Afterward, I lay on top of him and snuggled about two minutes, and then got up to get dressed. I was glad I didn't have any feelings for him.

"You can fuck all the women you want. I'm fucking other women too, and I'm not looking for a relationship."

"I'm too busy with work to be fucking around."

I believed him.

Rudy had to leave for his meeting and I went to work. That afternoon, he texted me some sexy messages and said I was beautiful when I had my orgasm. I welled up with tears. Nobody had ever said I was beautiful when I came. Rick had his eyes closed every time and had no idea how I looked. I told Rudy not to say things like that anymore because I didn't want to start liking him.

I was not attached to him, and he wasn't boyfriend material, because he seemed closed off emotionally and he wasn't funny. After work, I went to a lecture at the meditation center. When I got home later that evening, Wilson was still up.

"Hi Wilson, I'm home," I yelled out.

"Hi Mom," he said.

He was in his room studying. I went in and hugged him. Then I remembered the condom I had placed on my nightstand that morning. Had I thrown it in the trash? I went into my bedroom. The used condom was still on my nightstand. Darn! I went back into Wilson's room.

"Wilson, did you go in my room today?"

"Yes, mom."

"Did you see something on my nightstand?"

He grinned sheepishly, and then we both laughed. I didn't know if I should be embarrassed. Our situation felt natural, and I decided it was good for Wilson to know his mom enjoyed sex and was sexually active. I wanted him to have a healthy view of sex.

I threw away the condom and reflected on Rudy and what he meant to me, if anything. I didn't have feelings for Rudy. He wasn't sensitive or warm, and he wasn't funny. But I liked having sex with him. His cock was extremely hard and of good size.

HE MASTURBATED FOR ME

Ed, the man with the high libido who was getting STD tested before we met up, texted me and said his test results would be available in a couple days. He promised to go down on me, and, as he stated, "looking forward to your evaluation of my oral skills vs. the women you have been with."

He invited me to his townhome in Encinitas and served me the freshest juiciest salmon I had ever tasted. Over dinner, our conversation was about sex, particularly his massage table fantasy. Although he was handsome, I wasn't attracted to him. I didn't want to touch or kiss him.

"I don't feel like having sex with you or kissing you, but I'll watch you masturbate," I told him after dinner.

I had lost all interest in evaluating his oral skills vs. the women I had been with. I didn't want him to touch me at all.

He got up from dinner and ripped off his pants. I was sort of surprised. He sat down naked in his kitchen chair. I walked closer to him, but stayed about fifteen feet away. I watched as he stroked his cock, slowly at first, then faster and faster and faster, until his ejaculate shot all over the room.

"Did you see how far that shot?" He was beaming.

I really didn't care how far it shot, and it didn't turn me on at all, mostly because I had enough of men who were just into sex for their own pleasure, and also because I wasn't attracted to him.

"Yes, that was far."

I didn't want him to feel bad. I still stood far away and I just wanted to leave.

"That was hot, I think I'll go now."

He got dressed and walked me to the door.

A few days later, we talked on the phone about playing out his massage table fantasy. I was thrilled to finally meet someone who wanted to role-play! I thought he wanted to pleasure me on the table and I wanted to hear his fantasy and possibly come back for that, despite my lack of attraction to him.

"I'd like you to come over and give me a massage, then finish me off with a happy ending," he said.

Seriously? Why would I want to do that? He had to be deluded to think I would be aroused masturbating him, with nothing in it for me.

"I don't want to do that," I told him.

He seemed annoyed with me and said I had led him on and I did not keep our agreements, which would make it hard to build trust. I had no idea what he was talking about. I told him we were not a match and asked him not to contact me again. He didn't.

CHAPTER 11
GLIMPSE INTO THE LESBIAN WORLD

STRAP-ON HARNESS AND DILDO

After our brunch and sex between her car seats, Malory sent me text messages that often brought tears to my eyes. She told me I warmed her heart, made her ovaries swell, and other poetic beautiful thoughts that never occurred to me to say to anyone. It was all great, except that it seemed she was falling for me, and didn't feel the same way about her. I could tell she was jealous about Ed and Rudy.

"I'm glad you're exploring sexually, and that you like them," she said, but her voice did not sound convincing.

We changed the conversation to using a strap-on with me. I loved penetration by finger or cock, and I was curious how it would feel to have full-on strap-on sex with her in a hotel room. We set a date to meet at a hotel near her home, to minimize the time she would be away from her children.

She had already checked in when I arrived. She was beautiful as always. She greeted me and said she had two hours before she had to be back home to the babysitter. I couldn't believe it! She finally had me all to herself in that hotel room, she was a professional woman who could easily afford the childcare, and our date was going to last only two hours. My heart sank and my enthusiasm went with it. I didn't tell her about my disappointment, because I didn't want to ruin the mood, and after all, she had a right to do as she wished with her time.

"Come here, look what I brought," she said and led me to the bed.

On the bed lay a red velvet pouch with a drawstring.

"Hmmm...let's see which size you might like," she said, and pulled out three dildos of various sizes, materials, and colors: a 6" tall (1.75" wide) blue dildo, a 6" tall (1.5" wide) pink dildo, and a 4" tall (.75" wide) neutral toned dildo. I didn't know dildos came in so many sizes and colors, and I thought they were all very narrow and small. I was impressed with the assortment she carried.

"Wow!"

It was all I could say. I had no idea how to put all that into action.

She took her leather harness out of a bag, put it on, and adjusted the straps. Fuck! She looked so sexy. I wasn't thinking about being fucked by her anymore, because I wanted to do the fucking. I wanted to wear that harness. I hoped she would let me have a turn. She placed the 4" neutral colored dildo into her harness. It looked small, but I didn't tell her that. I was open to the experience she wanted to provide.

"I don't have sensation in the dildo, so I move by how it feels to you, not how it feels to me," she explained.

I lay on the bed and she climbed on top of me and we kissed. I wasn't feeling that into her anymore, especially because she reduced our big date to only two hours, and the dildo seemed very small. She put the tip of the dildo inside of me, and pushed gently, until it slid in, and then she used my wetness to push in deeper with each thrust. Once she was all in, she fucked me in and out, in and out. It didn't feel as good as being fucked by a finger or a penis. I was disappointed by the sensations, and I had no idea why it didn't feel so good. I tried to get into it. I held her tight and kissed her and focused on the sensations in my pussy. But I honestly didn't like it that much. She could tell I didn't like it so much, so after about five minutes she stopped.

"I'd like to try doing that to you," I said, hoping she'd offer me a turn to use the strap-on.

I didn't want to ask to use the strap-on, since it could be considered a personal item like a hairbrush or vibrator, something that is not passed around or shared. She didn't say anything at all, so I took that to mean she didn't want to share it. Maybe she didn't like dildos? I didn't ask.

"Lay down, let me go down on you," I suggested.

She laid her head on the pillow and looked at me. I climbed on top of her, kissed her breasts and stomach, and moved down to between her legs. Her pussy tasted and smelled sweet, she was engorged and wet, and I licked her clit until she was close to coming, and then finished off by licking her with steady rhythmic strokes on the little button part of her clitoris until she came.

She went down on me and I came very close to coming but couldn't. I masturbated and fantasized alternately about Malory going down on me and then about a man watching my clit and pussy, until I came. After we both had an orgasm, I just wanted to leave.

That evening, Malory texted me the link for the company in Canada where I could buy my strap-on. She told me leather gives and takes well as I move, and recommended I get a cock that fits the harness and is long enough so I can move and have fun with it. I told her I had an 8" dildo at home. She was surprised to hear I was *a size queen*, and wondered if she had been too small. She recommended the Aslan Jaguar leather harness, and that's what I purchased.

When I got off the phone, I made dinner. I had found a favorite recipe: sautéed salmon, brown rice, and sautéed leeks, with a glass of cabernet sauvignon.

But after dinner, I got lonely. Nights were hard, because I was used to snuggling up beside Rick and I did not like going to bed when I was there all alone. I stayed up until I was really tired, and then I went to bed.

In the morning, I ran the hilly dirt trails by my apartment. The outdoors and heavy breathing cleared my head. I was panting and dripping sweat when I was done. After my shower, I fell into the deep silence of meditation. Time to get ready for work. Makeup…a pretty dress and heels and pearl earrings….a spray of perfume… and then I got to drive in my beautiful car. It was ten years old, but I loved that BMW. I stopped at Starbucks on the way to work. I opened the sunroof, blasted my hip-hop music, took a snapchat that I also posted on Facebook, and smiled. Life was good!

HIS SISTER FETISH

I told my sister Sarina about Rudy. She was also on match.com, the site where I had met Rudy, and we often talked about our profiles and how to improve them. She asked for his handle and looked him up.

"He's hot!" she said.

The next time when Rudy and I messaged, I told him about Sarina, and when he asked about her match.com handle, I gave it to him. I never gave any of this another thought.

The next time I saw Rudy, he stayed for a sleepover. While I went down on him, we talked about not using a condom, since bare skin felt better for me as well as for the man. Rudy didn't think we really needed a condom, since he had been tested for STDs just a few months prior, and he hadn't had sex since then.

"I only have sex in relationships, and I haven't been in a relationship in about six months," he said.

I seemed an exception to his relationship rule. But it didn't matter, since the condom would protect me. My views on getting an STD had evolved. I was no longer afraid of STDs, because I did not know anyone who had an STD, although most of the sexually active people I knew never used a condom at all, including my friends and the swingers I had met. I had read up on STDs on the Internet and the CDC website, and couldn't get clear answers on how anything was transmitted. The articles recommended using condoms and oral dams, but there was still a risk of contracting herpes or genital warts through kissing and skin contact. I decided to go down on every man before I put his penis inside, and look for genital warts. I further reduced my risk by having sex with men with fewer sexual partners and men who were not bi. I was afraid that bi men were exposed to more STDs, although maybe that was an unreasonable fear.

"I don't go sleeping around," he told me again, and I believed him.

We did not use a condom that time. Or the next.

I started liking Rudy and his hard cock. He let me get on top, ride him just how I liked, and he stayed hard a long time. He would push his hard cock inside of me, and fuck me hard and slow. Then after about 20 minutes of penetration, when my pussy was swollen with arousal and completely wet, I asked him to ram his cock deeper inside. I clutched him and held on tight as I rode him like that. Skin to skin. My arms wrapped around his back, his warm hands grabbing my ass or hips. It was the greatest pleasure imaginable to me. Before Rudy (and even Eliot, my friend in Denver), I did not know I liked intercourse so much.

I started to like Rudy for more than the sex. I felt warm in my heart when I was around him or thought of him and when he held me. I wanted to tell Rudy about my fledgling feelings for him. I had to know if he felt the same way, and if he didn't, I needed to let go and forget him. I messaged Rudy one morning to tell him *I kind of like you and I want to see you again.* I waited for a reply. By early afternoon, he still had not replied. My heart sank.

A text message came. It was from my sister, Sarina. *"Rudy just sent me a match.com message saying I'm beautiful."*

What? I was confused. A few minutes later she messaged me again. *"Rudy says I'm very sexy."*

I was more confused. Why did he pursue my sister in Colorado, instead of me? I had invited him over. If he wanted sex, why not have it with me? I made him harder than most women, and we had good sex.

I called my sister.

"Rudy contacted you?" I asked.

"Yes, on match.com. He wants to meet me."

I was furious.

"That asshole! I just told him earlier today I want to see him again and I'm starting to get feelings for him, and he never even replied." I paused. "Do you want to see him too?"

"Well, he's very attractive and successful, so I am interested."

My sister and I were close, and I knew she wouldn't see him if I asked her not to, but I was till mad at her for wanting him, and allowing herself to be chased by my guy.

Mostly I was mad at him for pursuing her in the first place. How had I misread him like that? I didn't even know family men who contributed to society and loved their children could be deceptive. Maybe he was also deceptive with everyone in his life, not just with me? How had I attracted such a man to myself, and what could I learn from it? I purposefully had three dates with him to evaluate his character prior to hooking up. If I misjudged him after those three dates, how many other people did I misjudge?

There was also the issue of facing reality. My sister and Rudy were interested in each other, and why was I preventing that? What was I resisting? I admitted to myself I was jealous due to my own insecurity. I didn't want to be sexually compared to my sister and be faced with the possibility that she was more responsive in bed and maybe I was sexually inadequate after all. I didn't tell her that, because I didn't want to admit that, so I relied on the girl code instead. I told her he was my guy.

"If you two have feelings for each other and wanted to date, I would be really supportive, but you two just want to fuck. Go find your own fuck buddies. Come on, we don't fuck each other's guys."

"He's so sexy though," she continued.

I did not like her interest in him at all.

"Well, I don't want you to see him. I like him," I said.

"Okay, I won't see him then. But let's keep playing his game and see how far he will take it. I'll forward all his texts to you."

That seemed like a fun game and it made me feel closer to her. It was us against that player. It served him right to be strung along like that. We could have fun with him.

I was also mad at myself for having sex with him without a condom. He seemed to go after women so readily, and he wasn't honest. He obviously had sex outside of relationships, and he could be fucking a lot of other women besides me, and have given me an STD. I made an appointment to get STD tested.

An hour later, she texted me again. *"He wants to come to Denver to see me next month."*

I don't want you to, I texted her back.

Okay, I won't see him. My relationship with you is more important than some guy.

I was mad at Rudy, and couldn't keep pretending I didn't know. I texted him.

Hey, my sister says you want to hook up with her

Consider she contacted me first, he replied.

Aha, he suddenly found time to reply to me. But it didn't matter. I had already lost respect for how he went behind my back, but

I lost even more when he lied to me. I didn't understand why he would lie, instead of admitting he wanted to see her.

"Sarina, why would he lie like that, when he could just end it with me and then contact you?" I puzzled.

"Some people lie and it's how they go through life. They start with a lie, and they get away with it, and eventually everything becomes a lie. You can ask a guy like that where he's going and he'll tell you to the bank when he's really going to the gym."

I didn't want any people like that in my life, but it intrigued me. What was the point of lying about everything?

I was turned off about the lying, but I still lusted after his hard cock, and as much as I didn't like to admit it, I held out hope there was just a big misunderstanding of some sort and he didn't want my sister after all.

After that, Sarina became evasive when we talked about Rudy. She had told me she wouldn't see him, but the next time we talked, it was obvious she and Rudy were planning something

"Schahrzad, I told him to take you out to make it up to you", she told me on the phone.

Why was she coaching him on dating me? Weird. But it sounded like she was looking out for me. I wasn't mad at her anymore.

The next afternoon, Rudy called. I debated whether to answer the phone. I took his call.

"This is Schahrzad."

"Hi Schahrzad, it's Rudy. Do you want to go to the Marshall Tucker Band at the Belly Up on Friday night?"

That was a sold-out show. I loved the band and was impressed he could get tickets. Maybe he had changed his mind about my sister and wanted me instead. I told him I would love to go. He said he would get back to me. I thought he had to make sure he could get the tickets, but Sarina told me later the reason he had to get back to me was because he had bought those tickets months ago and had a date with another woman. He cancelled on her so he could take me instead. He just needed time to clear it with her first.

I was still online looking at profiles of both men and women. I looked at men's profiles on match.com. Whenever I saw a handsome man that turned me on, my body felt hot and flushed. I sent messages to those men, and rarely received a reply. I didn't like being titillated with a palette of men I could not have. I found a few men that interested me enough to meet, although none were super studs, and set up up coffee dates. Most cancelled at the last minute or didn't confirm. I attributed that to match.com itself. Rudy had told me "the purpose of match.com is to keep people on match.com", and I could see why. Each time I sent a message to someone, a screen popped up with profiles of several other people who were even more attractive. It created in me the sense there was always someone better out there. Perhaps that's what the men experienced too, and that's why they didn't go through with our dates.

I wasn't looking for a relationship although sometimes I wanted to be in love again. I missed the affection and closeness I had with Rick.

I felt ashamed about my sexual appetite. With lesbians, I was afraid to mention my past swinging and my male fuck buddies, because lesbians had such a fear of STDs from men. With men, I was afraid to talk about my male fuck buddies, because I thought men wouldn't respect me for 'sleeping around'. I had to be honest though and just deal with it. Besides, if the other person had a problem with how I lived my life, that person wasn't right for me.

People often asked, "what do your kids think of what you do?", as if I was doing something wrong. What did my kids think that I worked out or cooked or meditated? Dating was just a normal part of life, like other activities. Why was there any question about it? My kids knew everything I did, because I told them. My boys were fascinated by my sexual stories, however my daughter was put off. She wasn't used to all this sex talk. I persisted. I brought up sex and dating each time, even when she asked me not to. I had failed in teaching her about this important area of life as she grew up. I knew that with time, she would become curious about this part of her life as well. I was my children's teacher, and I wanted them to have the same sexual freedom I felt. I wanted to keep sharing my life with them, and to let them grow by observing me stumble, be vulnerable, and be excited about my sexuality, relationships, and dating.

"I feel like a butterfly," I told my son one day. "The whole world is my meadow. I want to land on this flower and that flower, that tree, that moss, that grass, that flower...the whole world is beautiful." He smiled as if he understood.

I talked with Malory almost daily, and I told her everything that was happening with Rudy, including his pursuit of my sister. I loved sending Malory sexy pictures of me, knowing I turned her on. She called me *Momma* or *Baby*, and said she could feel her hair brushing the inside of my thigh. I welled up with tears from her tenderness. Her words opened and warmed my heart, my pelvic area, and pussy. Nobody had ever talked to me like that. I remembered how my body opened up when I told Rick I loved him during sex. What else would my body do when I felt loved? Someday I would find out, with a man.

The harness came in the mail a few days later. I put on the harness and adjusted the straps. I slipped the dildo into the opening and looked at myself in the mirror. Fuck! I was so sexy! A real stud! I called Malory and told her I would ride my Girl the next time we were together. I wondered if she would let me.

A REAL DATE

Rudy confirmed our date for the Marshall Tucker Band, and invited me to sushi before the show. My STD tests had come back negative for everything so I could still fuck him that night. It was the first time since I had met Rick decades ago that I went on a date with a man <u>after</u> we had sex, so I was excited about the novelty of it. I went out with him despite his dishonesty, just because I wanted to go on a date and I liked his hard cock.

I assumed he was no longer interested in Sarina, since he had asked me out. I never asked him about his pursuit of Sarina, because I wanted to keep the date fun and pleasant. And what could I really gain from asking? It would seem I was causing drama or creating expectations of him, my fuck buddy, and he would probably lie anyway. I just wanted to have a fun date night.

At dinner, he talked about his misguided neurotic selfish money hungry wife, and their divorce proceedings that were years in the making. That turned me off even more. If I hadn't been so horny, I would have just ended the date right then. We walked over to the Belly Up, ordered drinks, and found a place to stand.

He stood behind me, his hard cock pressed against my ass, as we watched the band and moved to the music. I loved the band and being around all the people. I had not gone to a concert since I was in high school. I ground up against Rudy and he put his hands on my shoulder and hips. Sometimes I turned around and looked up at him. His head was turned to the side every time, as he looked out over the audience. I knew he was looking at other women, but I didn't care. His cock was hard, and I knew it was for me and I loved being the object of his desire. I just wanted the show to end so we could leave and I could have his cock all to myself.

After the show, we came back to my place and fucked passionately. Rudy was sweet and giving in bed, I couldn't help but like him again, but not in a relationship type of way.

The next day I received a message from my sister.

"Rudy wants to see me in Denver."

Somehow, that time, it struck me as hilarious. He didn't mean to be bad, but he just couldn't help himself! I called her, and she told me he had a trip planned to see her later that summer. The word rascal popped into my head and I laughed and immediately messaged him.

You have a sister fetish?

He didn't reply.

A few days later, I realized, to my utter dismay, I had grown attached to Rudy again, despite his lies. It was just about the sex. I didn't like that I got attached to him, because he lied to me. I had to figure out this attachment I got to my sex partners and how it happened, when I knew little about them outside the bedroom, or, as with Rudy, didn't even like who the person was. I had to figure out how not to get attached to someone who provided me with intense sexual pleasure. I set that as a goal for down the road.

I texted him to meet and he did not reply all day long, so that night I called and left him a voice mail message. No reply. I was mad that he ignored me, so I backed him into a corner. If he ignored my request to share my feelings, I did not want him at all.

"Please let me know if you can meet me tonight, else I can't see you anymore".

He found time to reply. His text came back two minutes later.

"Take your combat maneuvers elsewhere."

I felt powerful and free.

"I ended it with Rudy," I texted Wilson.

I didn't want Rudy to have the last word though. I wanted to humiliate him too, so I told him he was just a hard cock to me, nothing more. He didn't respond.

Sarina called me a few days later. Rudy had told her that "your sister lives a small life. I've been to over 50 countries and she's only been to three."

Who cared how many countries I had visited? What mattered was what I was inside: my inner being and energy, my accomplishments, even my education, and how I treated people. I was puzzled that he hadn't seen my value, and why did he speak poorly about me? What was the point? Maybe he was positioning himself to make his way into my sister's pants.

I was furious with my sister.

"Why are you still talking with him, when he's been so rude to me?" I asked.

"We're just talking. I'm not going to see him if you don't want me to. But you two are done, so there's no reason you couldn't let me see him."

That didn't sound reassuring at all. It seemed she was trying to convince me to give her permission to see him and I wasn't going to do that. Sarina and I were close and she loved me, so I believed her when she said she would not see him. Summer was coming up and she suggested visiting me.

"Yeah, that would be awesome!" I told her.

Sarina came out in early July. I just loved being around her! We talked, we went to the beach, we laughed, and we talked some more. She promised me again she would not have sex with Rudy, but a couple weeks after she left, she emailed me to say she and Rudy had a plan to meet in Denver. I felt betrayed. I did not talk to my sister for nine months. She kept calling me, but I wouldn't take her calls. Then one day, I got over it and I finally asked her what happened with her and Rudy. She explained.

"I thought you and Rudy were done. He said he wanted a relationship and if he and I connected, he would consider moving closer. He really led me on!"

"What?"

I couldn't believe he had lied to her in such a big way, and that she was so gullible.

"Yeah, you know I don't hookup. I only have sex in relationships and I wait months to get to know a man before I have sex."

"Yeah, true."

That was one thing about my sister. She did not hook up. Many of the men she dated were just friends. She took her time to get to know them. I couldn't remember a time she had ever hooked up.

"He convinced me about a relationship. He talked about skiing together and trips and our children being friends. I really fell for it."

"Damn! What a player. Did you at least enjoy the sex?"

"It was alright."

I wasn't mad at her anymore. I realized it was my own insecurity about my sexuality that was the basis for my jealousy. It was over between him and me anyway once he decided to go after her, and then it didn't matter who he fucked.

I didn't hear from Rudy again. About one year later, I went briefly on match.com. He sent me an online message, "*still looking good.*" I was mad for a few seconds, and then I had to laugh and replied simply, "*I'm into authentic people so we are not a match.*" By then, I was so grateful he had ignored me and he was out of my life.

MY FIRST PHONE SEX

It was June. It was the day I ended it with Rudy. I felt proud that I took a stand for myself. I felt free and powerful.

I was home alone eating my regular salmon and leek dinner when Malory called. She was telling me details of her sex life with past girlfriends, and it turned me on. I wanted to kiss and fuck her right then.

"Have you ever had phone sex?" I asked.

"Yes, many times," she replied.

"I never have. I want to try it."

"Yeah baby, let's do it," she said.

I took the phone into my bedroom. I slipped out of my panties and leaned against the wall, facing my closet mirror. I pulled up my dress and watched myself masturbate in the mirror.

"I'm rubbing my clit," I said.

She talked to me while I masturbated, and then we both masturbated. She told me all the things she was going to do to me and I got more and more turned on listening to her voice in my ear, until I came. I didn't think she came. She just wanted to get me off and then she got off the phone.

I liked her sexual openness, and how free I felt sharing my fantasies. I texted her the next day and told her I wanted to masturbate in front of my apartment window. She said it was hot and we could do that sometime.

I called my dad on Father's Day. I had not talked to him since our visit to Omaha two months earlier, and at that time I didn't mention anything about my failed marriage. I avoided it because I thought he wouldn't like hearing it, and I didn't want to deal with his reaction. I figured someone else would have told him by then.

When I called him, he already knew. A mutual friend had told him. He was mad that I left a 'nice guy' like Rick.

"Be grateful for what you have! Having seen your mom and me get divorced, you know that divorce is hard on kids. Rick gave you a stable life. What you have is due to him. Rick is a good man. You will never find someone as good as Rick again!"

I would have liked a little more support, but I was mostly surprised he thought everything I had was due to Rick, and I could never find anyone better! He really didn't know me very well. I was also mad that he lectured me for leaving.

"I had a purposeful independent life before I met Rick," I reminded him.

I knew there was no point in arguing with him, since he believed he was right. I was also afraid of him, since he was authoritarian and I probably was passive around him as a result. I did what I wanted, but just didn't tell him about it, and that's passive also. Instead, I told his wife and hoped she would tell him. My parents were not an active part of my life anyway, and I talked to them only once every few months, so I wouldn't have to face his reaction again for a while. By then, he would see how successfully I lived on my own. I knew he loved me. I told him I would call more often.

The kids were doing well. Wilson was coming over every other week. We ate dinner together and we talked about our day. He sometimes invited his friends over for sleepovers. The boys played video games or were on their phones. I didn't notice anyone drinking or getting high or bringing girls over. They stayed up too late and slept in. Christine moved back from college and we spent time together almost daily. We joined the Carlsbad Crossfit gym and she went to classes with me. I saw Matt about once a month. He sometimes stopped by and made dinner at my place.

⟫⟪

After the strap-on in the hotel, and the phone sex, I wanted more hot sex with Malory. Each time I asked her when we could get together for a date, she had a reason she couldn't see me.

"I'm so busy with work."

"You can get STDs from men, and it's not safe. I have children to raise. I'm just not comfortable having sex with you while you are having sex with men."

Other times, she would call me and want to talk for an hour. She talked to me about her children and what they were playing, and put her kids on the phone to say hi. She also sent me regular text messages, made comments about our engagement (her and mine), but then she wasn't available to meet for sex.

"It seems you are avoiding me. I want to get together again," I told her.

"I love you. I'm there for you. I have to reconcile my own issues before I can make myself vulnerable to you. I have opened up again and realized what love is, and started yielding to you, until you texted me an equivocation and then all my warmth turned sour and my ego took control. I know I failed you."

I had no idea what she was talking about or what she wanted, and I couldn't believe such a successful businesswoman was all over the place in her emotional life.

"Love comes when you want it and stop holding back, when you are open to a date, when you enjoy each moment. It sounds like you don't want to get attached. I found the best protection against attachment is having multiple lovers so my attention is not focused on just one person. Maybe that works for you also?"

I was frustrated with the situation. Malory was the first lesbian I met that was very good in bed, she liked me, yet she refused to meet up. I wondered when I would see her again, if at all.

NOELLE

I was immediately smitten with Noelle when I saw her profile on match.com. She was a 47-year old professional woman with radiant brown eyes that signaled confidence, passion, and strength. She had long thick hair. Her write-up indicated she was smart, witty, and educated. I sent her a message, and was thrilled when she replied. We messaged back and forth a few times, and she asked for my number.

She called me right away, and our conversation quickly turned to sex. She told me she was a top and 'always in charge'.

"I'm very confident sexually. Taking charge sexually is what I do."

I was drawn in.

"Wow, that sounds amazing! I like to be submissive, and I love strong beautiful lesbians," I told her.

A woman who was so sure of herself fascinated me. I was submissive and liked dominant women. What would she do to me as a "top", and how was she "in charge"? I asked her what she was looking for.

"I'm looking for fun. I don't want to be exclusive. I'm going to date several woman, and once it's not fun anymore, I move on."

Wow! She was the first lesbian I met who wanted ongoing casual sex with more than one woman. I liked her openness and sexual appetite. The man issue came up. Noelle said she was concerned about getting an STD from me because I also dated men. I didn't want to let sex with men come between me and her, but I wasn't going to lie. If she didn't like me fucking men, she didn't have to date me. I told her that hardly anyone could make me come, and that the lesbians I had been with were boring in bed. I hoped I wasn't offending her.

"I can get a woman off better than any guy. Best sex you'll ever have!"

She seemed so confident. What would she do to get me off? Did she give good oral sex? And sex was about more than getting off. Would she turn me on more than a man, and how would she do that?

"I am amazed by my beautiful feminine body, yet sexually I often feel like a man and completely relate to straight men in that way."

She went on to tell me that one night she spent two hours at a bar telling all her 'secrets' to a straight man on how to please a woman sexually. The man was so grateful, he almost kissed her feet.

My head was spinning. She seemed like a force of her own making. I was mesmerized by her sexual power, and male energy that put her in charge of a woman sexually the way I yearned a man to be in charge of me. I wanted to be on the receiving end of all she did to be a 'top', and tap more into my own male energy. What would it feel like to be in charge when it came to women? I'd seen The L Word. Maybe I could develop that kind of energy and presence? What would that take, and how would it look? She definitely had my interest!

I called Malory and told her about my interest in Noelle. Malory had already seen her profile.

"Well, now that our engagement is off, I am also interested in Noelle. I'm going to send her a message."

I didn't like Malory's talk about engagements and her jealousy, when I just wanted to see her and have sex. I also thought Malory's interest in Noelle was really bizarre, especially because both Malory and Noelle were tops, meaning they were dominant; they liked to take the role of doing the fucking. I felt pressured by Malory to see only her, and I didn't like it.

"Malory, I don't feel free when you get possessive and jealous like that, and it's a turn off. I just want to see you, be with you, enjoy you, and have amazing sex."

"Baby, we will. "

FISTING

I made a brunch reservation for Noelle and me for the coming Saturday at a restaurant with an ocean view. I texted her about the plans I made. She replied.

I like strong femmes. So HOT that u made a restaurant reservation with a view so I can see the ocean, but in reality I am always in charge.

Sex with a woman remained hotter, not necessarily because of the emotional connection between us, but because with a woman I could relax and not feel rushed or like a chore in bed. A woman gave me the attention and time I needed to climax and didn't seem to mind how long it took me to come. In fact, even when a woman couldn't get me off, she got super turned on trying.

Orgasms seemed more elusive with the men I had been with, at least in the past year. I didn't remember how it was before I was married. I thought that men just wanted to get off during sex, and were doing me a favor whenever they did something for my pleasure.

Noelle would be turned on getting me off. I'd be able to relax and discover new parts of me, sexually. I'd be able to please her as well. I knew how to make love and get a woman off orally. I was super excited about our brunch.

I found Noelle sitting in the lobby of the hotel, waiting for me. She was beautiful, with thick long curly hair, creamy colored skin, strong and also feminine, just like her picture.

"Hi. Noelle?"

She smiled. A smile that lit up a room.

"Yes. Schahrzad?"

She got up and we hugged. She was about 5'10", with a strong toned body. I liked how she felt in the hug.

Over brunch, she told me about some of her prior lovers, her work, and what she was looking for. I was fascinated by her experience and love of life. After brunch we went across the street and walked on the beach. I felt proud to be seen in public with such a beautiful woman.

Then we took a drive drove up the coast. Noelle kept putting her hand on my legs and saying we had chemistry. I didn't feel the chemistry yet. Noelle said she was concerned about STDs, especially AIDs. She asked about my sexual partners. I told her everything.

"I brought latex gloves that I will use when we have sex," she told me.

I felt a little hurt and disappointed about the gloves, but I heard her say she had brought gloves for "when we have sex", so it sounded like I was going to get laid that afternoon. Besides, I wanted to be open to new experiences. Maybe the gloves would not detract from sex, or maybe they could be a turn-on. I also wanted to honor her need to keep herself sexually healthy and safe.

"Do you want to come over?" I invited her.

"Yes, of course!"

We drove back to the restaurant, so she could get her car, and then we both drove back to my apartment. She had her overnight bag with her. I offered her some tea, and while the water boiled, she walked over to me, grabbed me, and leaned down for a kiss.

Her kiss was delicious, strong and tender. She was strong like a man, yet soft like a woman. I felt safe and trusted her, which turned me on even more. I moaned softly in response to my arousal. As our kisses grew more demanding, my moans turned to almost a whimper. I just wanted to rip off our clothes and go on my bed, where I thought sex was the most comfortable. We went in my bedroom, and she tenderly took off my clothes.

I lay on my bed, naked. She kissed me and then she moved down to my hips, sat between my legs, and put on the latex gloves. I didn't mind the glove. I liked that she was sitting by my vulva, looking at it, really present to giving me pleasure. My pussy felt so wet! She rubbed my labia for a while then slowly inserted one, then two fingers into my very wet cunt. Her touch was very gentle, not at all like the rough touch I'd had with some of the men. It felt good and my moaning increased. Her fingers started moving in and out, gently, slowly, and I really liked how it felt. It felt so good, I forgot where I was. I was moaning quite loudly. I lost sense of space and time. I went into some kind of zone and lost track of everything but the feeling of pleasure deep in my vagina. I realized I lost myself and I had to catch my breath. I came to enough to raise my head and ask Noelle what she was doing.

She smiled, "I'm fisting you."

I was alarmed. I had seen fisting in porn. It seemed gross and violent and painful. But here I was having it done, and it felt good. I couldn't decide whether I should be scared and ask her to stop, or let her continue because it felt so good.

"It feels really good, so just keep doing it," I said, and I sank back into the pillow.

Noelle kept pleasuring me with her fist, then she took out her hand, slipped off her glove, and licked my clit in circles and back and forth strokes until I came. Then she came up to my face and kissed me and we held each other a little while. I wanted to go down on her too, so she lay on her back and I sat down between her legs.

Her vulva was beautiful. Her dark curly pubic hair framed her thick outer lips. Her inner lips were purplish, her clit large and engorged. She smelled sweet. I started licking her for a while, sometimes looking up at her face. She lay there so beautiful. Her head was turned to the side; her long curly thick hair fell next to her on the bed. She looked relaxed. She started moaning more as she came closer to orgasm, and then she grimaced and smiled and moaned loudly in an orgasm that seemed to last for a full minute. She was gorgeous when she came. I wondered if I looked that good when I came. I was sure I did not.

It was late. I turned off the light. I lay on top of her and kissed her. I started rubbing my body against hers, and getting all turned on again. I was too tired to have sex again, but turned on. I wanted to just masturbate while she held me. I buried myself in her arms and rubbed my clit. I pushed her out of my mind and started fantasizing about a man watching me.

"I want to continue this with you, what we're doing, but I can't when you remove yourself and don't stay connected," she whispered to me gently.

What? It had never occurred to me that going into my own head and fantasy was pulling away, and much less that someone could sense that. It was pitch black in our room, and I was physically as close as I could get.

"Oh, you could tell? What do you mean? How can I fantasize?"

"Fantasize, yes. When you're with me, include me in your fantasy, make me a part of it," she explained.

That made sense! If it were daylight, I could open my eyes and look at her. Or if I fantasized, I could have her and the man watching me. I could have her watching me. In that instant, I came up with many scenarios that included her.

I closed my eyes and masturbated with her in my fantasy also. I was so tired though that I kept drifting off to sleep, then waking up and masturbating, then drifting off to sleep.

"You're moving away again," she reminded me gently.

"Yes, I'm just so tired. Let's just go to sleep," I said.

"I'll get familiar with your body while you sleep." She turned on the light on my nightstand. I snuggled up against her and was asleep within seconds.

The next morning, I awoke to that beautiful woman in my bed. Noelle said she had noticed the dimple in my elbow, my smooth skin, and the mole on my back, my fingers. Nobody had ever wanted to know my body in that way. I wasn't sure if I liked having this much attention given to me by someone I had just met the day before. I tried to be open-minded to being more loving and in the moment. But I didn't want to explore her body like that. Maybe I was just too selfish.

We had more hot sex that morning. I thought we could keep having sex that entire day. Women could have sex for hours on end. We didn't have penises that had to get hard and recharge. Lesbian friends told me about spending days on end in bed having sex when they first started relationships.

Noelle and I got out of bed, because she had plans for later that day. I checked my phone. Malory had sent me about 30 text messages, because she was upset she couldn't reach me. Her neediness was a turn-off and I wanted to figure out how to get rid of her. I didn't even want to reply. I just liked being with Noelle. I felt free and easy around her.

I made us a delicious breakfast and we talked as we ate eggs and fruit and drank hot strong coffee. Then she said something surprising in regard to my husband.

"You've been deeply hurt," she said.

"I don't feel hurt. I'm happy." I said.

But her words were unnerving. Perhaps she knew something I did not. When someone made a confident declaration about me,

I often listened as if the other person was some kind of authority or knew something about me I did not. Other times I ignored it or pushed back. Noelle sounded so sure of herself. Perhaps there was something I had withheld, something hidden so deep it had not come to the surface before. I wanted to look and examine all of myself, so I could keep growing mentally and emotionally. I decided I would make another appointment with the counselor.

After breakfast, Noelle told me I was smoking hot and she wanted more of the hot sex we had, and then she left. She texted me later that afternoon to say my scent was still on her and brought up memories of being so deep inside me. I felt so beautiful when she wrote that she liked the sound of my moans, the feel of my tongue on her lips, and the expression on my face when I came. Nobody had ever said that to me. I felt moved and inspired. I had such little experience in what was possible between two people.

These messages were much different from the way I was used to communicating with men. Men did not learn about my body, send me long emails and talk about my scent and how beautiful I was. Not men in hookups, not my husband either. Sex with Noelle had been amazing and memorable. She took charge. She knew how to touch me. She knew a woman's body. I felt comfortable, safe, and sexy with her. I could really let go. I didn't feel like anything she did was just a favor. I felt like everything she did to me, she wanted to do. I could tell what she did to me also turned her on, so I could get more turned on and I could relax. I was hungry for more.

I went back to the counselor. At the appointment, the counselor asked me about my kids, my work, my husband, and my dating. I told her what was going on in my life. She encouraged me in all I was doing. After about 15 minutes I was just looking for issues to discuss and couldn't find any. The counselor said, "Don't invent problems". I agreed. We ended the session 15 minutes early and I never went back.

I learned an important lesson: just because someone else sees something in me, doesn't mean she or he is right! I learned to not doubt myself so much.

Noelle had mentioned her experiences with strap-ons, role-playing, and dominance and bondage. What else would she do to me? What could I do to her?

Noelle and I were not moving to anything exclusive. She was dating other women, and I was still online looking for bi women and couples for sex. So I was surprised when Noelle said she could only keep dating me if I really wanted to explore the lesbian world and put dating with men on the back burner. It wasn't that she wanted a relationship with me; it was more that she only wanted to date women where a connection existed such that a relationship was at least a possibility. Neither of us had feelings for each other. We were truly friends who liked each other and had hot sex too. Her suggestion resonated with me, because dating both sexes was stretching me and confusing. I wanted to focus. I told her I would just date women.

Then we booked tickets to fly to Las Vegas.

MY MALE ENERGY

Noelle's male energy and how she got turned on penetrating women intrigued me again to explore my own male energy. I wanted to dress like a man too, and take a woman sexually like she took me, and be strong and powerful like she was.

I already had a harness and dildo I could use on a woman, but that wasn't enough. I wanted to wear men's clothes and cologne, and see how it made me feel. I longed to take and pleasure a woman the way a man took and pleasured me. I would make love to her and finger fuck her slowly and deeply. I'd watch her arch her back and moan from the touch of my hand. She would submit to me in utter sexual pleasure, and get lost in me. Doing all that to a woman would require getting into her mind and heart first. I already had the confidence to do that. I just had to make her feel beautiful and desirable. The entire fantasy was purely a sexual quest.

Most of my turn-ons about wearing men's clothes were about my love of men and the strength of a man. I missed having a man in my home. I used to smell or wear Rick's shirts when he was at work and I missed him. I wanted to wear a man's shirt, just for the feeling of being near a man.

I went to the men's department at Nordstrom's. Bright racks of shirts and carousels of colorful ties beckoned. As I walked into the department and selected clothes to try, I found myself turned on. I walked up to a salesman.

"I'm looking for a man's shirt for myself."

I waited for his reaction. He was matter-of-fact.

"Let's look for a narrow size 14. I have a wonderful new shirt that will fit you well."

And he brought out a lightweight blue and white-checkered Hugo Boss shirt.

"This is a wonderful shirt. Notice the spread collar."

He showed me into the dressing room.

"Put it on, and I'll call alterations when you're ready. Just come out."

I went into the dressing room. The buttons were on the right side of the shirt, opposite of a woman's shirt, and it was huge on me. A seamstress from the women's department came to measure me for the alterations. I asked her to include darts. She spent almost 20 minutes pinning the shirt to fit my petite body. I also bought a pink bowtie.

A week later, my shirt was ready. I was a little nervous wearing a man's shirt. I didn't want to look like a man. But the shirt was fitted. Maybe nobody would notice it was a man's shirt. Could I wear it to work?

I wore my new man's shirt with a fitted brown pencil skirt, pink sapphire necklace, and high heels. I felt immensely sexy! And nervous. On my way to work I stopped at the dry cleaner and Starbucks. It seemed like more men noticed me, and looked at me longer. It seemed that other people could sense something sexy about me. Did they know it was a man's shirt? Perhaps the spread collar gave me a powerful look.

"I love your shirt!" the barista at Starbucks told me.

"Oh thanks, it's a man's shirt," I boasted.

I was nervous going to work in a man's shirt. When I walked in the door, one of my co-workers complimented me on my shirt. That afternoon at a meeting, around the conference room table with men, I felt more powerful. It seemed they treated me with more respect.

I went to lunch. Again, more looks. I started to feel confident in my shirt. Throughout the day, I noticed women looked at me more, and talked to me a bit flirtatiously.

When attractive men looked at me, I felt lusty. In my man's shirt, I challenged a man to be more manly and dominant than I was. It was almost daring him to be manlier than I, and that was a huge turn-on because I liked dominant men.

That afternoon, I took a selfie and sent it to Noelle.

She texted me, *"Your lesbo look is adorable and sexy and makes a girl like me hard! I can't decide whether to scoop you up in my arms and kiss you, or throw you down on the bed and fuck you."*

Fuck! I finally found a hot lesbian girlfriend! Noelle turned me on like nobody had. I wanted to be like her. I wanted to feel all my male energy and wear my man's shirt but next time with pants and a dildo inside, and throw women on the bed and fuck them. I liked Noelle's confidence, her strength, her knowing of herself and what she wanted. She definitely didn't fit that mythical lesbian joke of "What does a lesbian bring on her second date? ....A U-Haul." Noelle was way too powerful to be so easily uprooted from her own life and into someone else's. I felt free around her, and it boosted my confidence that such a sexually experienced, smart, and capable woman found me sexy.

HER NEEDINESS TURNED ME OFF

I didn't have that same feeling of freedom around Malory.   But I kept seeing her anyway because she was sexually experienced and I respected her as a professional woman and mother. She finally scheduled a trip to see me. It would be the weekend of Gay Pride in July, and she would bring her kids. I didn't want her to bring her kids. First, I didn't think it was good for them. Many dating situations fizzled out after just a few dates, and children did not like seeing a revolving door of lovers and forming multiple attachments with people who kept leaving and never coming back. And second, I wanted time alone with her so we could fuck and do whatever we wanted. Fortunately, my ex husband and kids had said they would babysit for her.

Malory and her kids arrived several hours earlier than I expected, leaving me scrambling to rush home from work and clean my apartment. Malory had reserved a hotel suite near my apartment, since my mom was staying with me and I didn't have room for more guests. We talked with my mom, and then I went with Malory and her children to her hotel suite.

She put her kids to bed in one bedroom of the suite. Her children were used to sleeping with her, so she had brought them an iPad to play to entice them to stay in their own bed that night. They were certainly old enough to do so.

"Now you kids can watch TV or play with your iPad, and remember Mommy told you to stay in your room so Schahrzad and I can go to sleep."

The kids stayed in their room and giggled and talked awhile, which made me a bit uncomfortable while we were having sex. I didn't want to think about children or worry about them needing something and calling for their mom while we were having sex. That was part of the reason I couldn't relax to have sex when my children were young. (I could masturbate anytime, but I couldn't give myself to another unless I knew our time together would be protected from outside distractions.)

The next morning, my ex-husband, mom, and daughter babysat Malory's kids while she and I went to Gay Pride. While we were walking into the event, she took my hand and held it, just assuming I would want that. I didn't like holding her hand. At first I just let her do it, just to try it out and because I thought I was wrong for not wanting to hold a friend's hand. But after a couple minutes of walking like that, I pulled away. We only stayed about an hour at the event, and then it was time to meet Noelle for coffee. We had planned that coffee date so Malory and Noelle could meet.

Seated with my two lesbian lovers in the bakery, I felt very wanted. Noelle was easy going and I liked being around her, but Malory acted jealous and it just made me uncomfortable. Afterward, Malory and I went to dinner at a nice bistro downtown, but since I wasn't feeling that interested in her anymore, my eyes kept moving to handsome men seated nearby. I longed to be with a man instead. I didn't know how to get one at that moment, and I wanted to explore lesbians, but I couldn't wait to someday be with a man again.

At the end of the evening, by the time we got back to the hotel near my apartment and with two young children, I was tired and exhausted and didn't really want to be with her anymore. Since I had invited her down, I felt obligated to go. I was uncomfortable telling her I didn't want to be with her that evening. We had good sex. Malory was lusty and good in bed, and she could make me come easily. She was really a good mom, and her children were happy and well behaved.

Still, I didn't feel a connection with her and I was glad when she left. I really didn't care if I ever saw her again. I texted her I just wanted to be friends and we were not a good match. I didn't tell her all the things I didn't like, because another woman might like those things in her, and I didn't want to make her feel less valued.

"Why aren't we a good match?"

"You're just too needy."

I was being honest. It would have been better if I had told her in person before she left, but I just didn't have the courage. Malory was mad at me. She said I never really wanted her to come down, and it all felt yucky and she felt used.

I was furious with her. It sounded manipulative. I had wanted her to come down and I gave her love and affection and good sex. I had the right to change my mind about my interest in her. When I changed my mind, I didn't want to be put on a guilt trip about it either. I wish I could have helped her be less needy, but I really didn't know how. She blocked me after that and we never spoke again.

"LET ME SEE HOW WET YOU ARE"

Noelle and I took our trip to Las Vegas the end of July. Noelle brought a big suitcase with several changes of clothes and a half dozen stylish sunglasses. She was a woman, after all. That night she wore her Armani suit, and she looked like a man. She was hotter than fuck. That was the first time I went out with a woman dressed like a man. I felt proud to be seen walking around the town with a beautiful lesbian who was strong and felt like a man inside.

Talking with Noelle was easy. We both liked quiet time in the room, and time out with people. We could be together in silence, as well as talk seriously. We were friends and lovers, but without expectations or romantic attachment.

One afternoon, when we had returned to our room, I started changing into my bikini to go to the pool. Noelle sat on the bed and watched me undress. After I took off my panties, she commented on whether we should wait to go to the pool. I looked at her, and she smiled at me sweetly.

"Go sit on that chair," she said.

I walked over to the armchair facing her bed, and sat down.

"Spread your legs. Let me see how wet you are."

A rush of electricity shot through my clit and my body felt hot. My pussy was wet immediately. I lifted my dress and spread my legs for her as she watched. She looked at my pussy. I was turned on. I hoped I was wet enough for her. I trusted her. I was certain the wetness was not visible to her, but maybe she knew how aroused I was.

"Come here," she instructed.

I walked over to the bed, full of anticipation of what she would do. She grabbed me and kissed me.

"You're such a good girl to be so wet for me," she whispered in my ear. I felt weak in my knees and leaned forward into her.

"You're so beautiful, so sexy. I brought something special for you," she told me.

"Oh, really? What is it?" I was touched that she had brought me a gift.

"I brought a dildo that I picked out for you."

Wow.

A dildo just for me? And she had spent time deciding what I might like? I wondered what she determined would be a good dildo for me.

She reached into her bag and took out a harness and the most beautiful dildo I had ever seen. It was thick, blue, and translucent. A cock with girth. Yum! I took off my dress and bra as she put on the harness. She placed the dildo inside and then came over to me with her big hard cock. She got me more warmed up and wet with kissing, and then she fucked me with her thick blue cock in the missionary position. I didn't enjoy the dildo penetration as much as finger fucking or a penis, but I tried to get into it. I moved my hips and held on tight.

She moaned to the rhythm as she fucked me slowly, deeply, and then harder. She moaned more as our fucking picked up. Fucking me turned her on. I grabbed her tight and moved my hips up to get more of her cock inside me.

"You're really turned on by this, but you're not being stimulated."

"I'm feeling pressure against my clit, and fucking you turns me on."

I found the whole idea of a woman with a cock a huge turn-on, but physically the dildo didn't feel that good, and I didn't get completely lost in the experience. I wanted her to finger fuck me instead, and I also thought about using that dildo and harness on her.

Noelle put away her harness and went down on me. When my breathing quickened and she felt me closer to coming, she put her fingers inside me. I felt my pussy got tighter and clamped down on her finger. My body was preparing for an orgasm before I even knew it was close. My pussy felt wetter, my breathing got louder, and I felt my orgasm was inevitable. It was about to erupt out of me. I came with a loud moan while I contracted and pulsed on her finger. My face pulled into a long grimace and I hoped she saw it. Then I looked at her and smiled. That was awesome! She took her finger and put it up to my lips. I licked it. I tasted so sweet.

Then it was my turn to taste and pleasure her. Noelle had a beautiful vulva with a sweet taste. I loved how she turned her head to the side as her pleasure grew, how she smiled when she came, and her orgasms that lasted almost an entire minute.

We lay together and cuddled. I asked her if I could use that dildo on her sometime. She told me she only received penetration in a relationship. It made me wonder whether women got more easily attached after sex because we were the ones being penetrated. Maybe there was something vulnerable about having someone go inside our bodies?

We fell asleep in each other's arms.

PLAYING OUT FANTASIES WITH MY LESBIAN LOVER

The next morning we walked across the street for breakfast. I told her about my fantasy in which I masturbated in front of a window. It was a replay of a fantasy I had since I was five years old, when I first felt aroused by standing naked in front of my bedroom window. I had never done it though. I had not mustered the courage to do it alone, and my husband was not into role playing or taking those kinds of risks. He'd always close the blinds when I walked around naked, so others couldn't see me. After I moved into my apartment, I wanted to do it, but I was embarrassed to be seen by a neighbor. There in Las Vegas, surrounded by strangers and with Noelle, I felt safe and bold. I didn't just want to talk about it. I wanted to do it. So I asked.

"Will you watch me masturbate in front of the window?"

"Yes," she smiled sweetly.

I loved how she was up for anything. After breakfast, Noelle sat on the bed and I took off my clothes. I walked to our large hotel window overlooking the back parking lot. Nobody was around. I reached down and touched my clit. I started to rub myself. It felt good. Then I saw people walking. I stopped. I didn't want them to see me. Or did I? Then, a family walked to their car. I couldn't do it then. I didn't want kids to see me. I waited for them to get in their car and drive off. I resumed masturbating. I was nervous, and not turned on. Why wasn't I turned on? Maybe some fantasies are just fun in my mind, and not a turn on in real life? I was determined to see it through, although it was hard to let go, because I was so worried about people who could again appear in the parking lot. I had to really focus and forget everything, and I kept rubbing my clit until I came, while she sat on the bed and watched me.

That was hot! I wanted to role-play more.

"Can we play doctor and nurse?" And we did.

"Let's masturbate together and talk about my favorite fantasy." And we did.

"Let's find a guy to watch us fuck." We looked, but didn't find anyone.

Anything I wanted to do, I felt free to do with Noelle. She was calm and powerful, like me. And yet we didn't have romantic feelings for each other. Just a deep friendship. It felt really good. It was a wonderful weekend, and I wanted to spend more time with Noelle.

"I need to tell you something," she told me after our trip. "You remember the woman I told you about. I like her a lot and I'm going to be monogamous with her."

I was happy for Noelle, and sad for myself. I didn't think she would want to keep our friendship going, and even if she did, she and I wouldn't have sex anymore. I wanted to meet more women who were hot and sexy and free spirited like her.

I didn't want to date any of the women I had met so far, so I went back in earnest on match.com. I had not heard of Tinder yet and it seemed more women were on match.com than the free dating sites. Still, it was hard to find women to hook up. Most were unattractive. Others wouldn't hook up with me, because they wanted a relationship. The hot ones lived far away. Mostly, it was very time consuming to keep checking profiles and correspond with so many women. Most women started with a "wink" or marked me as a "favorite", instead of sending me a message. I had several more lesbian dates with women I did not want to pursue due to their looks. Then I took a break from dating, because browsing profiles, messaging, and meeting women took a lot of time from my life. Instead, I started going to events and meetup groups.

SACRED SNUGGLE PARTIES

I learned to ask for what I want and to deal with rejection at the most unexpected place: a snuggle party. Sacred snuggle parties were hosted by Kamala Devi and Michael McClure, the couple featured on the Showtime series Polyamory: Married and Dating. According to www.Kamala Devi.com/events:

A Sacred Snuggle Party is a sweet sensual event where we gather to flirt, touch, massage, run tantric energy, play, laugh, cry, share intimacy, vulnerability or whatever else spontaneously arises. It's a drug and alcohol-free party where we can relax and connect with like-minded people. More specifically it is a social laboratory to practice expressing what feels good and what doesn't, asking to get your needs met, setting boundaries, and perhaps even overcoming rejection!

The full list of rules can be found at: http://www.cuddleparty. com/rules/. The biggest difference was that cuddle parties were non-sexual events whereas nudity and sensual play was welcome at sacred snuggle parties.

At my first sacred snuggle party, about 30 people sat in a circle on pillows in Kamala Devi's living room. After introductions and ice-breakers, Kamala Devi and Michael gave us instructions for our sensual play interactions. Throughout the evening's play, the rules were the person who was asked to be touched could say yes or no as follows:

1. If you're a yes, say *'yes'*
2. If you're a no, say *'no'*
3. If you're a maybe, say *'no'*.
4. When I am told *'no'*, I say, "*Thank you for taking care of your-self*" to honor that the other person was just doing what was right for them.
5. You can change your mind at any time.

It was okay to change my mind? These people really under-stood me. I changed my mind often on things, even on such ba-sics as whether I wanted a relationship or just sex or whether I would get dessert after dinner. It didn't mean I was weak and un-sure of myself. Maybe it was just part of human nature to change our minds and we could acknowledge it instead of pushing it away? Maybe "seeing it through" wasn't working in people's lives if their heart wasn't in it. I was drawn to this honest real way of communicating.

Kamala Devi and Michael stood next to each other and demonstrated.

"If you want to touch someone, you ask for permission. Let's say I want to touch Michael's arm. I will ask him. If he wants his arm touched, he will say yes. If he doesn't, he will say no, and if he is a maybe he will say no."

She turned to her husband.

"Can I touch your arm, Michael?"

"Yes, you can touch my arm," Michael answered.

Kamala Devi put her hand on his arm. I was struck by how respectful that was. I didn't like how men I met for coffee just grabbed me for a hug, without even knowing if that's what I wanted. Kamala Devi said we had to ask for each experience we wanted with that person, unless we already had a relationship that implied we could touch them anywhere, or the person had explicitly said so.

"Michael, can I hug you?"

"No," he replied.

Kamala Devi looked at Michael and said, "Thank you for taking care of yourself."

She turned to the group.

"Notice when he said no, I was left free to go find someone who wanted a hug. I'd rather hug someone who really wants it, than someone who said yes just to please me."

That made a lot of sense. It seemed sometimes people said 'yes' to avoid disappointing the other person, and thus got into inauthentic situations and avoided reality. I wanted reality. I didn't want avoidance, withdrawal, or pretend.

Michael joined in.

"This is how we deal with rejection. When I said 'no', Kamala Devi thanked me for taking care of myself. When you thank the other person for saying 'no' to you, you acknowledge that 'no' was only to take care of themselves. The 'no' has nothing to do with you. There could be many reasons I don't want a hug. Maybe

I have an injured back, maybe I was worried I smelled bad and didn't want anyone too close, or maybe I just don't like hugs. It's so important to say 'no' if you are a 'no'. If you never tell me 'no', how do I know your 'yes' is real?"

He had a point!

Kamala Devi nodded her head. Michael spoke again.

"Kamala Devi, I changed my mind. I want a hug," he said and turned playfully to his wife.

The couple laughed and hugged each other.

After the instructions, each of us stood up and said one experience we wanted that evening, and one experience we did not want. I was drawn to their clear way of talking, and of thinking about what we wanted and sharing that. After the demonstration, we broke into groups of three and started sensual play. Within minutes, the room was alive with people taking ownership of their experiences.

More men than women attended. I noticed several men sitting alone on the perimeter of the room. I wanted to give them love. It wasn't right that just because they were physically unattractive, they were excluded. I asked one very large man if I could hug him, and he said yes. I asked him to scoot over, so I could hug him from behind. I sat behind him. I wrapped my arms around him and then I closed my eyes. His body felt warm, strong. My heart warmed and I felt happy. I forgot he was large and otherwise unattractive.

"I like this," I said.

"I haven't been hugged in years," he told me.

He told me he lived alone and broke up with a girlfriend about three years earlier, and had not hugged or had any intimate touch since then. I was surprised that anyone went that long without touch. I was sure he wasn't the only one.

"Will you hug me?" I asked him.

"Yes."

I sat in front of him on the pillows and he put his arms around me. I leaned back and relaxed into his strong arms. I felt comforted. Why did I choose people based on their looks, when the hugs had nothing to do with looks? If I were blind, maybe I would be dating unattractive people. Just because I had eyes, the man had to look a certain way. That's the way it was for me though.

Sometimes I went for weeks without hooking up, and eventually I longed for human touch. That's when I went to snuggle parties. When I wanted sex, I went online.

CHAPTER 12

DISCOVERING A LUST FOR YOUNG MEN

22 YEAR OLD MARINE: "YOUR PUSSY IS SO TIGHT"

It was the first week in August. Since my trip to Las Vegas with Noelle the month before, I had not hooked up with anyone. I was online on two dating sites, looking for beautiful, smart, sexually adventurous women like Noelle or Malory. But I had not met anyone to date and my social life was boring, so the next time my friends went downtown dancing, I asked to go along.

I was not interested in meeting men or hooking up. I just wanted to dance, or maybe pick up or meet a woman. I watched groups of women dance, and sometimes I joined them.

"Do you like girls?" I asked some of the women.

I wanted to know if that particular woman could be a hook-up potential. Some did, but I couldn't picture myself kissing her. Others said no. Whenever a guy came up to talk, I told him I was a lesbian, to get rid of him and also get his reaction. I danced either with women or alone the entire night. Towards closing time, a very young, handsome fit man, about 6'4", came up to me.

"Do you want to dance?" he asked.

I looked up and couldn't figure out why a man clearly in his 20's asked me to dance. He could have been my kids' friend. I never considered flirting or dancing with someone my kids' age. I never considered a man that age would even find me attractive.

"No," I said, almost mad, yet feeling a bit flattered.

Then I turned to my friend Mary.

"Mary, that guy just asked me to dance. He's so young!"

"He's cute," she said. "Not as cute as his friend, but cute."

I looked back at the young man. He had not walked away. He was talking with his friend, looking around the bar. Perhaps he looked around to find other women he could ask for a dance. I looked at him closely. He was fucking sexy! His friend was hotter, but he was definitely hot too. He wore a plaid shirt and tight jeans and he looked strong and lean, just the way I liked. Did a young man like that really find me attractive? Maybe I looked better than I thought. I was flattered and curious.

I walked closer and stood right against him. I lightly stroked his arm. Damn, his arm was strong. I was immediately turned on and my body felt hot.

"How old are you?"

He leaned down to hear me better. I had to talk into his ear, because of the loud music in the bar. I liked being that close to him.

"22, Ma'am," he answered.

He smelled like alcohol, but barely. He seemed sober enough that I wanted to continue the conversation. I loved that he called me Ma'am.

"I have kids your age," I told him.

He smiled. I told him the ages of my children.

"How old do you think I am?" I asked.

He looked at me closely. It was dark in the bar, but he could see my face.

"38, Ma'am," he finally said.

I laughed. I was definitely flattered.

"I'm 51."

He looked down at me and smiled.

"What's your name?" I asked.

"Nate."

"I love your name! I'm Schahrzad."

He asked me to repeat my name and then he repeated it after me, and smiled at me again. I wanted to be very close to him and feel his arms around me.

"I'll dance with you," I told him.

He took me by one hand, my friend by the other, and twirled us out on the dance floor. I was impressed that a man so young had the confidence to take not just one, but two women over age 40 on the dance floor. I didn't like him dancing with her too. I wanted his arms around me, his eyes on me. I wanted him to hold me and desire me and make love to me, fuck me, long for me, be with me. I forgot all about women.

A slow song came up next.

"Dance with me," I asked.

I wrapped my arms around Nate's neck and he held me tight around my back while my friend vanished somewhere. We danced together, slowly. He was tall and strong, and he felt good. He held me tight and looked at me.

I couldn't believe I had landed such a hunk! I thought my days of having hot men were way behind me. I had noticed young attractive men like him, out with their equal-age women, when I was married with children. That was a life I could never have, I thought. I had my middle-aged man. I was married. My die was cast.

But there I was separated, and new possibilities beckoned. Nate looked like a model. I was seriously turned on. My pussy was so wet, my panties felt damp. I just wanted him to grab me tight and kiss me and put his cock inside me. How would he make love to me? Would he be tender or demanding or dominant? He could take the place of Rudy, the man with the sister fetish. He was a young man, he was probably horny all the time, and we could have sex daily or as often as he could come over. It was perfect.

"Let's go outside to talk," I suggested.

I wanted to present my idea where it was less noisy. He led the way, and I followed him outside. He lifted me up in the air, and I wrapped my legs around him, and we laughed. He kept calling me "Ma'am".

"I want to ask you something. I just lost my fuck buddy, and I need a replacement," I explained.

"I can help you with that, Ma'am," and he smiled and hugged and kissed me.

I was thrilled to replace Rudy with that strapping young hunk. I asked him what he did for work. He told me he was a jet engine mechanic for the Marine Corps. I had been anti-military most of my life, but had become open minded and more loving over the past few years. I did not mind he was in the military, and he seemed sweet, so I invited him over. He eagerly agreed. Nate told his friend good-bye and left with us.

"Why do you like older women?" I asked as we walked to Mary's car. "Younger women have younger bodies, no wrinkles, and more in common with you."

"Having sex with a young woman is like having sex with a plastic doll. I prefer sex with older women."

Did that mean they just laid there and did nothing? That was an exaggeration. But I knew I was more sexual and more confident than in my early 20's, so I was probably more exciting and passionate in bed than many young women. Did he just fuck women my age, or also date them?

As we drove to my car, which was parked near Mary's house, I kept thinking about our age difference and that I was about to have a young stud in my bed. I hoped he wasn't going to change his mind. How long had he been doing this and how many other men did it?

"Is this a common thing, for men your age to want sex with older women?" I asked.

"Yeah, almost all my friends want to have sex with older women, but not all have the confidence to go after it."

Fuck, no way! Oh my god, why didn't I know about that? I remembered hearing the term *MILF*, or Moms I Love to Fuck. The term implied bored housewives with breast implants and bleached blond hair that would fuck anyone, including young men. I never wanted to be so indiscriminate in my fucking. I didn't ever want to be a MILF. I had also heard *cougar*, which implied being a bully, hunting prey, and taking advantage of someone. I didn't like that term either. I wasn't going to take advantage of him. I had also heard of rich older women who had boy toys, but the man was only there because she paid his way. I didn't want to have a man because I paid for him.

If many younger men liked fucking older women, why had I never heard about it happening outside of porn and occasional tabloid stories involving rich beautiful actresses? Maybe it was rarely done. I found the idea extremely exciting. I had never considered it until barely an hour earlier. I still hoped he wouldn't change his mind about fucking me.

By the time we got to my apartment, it was 2 a.m. and I was so tired, I could barely keep my eyes open. I went into the kitchen to get us some water and a fruit plate. He walked over and kissed me in the kitchen and I just melted into his strong body. He kneeled on the floor at my feet, pulled down my jeans, and licked my vulva and clit. I looked down at his handsome young face on my pussy. He got up and took a piece of cantaloupe off the plate. I thought he was hungry, but instead he kneeled on the floor again, rubbed the piece of cantaloupe all over my vulva, and then he ate it. Fucking hot!

He slapped my ass and smiled up at me. I didn't like spanking. It reminded me of one of the two times I was spanked as a child, and it had felt humiliating. Most girls must have liked that, because he reached his hand back and wanted to slap my ass again, and I told him again I didn't like it. He was so used to doing it, and he had forgot. He apologized.

"Did you bring a condom?" I asked.

"No, Ma'am."

I loved that he kept calling me "Ma'am". So he just went around hooking up without condoms. He wasn't concerned about STDs? I had plenty of condoms.

He stood up to undress. I helped him. I unbuckled his belt, then unbuttoned and unzipped his jeans. I gasped when he took off his shirt! He was fit and lean like the statue David by Michelangelo, and he had six pack abs. I pulled down his pants and boxers. His cock was stiff, extremely stiff, at more than a 90-degree angle. His cock pointed to the ceiling. Nice!! He was extremely turned on, even though I was so much older. His large balls hung down, and I couldn't wait to have it all in my mouth. I took off the rest of my clothes, and then he carried me into the bedroom.

"I'm not too heavy for you?"

I hadn't been carried into a bedroom in decades. I weighed 128 pounds.

"No, not at all."

He laid me on the bed, on my down comforter. I scooted back and my head dropped on the pillow. He went down on me again. His tongue moved all over my clit. First in circles, then in up and down strokes, then more circles. He was so young, and so skilled.

"Wow, that feels amazing," I said.

I rose up on my hands to look at him. His handsome face was pressed against my pussy. That was the way to do it. Pressed right up against me, not inches away with the tongue pushed out. His short hair turned me on even more.

He looked up at me with his beautiful brown eyes, while he circled my clit with his tongue. *I must be dreaming*, having such a handsome man between my legs. I took in the beautiful scene, his strong back and round ass, his muscular legs stretched out on my bed. Damn! I looked down at my landing strip, the strip of pubic hair I left in place when I shaved. I wondered if he liked it. I was glad I shaved every morning in the shower, even though I wasn't expecting sex. I lay back on the pillow, closed my eyes, and let him tongue me more. I let myself receive pleasure. My 31-yr old single friend had said she never knew a marine who didn't like eating pussy, so I figured he liked doing it. I just let him do it a few minutes. Then I wanted a turn to pleasure him.

"Here, lay down," I offered.

He got up. His mouth and chin glistened with my pussy juices. He wiped it dry with the back of his hand, and we laughed. He lay on his back. I kissed him, and then I went down on him. His balls smelled so manly! I inhaled to get all of him. I ran my tongue down his perineum, licking back and forth and I pushed my tongue down to rim his asshole. He gasped. I licked all around his asshole, in circles, back and forth, and I sucked his inner thigh. I kissed, nibbled, and sucked gently on these harder to reach areas, which turned me on a lot and I was wet and moaning. I worked my way back up. I licked and sucked his beautiful large cock. He was good sized. Sucking him turned me on to want him inside me.

I got a condom out of my nightstand and put it on him. He didn't complain about the condom. And then I got on top and he pushed his hard large cock inside me. Fuck. He felt so good! I was so wet. I liked a man to slide in slowly, but he went right in, I was so wet. I just rode him and rode him, moaning louder and getting wetter. We kissed passionately, our tongues moving in tandem with each thrust. I sat upright and looked down at him. He wanted to slap my ass, and I reminded him I don't like that.

"Just grab my ass, I love that."

I was so wet from riding him already, but when he grabbed my ass I really went wild. He put one hand on each cheek and squeezed hard, just like I liked. He pulled me up and down on his cock, with his hands on my ass. I got more excited and I rode him hard until my legs got tired and I was really sweaty, and then I still kept going. His cock felt amazing! I pushed my tongue in his mouth, in rhythm with pushing his cock deep inside me. I tongue fucked him. I felt rough and lusty and I didn't care.

"Your pussy is so tight!" he told me.

Wow, I had a tight pussy. What a compliment! I had not heard that before. I asked Rick once if my pussy was looser after child-birth and he said he didn't know, since he wasn't sure how it felt before. Nate was used to fucking young women. Was I tight like young women?

"Really, I'm tight?" I asked him.

"Yeah, you're really tight," he said.

I remembered all the Kegels I did on my runs. I didn't know all those Kegels paid off.

"And your skin is so soft," he added.

I did have soft skin. Was that from drinking cod liver oil? Maybe. Why did he mention it? Was it soft for my age, or soft in general?

He flipped me over on my back and got on top and kissed me. I loved how a man handled me and moved me around in bed. I grabbed him tight and let him fuck me as he wanted. It all felt so good, I wanted it to last forever. I looked up. Fuck, there was that strong young body thrusting in me. His charming smile, his hip bone moving up and down, his hard thick cock sliding in and out of my pussy, his tender demanding kisses, it all seemed too good to be true. I liked Nate's passionate dominant style of fuck-ing. Everything he did felt so good! He wanted to come inside me, in the missionary position, and he did. Hot! It was how I liked a man to come.

The sex was amazing, except I hadn't come. I masturbated while he held me and kissed me and played with my nipples. I came and moaned loudly and I thought I woke up the neighbors.

He spent the night and we had sex again in the morning. I made him breakfast and drove him back to the base. He asked for my business card. I wasn't sure if I'd ever see him again and that was fine. I didn't have any feelings for him.

But a few weeks later, as I kept thinking of him and he had not called, I wished I had his number. I hoped he would call me again. Or maybe I could find more hot men like him? Maybe someday. I was still online looking for women.

CAN WE TALK ABOUT IT?

It was mid August, and I felt at the top of my game, going after what I wanted and talking about it. There was no reason to keep my exciting sex life to myself. I became even more outspoken about sex to my friends, and on Facebook. I made Facebook posts about what I was doing sexually. People were interested in my stories. It seemed people liked being around someone who was open about her life, especially someone who was open about enjoying sex. My friends said I had no filter. I called it being open and self-expressed.

Some of my friends from years ago didn't like it. My friend Myra, whom I knew for twenty years, didn't like all my sex posts on FB. One day, she sent me a FB message. She wrote she blocked me because she did not want to read about all of my "broadcasted sexual activity". She said she found it annoying, and sex is something private between two people. Some of her FB friends asked about me, presumably because they went to my page because of comments I left on her posts, and she had 'no energy' for that. She wished me all the best and told me I was an amazing and sweet person. I was hurt, and yet I also understood. A few days later, a friend who had worked with me at the escort service unfriended me for the same reason – his aunt was asking who I was and he didn't want to explain it. Explain what? Couldn't a man in his late 40's decide whom he wanted on FB as a friend? Why did people hide who they were and who they wanted to talk with?

That's when I realized my friends had changed from married moms in their 50's to single women and men mostly in their 20's to 40's. I had been attending events, meetups, and meditation groups, and I was drawn to single people. I was not as interested anymore in being with couples and married women, since all I wanted to talk about was sex and dating.

Why did I only want to talk about sex and dating? What had happened to my interest in my career, economics, cooking, and making a home? Was my friend right to say I was too open talking about sex? Was sex something to be kept private between the people having it? Then why were some people so drawn to me, and anxious to hear more?

Other friends and even salespeople at department stores encouraged me, and sought me out. I felt a hunger from people to hear authentic discussion about sex. Their curiosity and interest in me lowered any shame I had I about the morality of my hookups. Some men said my openness reduced their own shame about lusting after women. They said they felt 'dirty' for wanting a woman's body because women seemed to get mad about it. Men had shame too? People were telling me their secrets. All my hooking up and being open about it made me and others feel free. Besides, I had nothing to feel ashamed of. My life and my inner joy were proof my life was working.

I wasn't serious about a relationship. I didn't want a partnership. I wanted sex and intimacy and cuddling and vulnerable conversation. Attractive people occurred to me as sex objects, not as people with feelings and goals. I usually wanted to leave after the sex was over, especially with women.

My whole life I heard women complain, "he just wanted sex and then he dumped me." There I was, just wanting sex and dumping women. I wasn't a cold person. Why did I leave? Was it the same reason men left? Did men really 'use' women if the women enjoyed the sex and got something out of it? Why had my friend said she felt used after sex? Did I really use people? I came up with these reasons that I left, and that I thought men left women as well:

1. The sex was not hot enough.
2. I can't imagine you in my daily life
3. I don't want a relationship (maybe not now, maybe never). And you are not going to change that!!

ABSTINENCE

I met lesbians for coffee, but I wasn't interested in hooking up with the women I met, because they were not attractive enough. Erica was an exception. She was in her late 40's and overweight, but she had something I wanted: years of BDSM experience in a long-term lesbian relationship. I was really curious about having a lesbian dominate me sexually. As we sat talking over coffee, I tried to imagine myself kissing her, but I was repulsed at the thought. I debated whether I could have sex with her anyway. It wasn't easy to find a lesbian into BDSM. I decided I could have sex, but I couldn't kiss her. I felt a little odd telling her that, but she was horny and was fine with it. I invited her over.

She wanted to go down on me first. Erica was amazing at oral sex. Her tongue moved and slid on my clit in all the right places. I moaned louder and I knew she could make me come. She was so turned on, she moaned and got really sweaty, and that helped me relax. My orgasm built and I came, and came hard. I returned the favor and then I couldn't wait for her to leave. I was still repulsed by her. I was surprised I could orgasm from someone I wasn't attracted to. Maybe her unattractiveness made me more at ease and let go? Maybe that was part of it. But mostly it was her skilled oral technique and her enthusiasm for pussy. So I did not need to feel emotionally connected or attracted to someone to come. I just needed to know the person enjoyed it so I could relax.

Nonetheless, the tryst with Erica seemed like a low point. I wanted to put a halt to the meaningless hookups. I decided to take a break. I didn't know how long it would last. I just needed a break. I called the break celibacy, but a more correct term was abstinence.

The break wasn't always easy. After one week, I already missed having someone to hold and cuddle, and giving and receiving affection. I questioned my abstinence on days I felt horny. I remained steadfast anyway.

About two weeks later, I finally heard from 22-year-old Nate. He texted me, and asked how I was doing. My abstinence was more important than seeing him. I told him I was celibate. I just wasn't interested in fucking anyone, and I didn't want to break my abstinence out of the blue for no reason. He wished me well.

I remained abstinent because I did not know what I wanted. I liked dominant lesbians, and I wanted a hot chick that could fuck me like a guy and throw me up against the wall. What made me want a woman was more about the pressure I felt with a man to be quick to orgasm. It wasn't that I wanted to be with a woman in a relationship.

I was attracted to men. I thought of switching teams and going back to men and working through the issue I had with thinking I was work in the bedroom. I still liked single dads in their 40's and family life, and thought about raising children again. I also liked younger men.

Lesbians, single dads, and younger men....all those things I wanted were mutually exclusive, and since I wasn't sure who I wanted to bring back to my bed, I took a break from hooking up. I wasn't dating either.

I still had regrets at times that my marriage ended. It seemed like such a shame, since we had both loved each other so much. I didn't want him anymore, but I wished he had been different so we could have stayed together. We talked about the breakup sometimes.

"Mom, you changed and he didn't," my daughter said.

It was true. It also meant he didn't do anything wrong. He was exactly the man I married. I changed. I broke the rules in a way.

The kids told me he hadn't been sleeping well. They said his bedroom lights were on all night, and he had big circles under his eyes. I called Rick and asked how he was doing. He said he was trying to find meaning in life and move on.

September came. I was still abstinent, and no longer saw the point of it. I went back online to meet women.

I met Ashley for a sushi dinner date in mid-September. She was a 34-year-old horse trainer, blond, with radiant eyes, a warm smile, flawless skin, and a body toned from working with horses all day. Our conversation was easy and comfortable. I liked her confidence. Ashley was lesbian, yet she had no issues with me also seeing men. As I sat across the table from her, I was struck by her vivaciousness and beauty. I wasn't attracted to her.

How could I not be attracted, when she was so hot? Maybe I would get turned on once we made out. We took a walk after dinner, and we stopped and I stood close to her, and nothing inside me made me want to kiss her. She must have felt the same way, because neither of us made a move. She walked me to my car, and then we finally kissed, and I didn't feel turned on.

I liked Ashley, so when she called me a few days later to invite me to cook vegan with her, I asked her over. I suggested that she come on a night that Wilson and Christine were over, so they could meet her. The kids didn't like me having men over, because they didn't like the idea of a revolving door of men, but they had liked meeting my lesbian dates Noelle and Malory. It really made no sense, but it was probably based on the meanings they attached to my relationships with women versus men. They probably knew that women did not compete emotionally for my attention, so they weren't jealous or uncomfortable. I checked with the kids, and they said Ashley could come over, and they wanted to meet her.

Ashley brought all the ingredients and cooked a 10-minute vegan recipe, mostly with healthy packaged food from Trader Joe's. The kids ate with us. During dinner, I debated whether or not I wanted to have sex with her. I definitely wanted to go down on her. I was still abstinent though. Would going down on a woman end my abstinence, and did I mind? Could I have sex with her while my kids were home? Yes. I would clear it with them first. After dinner the kids went in Wilson's bedroom and Ashley and I cleaned up the kitchen.

"Do you want to go into my bedroom?" I asked.

"Maybe," she glanced over at me. "Are you sure your kids are okay with this?"

"Yes, they're fine, come on."

Ashley wasn't convinced. She disagreed with me and we went back and forth until I convinced her the kids wouldn't care. I went into Wilson's room. He was playing a video game, and Christine was reading a book.

"We're going in my bedroom," I told them.

They looked at me quizzically, but didn't object. I knew they didn't want me having sex with a man while they were over. I didn't think they would mind if I took a woman into my bedroom.

I had a different way of viewing sex with women, that didn't make sense to other people. My mom said since I was young that women were more refined than men, and that men just wanted sex and sex was bad. I had always believed sex with women was good. It wasn't something to be hidden away as sex with men had to be. I had also heard of the emotional damage to children who saw their moms bring in a revolving door of men, but had never heard that in regard to women. I came back out to Ashley.

"Yeah, the kids don't mind," I said.

We went in the bedroom and closed the door. I still wasn't attracted to her, but I couldn't wait to go down on her. I asked her if I could, and she said 'no'. I respected her no. I wasn't going to try talking her into it. I learned at the sacred snuggle party to respect and even encourage others when they were a "no". She wanted to go down on me, and I let her, but she wasn't good at it and I didn't come. I wanted to masturbate and let her watch, but she said she was tired and had to go.

"Send me a picture of you masturbating," she told me.

I finished myself off masturbating after she left, and texted her some pictures of myself naked on the floor, in front of my closet mirror, with my fingers on my clit.

The next morning, Christine said, "Mom, we didn't like you having sex in your bedroom while we were home. That made us really uncomfortable."

Wilson agreed.

"Ok, I'm sorry, I thought you wouldn't mind since she was my friend. Thanks for letting me know."

The kids had a point. I also realized that as much as I wanted to combine dating and motherhood, I hadn't accomplished it. Could it ever be done? I had always disapproved of moms who brought their revolving door of men into their children's lives, and decided I would never do that; however, was I doing that to them? My kids were 17 and 22 years old and no longer children. Would I ever have sexual freedom?

There was more. I wanted my kids to be comfortable with sex. I had regrets for the missed opportunity in teaching my children about sex and connection while they grew up. It was a major omission, and I knew I had to correct it. When I talked about my lovers, or I had Ashley over, I taught them by example how I dated and how it worked for me. They weren't used to talking about sex, so it was natural they would be uncomfortable at times. I just needed to be persistent and not let the discomfort stop me.

I felt a deep sense I was doing the right thing not only for them, but for also for me. I had to go on an adventure inside myself, and unlike my spiritual and educational adventures, which were family-friendly, this one seemed to be anti-family for some reason. I really thought it was just the way society and kids viewed sex and our human need for touch and connection. Maybe we were all too sterile about it all.

I WAS A PIT STOP ON HIS WAY TO THE GYM

That night with Ashley ended six weeks of abstinence. A couple days later Nate, the 22 year old marine, texted me while I was at work and asked how I was doing. That time, I wanted to see him. It had been a couple months since I had sex with a man. I was curious what it would be like for me. I remembered his young hard body on mine, how he called me "Ma'am", and it really turned me on. Nate said he was no longer a marine. He worked in a warehouse and went to the gym several hours a day, so he could be in top shape for his modeling photo shoots. I invited him over.

He said he was free Thursday after work. He said he would come over straight from work on his way to the gym. I didn't like that at all. I liked a man to get showered and dressed up for me, and the gym comment implied he wouldn't stay long. But I wanted to see him badly, so I agreed to Thursday after work.

He texted me when he left work. I got ready. I put on a sexy dress, heels, and my favorite perfume. I was turned on and excited. He knocked on my door. I opened the door and there he stood and I blushed. Although he was wearing his t-shirt and plain jeans and work boots, he was tall, strong, and handsome, just like I remembered him. He was sexy as hell!

"Hi, how have you been?" he asked in his soft deep voice, and smiled at me.

"Great. It's so good to see you."

"You look amazing!" he said.

He came inside and shut the door. I walked over and wrapped my arms around him. I pressed into his strong muscular stomach and held him tight.

"Wow, you feel so good!" I told him.

I looked up to kiss him and his warm lips met mine. I moaned softly. Kissing and moaning, and getting all wet. Nate reached behind me, under my dress, put his hand down the back of my panties, and slid his fingers easily inside my wet pussy. I moaned louder.

"Oh my god, that feels so good!"

I lost my balance and he held me with his other arm and his fingers probed deep inside me. I didn't want him to ever stop fingering me. I writhed my body to meet his probing fingers. *Deeper, deeper, don't stop, just please don't stop.* I felt selfish for just taking all that pleasure. I thought I needed to reciprocate.

"Come, let's go in my bedroom," I invited him.

He scooped me up and carried me into the bedroom. I giggled. "Aren't I too heavy for you?"

I had asked him that before. He laughed.

"No."

He put me down gently on my bed. Then he took off his clothes, and I noticed his colorful large tattoos and his strong lean body. I had not noticed the tattoos the first time. I didn't have tattoos, but I loved them on men. They turned me on. Nate was hard as a rock. Stiff and erect.

He laid me on my back and put his head between my legs and I spread my legs wide with anticipation. His warm tongue licked circular strokes on my vulva, settled on my clit, and then he sucked gently. I didn't recall him sucking the first time. It felt amazing! Wow, such delight. He licked more. I rose up on my elbows and looked at his brown hair and young face buried between my legs. He looked up at me. Kept licking, while he looked me in the eye.

"Damn, you're so good at that!" I told him.

He smiled.

"Here, lay down," and I patted the bed.

He lay down my bed. I licked his large soft balls and ran my tongue up his shaft while I looked him in the eyes. I brushed my face against his hard cock. Then I asked him if he brought a condom. He didn't. I thought he probably never used a condom. I had so many in my nightstand. I slipped a condom on him. I started riding him, but in less than a few minutes he flipped me around and sweetly and tenderly turned me on my back. His young hard cock filled me up and then went out, filled me up and went out, over and over and over and over, and I never wanted it to end. I clutched him tight and we kissed while he fucked me tenderly.

"Can I come inside you? Without a condom?"

"I love a man coming inside of me! But I can't do that with you without a condom. Why do you like coming inside a girl?"

"It's more intimate."

"Yeah. Well, come inside me, with a condom."

Nate turned me over and fucked me from behind. I pushed my ass up in the air to take him in deeper. He stayed hard a long time, and he fucked me well, and then he came in the doggy style position and he was distant. He didn't hold me close or kiss me, and I felt all alone. I masturbated to orgasm while he just lay there. That was a huge turn-off. Maybe he had things on his mind or he was tired, but I was disappointed.

I wondered if he would open up more if we dated. He had said he liked older women. Did he like older women just for sex, or also for dating? Was I too old for him? I used my courage and asked him.

"Can we go out sometime, maybe to the beach or something?" I asked.

"Then it would mean something," he said. "I don't want to be in a relationship." He told me about his calendar shoot in Dallas while he got dressed, and then he left for the gym.

I felt deserted. I didn't feel used. Nate was tender and sweet to me, and I enjoyed myself. But I wanted more. I longed for a deeper longer connection, and I was just a pit stop between work and the gym.

I let myself feel sad and then I sobbed. When I finished crying, I sat down and played piano. I had not played it once since I moved into my apartment. The tender music of Chopin filled my heart in all the places he had created and left empty.

THE STRENGTH OF A MAN

The next morning, I almost forgot about wanting to date Nate, the 22-year-old former marine. I did not like how I went back and forth. Mary first pointed it out, "You don't know at all what you want!" she'd say, and I got defensive because I wanted to be a woman who knew what she wanted and went after it. I guess I did, it's just that what I wanted kept changing. Sometimes I wanted a connection and a relationship. Other times I wanted to stay single so I could be free without thinking of anyone else's needs and had the option of seeing if someone better came along.

But after Nate, I was finally very sure of one thing: I no longer wanted sex with women. I wanted to fuck men. I missed the strength of a man. I missed the smell and touch of a man, the way a man moved, picturing him doing his favorite outdoor activities, his cologne, the way I just melted into a man's strong arms. Sexually, I preferred riding hard cocks to having a dildo inside me. I was curious if I could get more young men. Was Nate an exception? I texted Nate to ask what he liked about older women. He replied right away:

I love older women because they know how to appreciate my young hot sexy body- I'm 6'4" and I'm muscular. They know how to enjoy a nice glass of wine and they know how to actually have passionate intimate good sex. I don't mind that you're 51 - that's hot. I love the way u look.

Damn, that was hot! If he felt that way, surely more young men did too. I wanted to fuck more young men. I didn't want to go on coffee dates and have oral sex and maybe a dildo or fingers with a woman. I wanted to be taken and dominated by young hot hunks with hard cocks. My lust and animal forces were awakened. I wanted to play with it, give it life, and see where it took me. I also yearned for freedom from the weight I carried inside of feeling sexually inadequate and of being work in the bedroom, carryovers from my marriage. I was curious about how different men made love, and what I could learn about sex, men, and myself. And of course I was lusty and really enjoyed fucking.

Yeah, I loved fucking.

Could I say that in polite company? "I love to fuck".

There, I said it.

And then I started telling my friends. I started saying words to my friends I had never heard myself say:

"I like fucking. I'm horny and I want to fuck."

There were no reasons to hold back. Reasons like: "I need to have feelings for a man before I have sex," "good girls don't", "he won't respect me if I do", "I can't let him see me naked", "I'm afraid of meeting people online", "I'm afraid of STDs", "I'm afraid what others will think", "what if I get pregnant?" I didn't have any of that. I just needed to look up to and desire the man, and I needed to feel respected, valued, and safe. That was all.

I needed to find fit, successful, tall young men, but I didn't want to go to bars. All my sex had been sober sex and I liked it that way. I liked to feel. Alcohol numbed me mentally, emotionally, and physically, and I wanted to connect. When I drank, it took me longer to come, and men who had been drinking were less attentive in conversation and less hard. Bars were not the place to meet a man for a hookup. But where?

Although I often went out socially and through work, I rarely saw hot men in real life. And when I did see a man who was attractive enough, he was at the grocery store with a girlfriend, or at coffee with the wife and kids, or he didn't return my glances when I checked him out.

So I resorted to going online. I went on OKCupid and I made an online dating profile specifically looking for sex, with pictures showing off my ass in a bikini. I had a nice ass, and I knew it. Men who liked petite women with nice asses typically went for me, and I wanted to play up all my features. I wanted to attract men who liked the outdoors and sex, men who were open with their hearts and as passionate about life as I was. In the profile section I listed what I wanted sexually, like oral sex, intercourse, and eye contact. I set the age range from 22 – 55 years old. I did like some older men (40's and 50's), provided they had a flat stomach, confident posture, and a spark in their eyes. All that was rare to find at my age, so I focused my browsing on the young men.

Why did men lose the sparkle in their eyes and their fitness as they aged? I never wanted to let myself go like that. I wanted to stay playful, curious, innocent, and lusty. That meant doing things differently and stretching myself. Why didn't I swing on that big tree swing at the end of the trail? Maybe I was resisting my own playfulness. What had happened to that playfulness of childhood? I wanted more of it. I went on the swing. When I ran and wanted to throw my water bottle in the air as I ran, I started doing it. I climbed a tree in the park and took selfies to send a guy who wasn't feeling well. I hugged a tree, even though I felt awkward wondering what passersby would think of it. I bought a brighter lipstick, a new outfit, ran a new trail, had my pedicure at a different salon. Every time I did something new, even something so small, I felt more alive and stronger. No wonder I was drawn to young men. I was young inside!

Online, I saw so many hot young men. They were available and single, and easy to approach. I loved looking at their strong young hard bodies. Seeing those young men with their shirts off, with a charming smile, backwards baseball cap, and hiking with their dogs was a huge turn-on. I notice as I browsed their profiles, my body got so flushed and hot for about ten seconds, I had to take off my sweater or turn on the AC. I hoped at least some of them liked older women.

My plan was to meet for coffee, as I had done all along. It worked well. A coffee date was a simple way to gauge our mutual interest, without the distraction of eating or the interruption of waiters checking on us. It would be easy to leave at anytime, since there was no obligation to sit through a meal. And it was cheap. Why should men get financially burdened just to meet people and connect? Coffee was familiar from meeting with real estate clients and friends over the years. Besides, I loved coffee. Coffee was the way to go.

I sent messages to every man who turned me on, and in their early 20's there were dozens. As men got older, fewer of them turned me on and by age 50 it was rare anyone was attractive to me. I rarely received a reply. Maybe I came on too strong. Maybe I wasn't their type. I did receive a lot of incoming messages, but all from men I found very unappealing.

FELL FOR A 20-YEAR-OLD COLLEGE STUDENT

Finally, one incoming message caught my attention. It was from JustinInSD.

"I hope you're still on this site in two years when I'm 22" he wrote.

I clicked on his profile and liked what I saw. He was tall, 6'3", and slender. He had a cute sweet face that looked like one of my kids' friends. His authentic request to meet me was touching. How could I resist his invitation?

But gosh, he was only 20 years old, so young! What did he want from me? Did he really want sex with me, a woman so much older? He had been online searching in my age range and found me. And could I really have sex with a man so young? Yeah, I could. In fact, I got aroused thinking about fucking a man my kids' age, mostly for the novelty and perhaps also for the taboo. I had never heard of a woman my age having sex with men so young. I also knew I was intensely attracted to a young man's hard body. I changed my lower age limit in my preferences section to 20 years old. I considered going to 18, but thought going that young could wait for another day. Then I messaged him back.

Justin said he wanted to meet me for a hookup. He said he liked older women. We set up a coffee date at Starbucks near my apartment for the following week on a Wednesday night. It was late September, the day before my 52nd birthday.

I didn't see him when I arrived, so I ordered a latte and sat in an armchair by the door. A tall young man with thick brown hair came into the Starbucks. Was it Justin? He wore a long wool coat. Long coats, suits, and a well-dressed man were huge turn-ons. It was hot and it warmed me inside and I smiled. I also loved his purposeful, strong, and energetic walk. He saw me and walked over.

"Hi, I'm Justin," and he reached out his hand.

He impressed me. I didn't like men coming in for a hug to greet me, since it felt like they were just groping me. Justin's handshake was classy.

"Hi, it's so nice to meet you!"

He sat down next to me, and turned his body toward me, and looked me in the eyes.

"How was your day?" he asked.

Wow. Nice opening. He started by asking about me.

"It was really great. Oh my god, you are soooo handsome!"

I loved saying what I thought and giving compliments and being forward like that. I asked him what he did, and he told me he was a full time marketing student at a local community college. He also worked 30 hours a week at a retailer, and he had to study after our date for a test the next morning. His discipline and work ethic raised my interest in him.

"I'm going to get a coffee. Go ahead and grab a table outside and I'll meet you out there," he said,

I liked that he took charge. I had not expected a young man to keep a good conversation and direct me where to sit. I found a table outside, and he came out shortly to join me. All I could think about as we talked were my wrinkles. Did he regret meeting me because I looked too old? I needed to reassure myself.

"So you like older women?" I asked.

His eyes lit up and he smiled.

"Yes! I do."

That was just hot. I was turned on knowing the age difference aroused him. I was probably part of some fantasy that excited him.

"What do you like about them?" I asked.

"They know what they want sexually. They are interesting," he paused. "What do you like about younger men?"

I looked him straight in the eyes. I imagined his naked body against mine, and his eager hard cock inside me.

"I like their strong hard bodies."

"Oh yeah?" he smiled.

It occurred to me at that moment that a man liked to be wanted just for his body. Women seemed to resent only being liked for their bodies, but maybe men liked it.

"You want to come over?" I asked.

He didn't hesitate.

"Yes."

I texted him my address in case we got separated. We drove to my complex. I met him outside my building, and we walked along the walkway and up the stairs to my second floor unit. As he walked behind me, I wondered if he was watching my ass.

"I like your apartment!"

"Oh, thank you!"

I walked into the kitchen, and he followed me in.

" Do you want some tea?" I offered and looked at him.

Fuck, he was so handsome!

"No."

"What music do you like?"

I plugged my phone into the speakers on my kitchen counter and put on Pandora on my phone.

"Play what you want," he said.

I put on my Passenger station. He walked over and tenderly leaned down to kiss me. His lips were soft and I melted into a warm soothing feeling that started in my heart and washed over my body. That was the emotional part of sex I needed. I felt open and receptive and I wanted to be taken so I put my hands behind my back. His strong hands gripped my waist and he pulled me closer. He tugged tenderly on my lips, and then his tongue met mine, and I kissed him back slowly. My body felt hot and I wanted to take off my sweater. I pressed closer into him, and then I felt his strong chest and abs. Fuck.

My hunger for him grew, and my kissing became demanding and harder. The heat in my body spread. I moaned louder and opened my mouth to get more of him, to fuck him with my tongue. I pushed my tongue deep in his mouth and reached for him and didn't care if he could handle me. But he did. He hungrily kissed me back. He held me tighter still. I felt weak in my knees. His rock hard penis rock pressed into my body. I was surprised a young man could be that aroused by a 51-year-old woman. I felt light headed and wanted to catch my breath.

"Have a seat on the sofa. I'll get us some water," I offered.

He sat on the sofa. I poured us some water and set our glasses next to him on the piano bench. I straddled him, wrapped my arms around his neck, and looked at his young face. His beard wasn't even fully in. Much of it was still soft hair. Yet he was a man. Damn, how did I get so lucky to land this young hunk at my age? Thank you God. He looked up at me and our lips met and we kissed. Softly. I snuggled closer into him, and pressed my chest tightly into his hard body and we just kissed like that, deeply.

My moaning got louder and I ground my pussy on his legs in circles. *Take me please*, I thought. I wanted his cock. He felt it too.

He picked me up off his lap and carried me into the bedroom and set me down on my bed. I turned on my nightstand light so I could see him and look into his eyes when we fucked. I liked to see.

He slowly unbuttoned my blouse, unhooked my bra, and slid off my skirt.

"You're so sexy!" he said.

He slid off my lacy thong, and then I helped him take off his clothes. I looked at his penis. It was curved, hard and erect, and pointed straight to the ceiling. Good. I liked a hard cock.

I lay back on the bed and let him decide what would happen next. He went straight for my pussy. Sweet licks, flicks, and sucking. He was really good! But I stopped him anyway, probably unnecessarily. Although I wanted a man to love licking me and to do it until I came, I had so many reasons to not let that happen. First, I didn't think any man really enjoyed pussy licking more than a few minutes. In my mind, he and other men did it as a favor, just because that's how it was in my last relationship (my marriage). I didn't want to offer my pussy as a favor; I wanted to offer it to someone who wanted it. I didn't want to spread my legs and make myself vulnerable like that, unless the other really enjoyed it. And there was indeed so much vulnerability in spreading my legs open for someone. Would he like how my pussy looked, how I smelled, how responsive I was?

Second, I didn't think I deserved all that attention lavished on me, unless I gave it back equally. I would need at least 20 minutes of oral to come, but a man would need only a fraction of that time. How did I deserve so much more time? It just didn't seem fair. I could only take that time if the man absolutely loved licking me.

Third, I wasn't sure if he was good enough to stay on the same spot and not move when I got close to coming. I had to trust that whatever he was doing that built my arousal would continue until my orgasm. My orgasms seemed elusive at times and often required me to fantasize or focus, so I would get frustrated when someone brought me just to the brink, then made a slight change in technique and the entire buildup was gone. The worst was when a man's tongue got tired and he slowed down and missed spots, which felt less good and also made me feel like a burden again. I would just rather masturbate than be frustrated in that way.

I had to be turned on, relaxed, and trusting to come. I needed a man who loved eating pussy and had good technique. That was something I could explore later with a boyfriend.

"Lay down," I patted the bed.

He switched places with me. I went down on him. I licked his balls, asshole, and cock, the way I always did with men. He got the same blowjob I always gave. It still turned me on to do it. I suckled on his cockhead while I looked at him. I just wanted to fill myself up with that cock in my mouth and then I wanted it in my pussy.

"I want you inside me. Did you bring a condom?"

He got up and took a condom out of his pants pocket. I helped him put it on. I mounted him and we both moaned as I took him inside me. He grabbed my ass with both hands and moved me up and down. I was wet and he slid in and out easily. I rode him in my own ecstasy, longer and deeper than I had ridden anyone in a long time. I wanted it deeper.

"Deeper, go deeper, deep, deep, deep," I moaned in his ear.

He pushed deep inside me with little pulses. Pulse, pulse, pulse. My moaning grew louder and I buried my head next to his on the pillow. I wrapped my arms around his back and moved my fingers in circles on his back, in rhythm with my thrusting. I wanted to scratch him hard but I held back. Maybe he wouldn't like it. I would do that later with a boyfriend, when I could talk with him and know him and really let go.

Justin's cock was pushing on pleasure spots deep inside me. Fuck, it felt sooo good! The pleasure wave grew, and I wondered if it could grow into an orgasm.

I had never had a vaginal orgasm. Although penetration was intensely pleasurable, I never came from it. Clitoral stimulation gave me a slow buildup to a powerful orgasm, and when combined with a dildo or nipple play my orgasms were deeper and longer. I would hold the dildo in place or barely move it, because if the penetration was too intense, it overpowered my clitoral stimulation. I still wanted to try masturbating during intercourse. I just didn't know what the best position was that allowed me to masturbate without the man's thrusting hips pushing against, and moving, my hand.

The pleasure wave stopped growing and dissipated. I sat up. Justin smiled. He flipped me over on my back and kissed me. He was still inside me. He fucked me deeply, then rhythmically, in and out. It seemed like a good opportunity to masturbate during intercourse, so I reached down to stroke my clitoris but I didn't have enough room for my hand. His thrusting pelvis hit my hand with each outstroke. I told him so. He said we could change positions, and he moved me sideways on the bed, and entered my pussy from behind. I rubbed my clit again, and it just didn't feel good from that angle. I just felt the pleasure of his penis stroking the sides of my cunt and I let go of my clit and got lost in my cunt. I loved that word. Cunt. I wished I could fuck myself like that; I'd do it all the time. My loud moaning brought me back to the room. I decided I could experiment more with masturbating during intercourse another time, with another guy.

He turned me on my back and got on top. I wrapped my legs around him and held him tight as he ground deep into me. I was lost in the most intense delicious pleasure I could have thought up. I wished it would never end. I was getting wetter and wetter. Our bodies were skin to skin, and his penis was buried deep inside me and we kissed. I clutched his back with one hand, his nice firm ass with the other. I just pushed him deeper into me. The room felt hot to us both, and he was really sweaty. I offered to turn the A/C on, but he said it was fine and I got lost in his cock again. After about 20 – 30 minutes of this, his breathing got heavier and faster, and his cock felt bigger and harder, and then he panted hard and came.

We kissed and I held him tight. He pulled out and took off his condom. I took it from him.

"I'll throw that way and bring you a warm washcloth."

He lay, relaxed, and watched me walk over to the sink. I threw the condom into the toilet and flushed it, and turned on hot water. I ran the hot water over the washcloth, wrung it out a few times to make sure it was very warm, and came back to bed. He watched as I patted his softened penis and balls gently with the warmth of the washcloth.

"Do you swallow?" he asked.

"I like a man to come in my mouth and I always swallow," I told him, and threw the washcloth in the sink.

"I have a fantasy of coming on a girl's face," he said.

"Oh, I would never do that. That's so degrading."

"You think men do that to disrespect women?" and he laughed sweetly.

From his gentle voice, I immediately got it was not disrespectful at all for a man to come on a girl's face. I realized then, it was a huge turn-on and an act of love and connection, because a man associated his cum with his orgasm. Men were proud of their cum, including how much there was and how far it shot.

"Next time, you can come on my face," I told him.

I wanted to try that, and see how I would feel doing that. I came back to bed. Then I turned on my back and masturbated, while he stroked my nipples. The way he touched my nipples turned me on even more. It went straight to my clit from the inside, while my rubbing was on my clit from the outside. I was getting double stimulation, and the extra physical sensation overpowered all those thoughts in my head about whether he was bored. I was too turned on to care. It took just a few minutes, and then I came also. When I opened my eyes I saw he was hard again. Maybe we could have another round then, or in the morning?

"Can you spend the night? I have a parking pass we can go down and put on your car."

"I still have to go home and study for my test tomorrow."

Bummer. I kind of liked him. He said he would spend the night the next time.

I gave Justin an A-. I felt happy that evening and all the next day. We gave each other pleasure and love and connection for just a few minutes. All that fucking was good for me! It was like food for the soul, nourishment. Why didn't everyone hookup? And why did some people look down on it? All those bible quotes about premarital sex being bad were just words meant for other people who liked those words. I was living life, and my life was good.

My dad was wrong to think my life was only good because of Rick. My life was good because of me. I had a job consulting on facilities in the public sector, I had new friends, I had close relationships with my children, and I had loving (although infrequent) interactions with my parents and siblings. The men I chose treated me well. I felt happy inside from the way I ate, exercised, and meditated. I made my own decisions, my bills were paid, and I had a high credit score. I was living off my retirement account because I didn't want to work more than 30 hours a week, and I knew it was unsustainable and my acknowledgment of the situation was good enough. I liked the woman I was. I created the life I had and I was proud of it.

There was something that bothered me though. I felt disinterested in Rick and I didn't want to see him at all. Usually the person left behind was angry with the spouse who left. Our situation was flipped. I was the one who was angry. Rick was loving and open to me, and I was still mad at him for not meeting my needs. I had not let it go. Sometimes he invited me to dinner. I still had a key to the house, and went over often to see the kids. He would greet me with a smile. He was dating a woman he was very interested in, and asked me for dating advice. I figured my resentments would just disappear with time.

I often yearned for a boyfriend and a man who loved me, held me at night, and brought out more feelings in me, a man who made love to me and didn't bolt after he came. I missed the tenderness and affection I had with Rick. I felt lonely and sometimes I cried.

"You should be happy in yourself before you get a boyfriend. I met my boyfriend when I wasn't even looking. When you're looking, it won't happen," most of my friends said.

Easy for them to say! Why didn't they dump their boyfriends then and get happy in themselves? Besides, maybe they were happy single because they were so relieved to finally get out of an unsatisfying relationship. I had times like that in my life too, where I was happy to be alone. But I had been in a loving marriage, and I knew what I was missing. I was sure I wanted a boyfriend. I asked my friends on FB to set me up on blind dates. I just hadn't seen any guys who interested me in public or online, and I so much wanted to give my love and affection to someone, and be loved in return. But the next moment, I wanted to hookup. I wanted the freedom to fuck this guy or that guy, and I wanted my dating to begin with sex. What I really wanted from men was sex. I just wanted their hard cocks and passion for a short time. It seemed that people who left a long relationship went out and got what they didn't get during the relationship, whether it was peace and quiet, travels, sex, or finding themselves. It seemed they spent a couple years doing this, and I was okay with just wanting sex from men. I knew it was a phase I had to go through, to discover myself and get all that sex I didn't get the past few decades, tap into my feminine body and explore its power.

No, I wanted sex and passion with one man, a boyfriend. No, just sex, and not be tied down. Well, I really didn't know what I wanted.

One thing was sure: I didn't like going to bed alone. The bed looked like an ice-cold empty lonely stark place. I waited until I was thoroughly exhausted, late at night, and then went to bed. I asked my friends for advice. I heard some good suggestions.

"Get a body pillow," one friend said.

"Get a bedtime routine that comforts you, like reading a good book with hot tea," another friend said.

"Make your room and bed a place you long to be," a friend offered. I pictured fluffy pillows, candles, and large teddy bears.

I didn't get the body pillow or the bedtime routine or the bed makeover. I just avoided my bed until late at night when I was exhausted.

What I wanted changed daily as I changed. I changed my OKCupid dating profile almost daily, to match what I wanted that day. The age range was still 20-55. I met men for coffee almost every night, and if they were hot enough, I invited them over and fucked them. If the man was not hot enough, I thanked him for meeting me for coffee and left. Most people over age 40 seemed to be out of shape or walked with a slouch, so most men I met were in their 20's and 30's. I had a type. I liked fit, confident men, at least 5'10", with a lean build, who were career driven, sensitive, and into outdoor activities. They didn't need to have perfect bodies or faces, and I didn't care about money. I did care about his career. I liked alpha men, men who chose to go into sales or started businesses. I had a type.

I became somewhat demanding and snobbish. Sometimes I got mad at people I saw in public for not being good-looking enough for me, as if the whole world revolved around me and my needs.

"FUCK ME, DADDY"

It was October. I was grateful to live in San Diego, where it was still in the 60's even at its coldest. It had been a week since I had seen the kids, so I stopped by after work. I still had a key to Rick's house, so I just walked in. Rick was home and asked if I had a nice birthday. I didn't want to see him or talk to him. I told him about my interest in young men and he shook his head disapprovingly. Yes, I always talked about sex and he didn't like that and that's why I had left him, no loss. I said hi to the kids and then I left and came home.

When I got home, I saw a text message. It was from Justin, the 20-yr-old college student I had met two weeks earlier. He asked if he could come over. He didn't ask me out. He wanted to come over. That meant sex. Only sex. I would have gone out too, but I definitely wanted the sex. I was insecure about my age, and especially my wrinkles. I felt beautiful inside, but not outside. I didn't like my wrinkles at all. I loved the beautiful laugh line wrinkles on other women my age, but not on me. So I thought he was probably embarrassed about going out in public with me, and that was the reason he wanted to come right over. We could have sex and nobody would see me with him. I was a little hurt about it, but it made sense and I was horny.

He came over. He wore that same long coat.

"Hi Justin," I smiled at him. "I forgot how tall and strong and handsome you are."

I flirted with him as I wrapped my arms around him and snuggled up against his chest. I loved complimenting a man. He liked hearing it.

"You look great too! I'm glad to see you again." He beamed a smile at me.

"Do you want anything to drink?" I offered.

"Let's drink a glass of red wine, and sit and talk," he suggested.

I did not want to drink alcohol before sex, but I also wanted to be flexible and not rigid, and open to new experiences. All my sex had been sober. Why not try sex on wine?

"Sure, that sounds great!"

I poured two glasses of cabernet sauvignon, and brought them to my dining room table. I lit candles and sat down across from him. We drank our wine and talked about his school, my kids, our work, and sex. I was impressed that a young man could have the confidence to come over to my home, and ask to talk with me, and keep me interested. I admired that he was calm and could carry on interesting conversation while keeping eye contact. I wondered if I could have pulled that off at his age.

"Do you still like older women?" I asked.

"I don't think it's something that ever goes away," he said, and looked right at me.

Fuck! That was hot. I was turned on knowing he was turned on by me and that something about me was such deep long-term erotic turn-on for him. I walked over and pressed close to him and we kissed. His lips were warm and soft. He yielded to me, and then I to him. I felt a warm feeling in my heart. Oh gosh, did that mean I was becoming attached?

"Here, let's go in my bedroom," I said.

I walked in and lit two candles and the lamp on my night-stand. I wanted light to see him, and to see us. He followed me in. I quickly took off my clothes. I jumped on my bed, and threw off all the extra decorative pillows, and fell back on my down pillow. I turned around and saw he was naked too. His cock was rock hard. I wanted him in me. I felt too horny for oral. *Let's skip the oral.*

He lay on top of me and we kissed. His kiss was sensuous and deep. He had a thin lanky build and he was only 20 years old, but inside he was calm and had a strong presence. I trusted him.

"I want you inside me," I whispered while I looked him in the eyes.

He took a condom out of his pants pocket. Good, he was responsible and came prepared. I looked up at his strong slender body, those tight abs, and his hipbones. Why did my friends like men in their 50's? I couldn't see any reason.

He got on top. I looked at Justin's face, his eyes, and he looked back at me while he fucked me slowly, first shallow, then deep, in and out. He looked at me, and I at him, and the eye contact made me feel closer to him. I trusted him and he had that strong presence, so I could look at him and let go. He leaned down to kiss me and then dropped his head on the pillow next to me. Slowly, deep, in and out, faster. I clutched him tight, lost in my moans and the intense pleasure inside my body. His cock took me to places I wished I could take myself so I wouldn't need a man to take me there. He was sweaty. It was October, but it was in the high 50's that night. I offered to turn on the A/C, but he didn't want me to get up. He said the temperature was fine.

I raised my head and looked down, and saw his cock going in and out of my pussy. It was sexy as hell. He saw where I looked and asked, "do you like watching?"

"Yeah."

I didn't know what else to say. I wish I could have said something really passionate and sexy, but I wasn't that comfortable or experienced with hot talk. What if I said something that sounded weird or turned him off? It was one area of my sexual expression I wanted to work on, but not with him, not then, maybe when I got into a relationship and could really let go.

I saw his cock come all the way out, and then just the head came in and out, in and out, and put pressure on my clitoral bulb. I glanced over at his hipbone moving up and down. That was one of my favorite parts of a man's body. I leaned back again and clutched him tightly and wrapped my legs around him and pushed my hips up. He was sweaty and I didn't care. I wanted him to fuck me deeply. So deeply.

"Do you want to come on my face today?" I asked.

"Yes!" He didn't hesitate.

He turned me around doggy style. I had to make sure he didn't ram me, because it hurt when a man went too deep right away from the rear entry position.

"Easy, easy, easy, start out easy, let me get warmed up first."

He slid in and out slowly, very slowly, and I relaxed and my body opened up and I took him in. I liked the feeling of being fucked from behind, but I also missed having someone to hold onto and kiss. I imagined he was looking at my ass, although I had no idea. I couldn't see him. Deep places inside my body came alive with pleasure. I wanted more of him. I pushed my hips back into him to get him deeper inside me. He felt so fucking good!! I moaned louder, "Yes, yes, yes." I ground my hips in circular motion, pushed up against his pelvis, moving his cock head all around deep inside my cunt. He liked it too. He moaned. I got lost in my pleasure and my loud moaning brought me back. Did the neighbors hear us? Probably. I got really loud.

I wanted to try something new with him, something I'd been curious about. I turned around and looked at him.

"Some of my friends call their lover 'daddy'. Do you like to be called 'daddy'?"

He smiled. "Yes!"

I loved trying something new, so I was glad he was into it. So I said it, just quietly at first, and then in a normal voice.

"Fuck me daddy, fuck me daddy."

He thrust deeper and he felt harder. I turned around to look at him. He had a big smile on his face.

"You like me saying that?" I asked.

"Yeah, I do. Say it again."

And I did. And he moaned and pushed himself into my depths.

It didn't turn me on to say it, but I felt playful and fun. Plus, it seemed to turn him on, and when he got more turned on, I got more turned on. I felt a bond with him, for having that new experience with him.

"I'm close to coming," he told me.

"Tell me where you want me, so you can come on my face," I told him.

"Just here on the bed is fine, just turn around," he told me.

He gave a few more thrusts, then pulled out and I quickly turned around to face him. He put his hard cock a few inches from my face. I was so turned on seeing him so turned on and his cock so close to my face, when he was within seconds of coming. I looked at his face so I could see him come. Maybe he wanted me to watch his cock and the cum about to come out, but I wanted to see his face. He stroked himself three times, then his face grimaced and he moaned loudly and several squirts of thick creamy liquid shot out of his cock and onto my face, neck, and hair. He beamed proudly.

My face was full of cum. I rubbed the creamy liquid in my face. He looked at me and smiled.

"Wow, that was hot!" I said.

"Yeah, that was amazing."

He lay down on the bed and I rested my head on his stomach. The dry cum pulled my skin tight, like a facemask. I did not feel degraded when he did it, but it didn't turn me on either. It seemed that men thought that women love their ejaculate or at least they wanted women to do so, but there was nothing sexy or arousing about the ejaculate itself. I was more turned on feeling a cock pulsing or hearing a man moan or watching his face as he climaxed.

I left the cum on my face while he and I talked. After about ten minutes, I washed it off. My face felt smooth!

He seemed like he wanted to get up. Would he spend the night this time?

"I need to go," he said.

I did not want him to leave. But of course he was free to go. I wasn't going to put a guilt trip on him. He was always at choice. He got dressed. I walked him to the door.

"I'll see you again soon," he said and gave me a kiss.

My heart felt a little tug when he walked out the door. But mostly I was happy about our time together. I got on FB and posted this when he left:

Justin gets an A+ tonight. He is 6'2", affectionate, athletic, handsome...and only 20 years old. My parents would not approve. — feeling happy.

The next day I sent him a picture of me in booty shorts, a loose top, and my new over-the-knee Ugg boots.

"Daddy likes your pictures," he texted back.

I appreciated his reply. Often men ignored my texts. It was hot that Justin was taking the daddy line to heart, especially since he was so much younger.

I was happy about my time with Justin, so over the next few days, I replayed the evening with Justin in my mind. I relived his kisses, his hard cock in me, and the way he grabbed and held me. Replaying the hot memories, especially while listening to sultry music, stirred my emotions and I grew attached. I had a crush on a 20-year-old college student! I texted him, and he texted me back. Maybe he liked me too? I texted him the next day to invite him over and he didn't reply. On Saturday he texted me that he would come over and I was excited. I was at the grocery store with my kids late that morning when he texted me to say he told his mom he would give his little sister a ride to her gymnastics lessons and he couldn't come over. I showed my kids the text and we all laughed. Maybe he'd come on Sunday? I texted him again, to coax him to remember me. I wanted to see him again. He said he was busy. And then he stopped texting me back.

I couldn't understand being too busy for sex, especially good sex. I really wanted to understand. I kept checking my phone every few minutes for a text from him. Nothing. I was heartbroken and yes, I cried. I cried over a 20 year old man I barely knew, just because I liked him and the sex and how he made me feel. I missed him more at night and when sad songs came on the radio.

I did not like being attached to Justin. I didn't like constantly thinking of him and wanting him, since I couldn't have him. I struggled with overcoming my attachment. I thought Justin liked me too but he did not return my text messages. I asked my friends for advice on how to not get attached. They didn't know either.

I realized by then that if I liked someone and the sex was good, there was a 10% chance I would get attached, even by the second time. What was the key to avoiding attachment after sex? I needed to explore that by having more sex dates and figuring out under which scenarios I got attached. That shouldn't take long, because I had a big sexual appetite and there were many young hot men online.

I was constantly horny. My lust and how much I wanted a hard cock, changed monthly during my cycle. When I was less horny, I wanted sex only with men in a relationship. I longed for a boy-friend and dating and I didn't want sex without feelings. But when I was very horny, presumably in the week I ovulated, I wanted to fuck anything that walked. I'd get a deep longing ache in my va-gina and/or a tingly feeling in my clit that lasted the entire day and distracted me at work. I felt my warmth and wetness deep inside my body, and longed to be filled with a hard cock. A dildo would not do it. I wanted real flesh. I wanted to wrap my arms around a man's body, kiss him, smell him, and moan in his ear. I wanted to be on top and ride him hard, long, deep, to fill every craving and desire deep inside my body. Maybe that's what made me different from women who didn't hookup. Maybe they weren't as horny as I got. I really didn't know.

No matter how horny I got, I didn't want to fuck just anyone and I preferred to have sex with a man I already had met and liked. Nate, the 22-yr old former marine, and Justin, the 20-yr old college student, did not text me back when I invited them over. I was mad at them for blowing me off like that. It seemed rude to ignore me. I wished they would have just texted me back to say they were busy or not interested that night, or never interested again ever. Anything at all. I hated avoidance and not knowing where things stood or why they didn't reply. I told myself they had a right to ignore me, and then I had a right to not see them again too. But for me, dating and communication was so much more enjoyable when everyone was just real and said what was on their mind! Other times, men would reply and tell me they couldn't hookup because they were busy, or working, or tired from working.

ASKING MEN OUT IN PERSON

I was horny, and I wasn't going to wait around for the guys I knew to get back to me. I had to find a new guy. I spent hours every day online, looking for a boyfriend or guys to fuck, depending on what I wanted at that moment. Being online so much was taking too much time and I had seen the same profiles over and over and just wanted to get away from it all.

I closed my online dating account and trusted that I would meet men in my real life. I started looking at the men I saw at my Crossfit gym. One day or so, I noticed a man who seemed to give me extra attention. He was handsome and fit and vibrant, and probably in his early 40's. After our workout ended, he walked out to his car. He had a BMW. I wasn't too materialistic but I thought a beamer was the sexiest car a man could drive. I caught up to him. He had just opened his car door.

"Hey, do you want to get a coffee sometime?" I asked.

"I'm married." He smiled at me and didn't move.

I looked at his finger.

"Oh you weren't wearing a ring."

I had not done anything wrong, so I didn't apologize for asking him out. He just stood there and looked at me.

"Well, I'm single and looking for nice guys to date, I didn't know you were married."

"Thanks," he said, and then he got in his car and drove off.

I walked back to the gym and I was happy I didn't take his *no* personally. I was proud that I had found the courage to ask, and that he didn't get mad at me or ignore me or embarrass me. I thought I could do more asking. I was proud of my move and told my friends. Almost all my male friends thought it was hot. They liked a woman coming on to them. Some of my female friends encouraged me, but others disapproved that I asked men out. They told me to never make the first move.

"Men are hunters and women are prey," they advised. "Let the man make the first move."

That just went against every grain in my gut. I didn't want to become prey or go through life as an observer, hoping someone would begin a conversation. I wanted to be empowered and in charge of my life. I wanted to ask for what I wanted, like I had learned at the snuggle parties. I wanted to expand my skills in picking up women and men, and to do something socially difficult. Asking the guy from the gym to coffee had made me stronger, not weaker. He was flattered, and I felt alive for taking the risk. Why did men always have to go out on a limb? Maybe they liked being desired and approached? Who came up with these dating rules anyway, and why was anyone following them?

The next step was talking to men at Starbucks. I was nervous. I worried what other people would think of about me going up to random guys, and how embarrassed I would be if the man told me to get lost. One of the men I had hooked up with, an outgoing salesman, told me that wouldn't happen. He told me the men would love the attention. I debated for a few weeks if I could actually go through with it, and then I mustered up the courage to make my move.

I started by changing my attitude. I had to be different in the store. I had to be bold and confident, and hold my head high. I used to avoid eye contact with men, especially men who were married. When I was in line at a store, I'd look ahead or down. I decided I had a right to look at people. I also had a right to take up space with my body, to put my shoulders back, and to look up. Why did I fold my arms when I stood in line? I changed how I stood in

line at the Starbucks and other places I went. I stood with my feet
a stance apart, arms at my side. I felt confident when I stood that
way. It seemed like a small thing to change how I stood in line, but
it was big. It meant I could shine. I didn't have to shrink myself.

I was ready. One morning, as I walked into the store, I looked
at the men who sat alone at tables by the door. I could spot them
on my way in the door, and they did not notice I checked them
out. Those men would also be the easiest to approach. The bigger
challenge would be to start a conversation with a man seated deep
inside the store, but I kept that challenge for later.

I forced myself to look at the other customers in the store,
while I stood in line, or waited for my coffee. At first I was very
uncomfortable doing that. It became easier with time. When
I saw a handsome man, I made eye contact and I held it. That
was often a turn on if he met my gaze. I started conversations
with men seated near the door. Once I approached a man who
worked on his laptop, started a conversation, and then asked if I
could sit down. I told him I was looking for men for hooking up,
and he didn't even blink as he asked me for my number. I gave
other men my number. None of those conversations ever led to
more than some texting. It didn't matter that nothing came of
it. What mattered was that I had the courage to start a conversation with a man in a store.

"SPIT ON MY COCK"

Meeting men in person was fun, but not useful for getting sex. I
had been horny all day. I got out my Fuck List and browsed it for
men to call for a hookup that night. I had about ten men on the
list. The older men I had met were not on the list. I had no interest in fucking old men anymore. I texted the men who had an A
grade next to their names. Most of the men did not return my text
within the hour, so I texted the B guys. The man who had advised

me on how to start conversations with men at Starbucks said he was at a basketball game with his mom. Seriously? He'd rather be at a game than having sex? Another man said he couldn't make it and gave no reason. Other men replied and said they were working late, or tired from working. I didn't want to fuck the C guys. Damn. I had no idea it would so difficult to find young men who wanted to get laid.

I didn't like the lack of access to sex. It was just like being married. Darn it. I decided I needed to expand my Fuck List and find men who liked fucking as much as I did.

I went back online, and that's where I met 31-year old Doug. It took many attempts before we finally got together. Often he called at the last minute with an excuse why he had to reschedule. We finally met at the Corner Bakery for lunch. We sat outside and I ate my salad while we talked. He was strong and tall, about 6'4", kind of muscular, just like in his pictures. He seemed extremely interested in me. He leaned forward across the table and he kept telling me how beautiful I was, how much he liked older women, how he could not wait to just be with me and have great sex. I had to get back to work, so we planned a second date for hooking up.

After several attempts and some rescheduling, we finally had our second date. I persisted in meeting him, just because he seemed so interested in me, and his excuses were work related and made sense. We went for a beach walk. He kept grabbing my ass while we walked.

"I love nice asses. Wow! Your ass is just beautiful!"

And then I ran in the water and back to him and hugged his waist.

"What a nice ass! I love anal sex. I can show you a really good time," and he smiled at me.

I liked his touch and flirtation, and I felt playful. I couldn't wait to bring him home. I wasn't sure about the anal sex that day, but it was something I wanted to explore more and if he was good at it, maybe I would do that with him. I invited him over.

Back at my apartment he changed a little bit. His eyes became serious and lusty. He no longer wanted to touch me at all. He wanted to be serviced. He became a little more determined, a little more sexually aggressive. He took off his pants and sat on my sofa. I just went over and started licking his balls and penis, thinking that was how he liked to start things off. I did not set my own agenda, because I was curious about different men's sexual styles. I wondered how he would take charge of me and what he would do to me. But he didn't take charge.

Doug just sat there and became more demanding. He wanted to be serviced. His eyes got really lusty.

"Spit on my cock, spit on it," he whispered in a low voice.

It seemed hot, although I was a little uneasy of his demanding tone. I spat on his cock a few times. It turned him on, as he got harder and moaned, and the look in his eyes became more lusty and distant. I suggested we go to my bed, thinking we could change things up there, maybe he'd want to go down on me too or have intercourse. He agreed. But moving to my bed didn't change anything at all. He sat up in my bed and demanded me to suck on his cock, to keep spitting on it. I couldn't tell if it was my spit, or the sound of my spit that got him so turned on. I noticed the louder I did my spitting and slurping, the more turned on he became. I was not at all turned on by it. I was doing it because I was curious about it and wondered what could be next. He was loud and demanding and kept asking me to spit on his cock and suck him. He came in my mouth with a loud moan and then immediately he got up and got dressed. I was taken aback. What about me? He had done nothing for me. He walked to the front door. I no longer wanted him. That wasn't enjoyable and I had to tell him how I felt.

"Hey, I just want to let you know, this was really one-sided. This was just all about you."

He looked over at me. "Next time, it will be all about you."

He called me at 1 a.m. a little over a year later. He asked to come over. I laughed to myself. I told him he was a bad memory and I never wanted to see him again. He kept talking and insisting on coming over, so I hung up. I never heard from him again.

CHAPTER 13
LIFE AND SEX, MY WAY

"ARE YOU A SEX ADDICT?"

The next time I was horny, I called my favorite hookup guys, Nate and Justin. Neither replied. I didn't want Doug, the man who liked spit. I had to find another man. In fact, I often had to find other men, and my Fuck List was growing. I didn't have so many men because I was insatiable. I had so many men because I was horny, and the men I fucked often didn't come back. If they didn't come back, it was because they got into a relationship, or they liked variety, or had a different sexual style and preference from me, or they were so career oriented that sex was low on the priority list, or they traveled or worked a lot, or the passion was too much and they wanted something more casual from a hookup, or they just hooked up once with a woman. I didn't always know the reason. I wished more men would reply to my invites rather than blowing me off, but that's how it was.

A good friend from Phoenix came to visit. She had been married 25 years and she was surprised at my many sexual encounters.

"Why do you have so many men? Are you a sex addict? Maybe you switched your addiction from pills to sex."

I laughed, but it was a fair question. It certainly was an interesting question, and I briefly thought of how to answer. I explained it to her:

"Addictions rob people of themselves, make them smaller. What I do is making me bigger, more alive. And both I and the men I meet are better off as a result of our interaction. Touch and sex are nourishment for my soul and my body."

"Well, I can sort of see that," she replied.

"There's more. People are usually ashamed of their addictions. They hide them. They don't want anyone to know. I put myself out there. I'm proud of what I do. I'm discovering myself."

"Yeah, but I just couldn't do that, have sex with all those men."

"I guess I just give myself permission to do it. I don't know any other women who do what I do. I'm not sure. "

People who were around me and knew me, like my kids, my family, my co-workers, and my friends who saw me in person, did not have those questions. They could see I was shining and full of life and happy.

But what was that force inside me that longed for a hard cock? It felt like a fire burning inside me, a hunger. I was sure other people felt it too, and decided to not express it. Again, I had no such restriction. If I had a hunger to be filled with cock, what would be a reason to push it away or ignore it? I could find no reasons at all.

MY EX CAME FOR DINNER

I wanted to get over my resentments with my husband and get along. I invited him and the kids to dinner. He came over for the first time to my apartment. Rick noticed my bare wall and three pictures slanted up against the wall.

"These pictures should be hung. Why are they on the ground? Do you want me to hang them up?" he asked and looked around for a hammer and picture hangers.

His excitement over hanging my pictures reminded me how he was excited about doing home improvement projects and not excited about being with me, how he would rather hang pictures than ask me how I was or what was going on with me or connecting with me. I was furious. I didn't like him telling me what to do, instead of asking me how I was.

"How dare you come in here and fucking tell me how to decorate my apartment? I put those pictures on the ground on purpose," I yelled at him.

My kids and brother looked at me in amazement. I didn't care.

I didn't tell Rick how I really felt. I didn't tell him I wanted to get along with him again, and I wanted to talk about what was happening with each of us emotionally in our lives. I didn't tell him what the pictures on the ground signified. They were a statement the apartment was temporary. I didn't want to be a single woman who spent the rest of her life in an apartment because that's all she could afford. The pictures on the floor reminded me that something better, more permanent, was going to happen one day. One day I would buy my own place, or move in with a man.

"You know, I'm just going to leave now." And he took his jacket and left.

I was a total bitch. I needed to get a handle on that but I didn't know exactly how. Maybe with the passage of time all my resentments would go away.

I texted him the next day to apologize. But I hadn't changed my view of him so the apology didn't change me and I still had that to work out.

FINALLY – RELATIONSHIP CLASSES

All those years I was married, I didn't attend relationship or sex workshops because my husband wasn't interested. I didn't have that stopping me anymore. I attended sacred snuggle parties, connection events, lectures, and other events my friends posted on Facebook. At one of the sacred snuggle party events, I was introduced to the Zegg Forum.

The Zegg Forum was an intimate container for a group of up to 50 participants who sat in a circle. The purpose was personal growth and understanding. The trained facilitator guided the process. A presenter stepped in the middle of the circle and while moving and walking, shared what was deep and meaningful in his or her life. The group listened. Any participants could enter the circle afterwards and act as a "mirror" to the presenter to share what was perceived. The participant could accept or decline the presenter's view. A typical session had up to ten presenters.

Aiden, a fit lean man in his late 20's, told us he had almost shot himself in the head one night because he was so depressed about not having had sex in years. It was four years since he had gone down on a woman. I was amazed that a single person had gone so long without sex or affection, and that a man could be depressed about not having a pussy to lick. I thought men were not into licking pussies.

I got up after him in the circle and admitted publicly what had been so hard for me to say to all but my closest friends.

"My husband never went down on me the first 22 years of our marriage, and when he finally did, he always asked me to wash up first."

I talked more as I walked the circle, and then when I passed Aiden, I turned to him and said, "Where have you been all my life?" Everyone laughed. Aiden laughed too. I wanted to find a man like Aiden, a man who really wanted to go down on me, so I could relax and enjoy it and see if a man could make me come that way. Other people got up and also said things that surprised me. The candor and the open sharing struck me. It was almost as if people dared themselves as to how much of their inner self they could expose. Aiden smiled the rest of the evening.

It had been three months since my last STD test, so I called my doctor's office and requested a full STD panel. The lab tested for gonorrhea, syphilis, Chlamydia, Hepatitis B and Hepatitis C, and HIV. And every two years during my pap exam I was tested for HPV. I requested the herpes test and was told it was not available. (A few months later I insisted and was given that test also.) My test results came back negative for everything.

POLYAMORY RETREAT

I heard about the polyamory retreat at a snuggle party. I immediately wanted to go. PolyPalooza 2013 was a clothing-optional take-over of a comfortable hotel in Desert Hot Springs, CA. About 100 people attended. I hoped I could learn more about Zegg Forum as well as have hot sex and maybe try something new.

On my drive up, I kept thinking about Justin, the 20-year-old college student who let me call him "Daddy". I had a huge crush on him. I would have rather been with him than go to a retreat, but he had been ignoring me. I was also extremely horny. My panties were damp for days leading up to the retreat, but I was busy at work and put off making sex dates, since I figured I'd get lots of sex at the poly retreat. I did like Justin, but not enough to stop having sex with other men.

I was assigned to a room with three other women. We laughed at the registration mix-up because one of our roommates was a man. He had a foreign name that sounded female. Who would sleep with him?

"I'll sleep with you in this bed, but we stay on our own sides. I don't want to have sex with you," I said.

And he agreed.

The retreat featured morning yoga, sex parties, bondage demonstrations, an elaborate rope tying demonstration, snuggle parties, BDSM and flogging demos, a costume party, STD and communication classes, Zegg Forum, and fresh vegan food three times a day. The Red Room, named for its red sheets and décor, was available 24 hours a day for anyone to have sex or watch others having sex.

I was horny, so I propositioned the only two men I found attractive for sex. Both men told me *no*. I felt more alone then. I envied couples who seemed so in love. I wanted a boyfriend. I kept checking my phone for a text from Justin. None came. No man propositioned me for sex. How did these participants get so many poly relationships, and I did not have even one? I envied them for getting all the sex they wanted, sex that presumably was good or better than the sex I was having.

The sexy-costume sex party was held in a large room filled with pillows, blankets, and soft lights. I wore my sexy schoolgirl outfit with my leather harness and dildo. I hoped someone would touch my dick. I felt very sexy. I was standing up talking with some friends, when I heard a man's voice.

"Can I suck your cock?"

I turned around and saw a large man in his 60's.

"What?"

"I'm Edward. We met at the last group exercise. I want to suck your cock. You're so beautiful, and I've always wondered what it was like to suck on a cock."

I wasn't sure whether to laugh at his playfulness, or be turned on getting a blowjob. I admired him for his courage to ask me and try something so new at that age.

"Absolutely! Here, let me lie down," I said.

I lay down. Edward kneeled between my legs and he sucked on my cock with vigor. He put my entire cock in his mouth and sucked up and down. I'd never had someone suck my cock. I let myself feel like a man getting a blowjob from a man, and I pushed my hips up and down in rhythm.

"Do you like sucking on my cock?" I asked.

He looked up.

"Yes, I do."

He kept sucking on my cock and I wished I had more sexual courage and could have pretended to come all over his face or in his mouth. When he was done, we thanked each other for the experience. The next day, Edward told me he realized he was bisexual. After our play event, he gave his first blowjob to a man at the sex party and he very much enjoyed it. I admired him greatly for making such bold sexual leaps in his 60's.

I walked around and saw one of the men who had refused to have sex with me. He wanted to play. What he wanted was anal play. Ah, my turn to be the dominant partner and deliver pleasure. He got on all fours. I got some oil, put it on my finger, and slid it barely into his ass. He started moaning. Since he liked it, I gave him more. I slid my finger in deeper, slowly. He moaned louder, so loud I was almost embarrassed. No, I was proud I could deliver so much pleasure. I moved my finger in circles and went in deeper, then in and out. His moaning got louder, and he stuck his ass higher in the air. I realized he had saved our sex play for the group party. Did he like being watched?

"All the people are watching you be fucked in the ass," I told him.

His moaning became a wail. I liked the power of turning him on like that and everyone seeing how hot I made him get. I finger fucked him, in and out, in and out, and then I got bored with it and told him I was done. He thanked me and we each got up to find something else to do.

I looked around to see all the other people having sex. I didn't feel like joining in. I just watched, and I was still horny. I finally found a man who was reasonably attractive and invited him back to my room. My roommates were in other rooms for that evening. The sex with him was boring, but it took the edge off.

The entire long weekend, I was struck by how easily and lovingly people shared affection and moved between partners. At the lectures and meals, participants switched readily with whom they sat. I wanted to feel that kind of freedom. I hugged one man from behind for about half an hour, then put a pillow in my lap so another man could snuggle in it for about twenty minutes then got up and sat with a different man, then got up and sat with a woman. I had no obligation to pretend I was attracted to only one man. The freedom to be and not pretend or restrict my attention and love was priceless.

I was attracted to a couple in their early 40's at the retreat, and approached them about a threesome. She was one of the most beautiful women I had ever seen. I felt nothing for him. They invited me back to their room. Erin was so in love with Bryce, that I was sure he was an excellent lover. I wanted to be part of that, to feel something new and learn from him what he did to get her to love him so much. He wanted turns at fucking us. I couldn't wait. How would he make love to us? What was that magic between them?

Bryce lay on the bed. He had asked us to spoil him, and do all the work. I put on a condom and slid Bryce's cock inside me. His eyes were closed. I rode him, but without the eye contact, there was no connection, and he didn't feel that good. He asked to fuck his girl. She was his favorite, he said. I couldn't wait to see how he made love to her. He must have changed his mind about being passive, because he asked her to get doggy style, and then he fucked her like a rabbit, in short quick thrusts with his eyes closed. My heart sank in disappointment. Is that how he did her, that beautiful woman? She deserved so much more! The scene was a replay of sex in my earlier marriage…my husband fucked me just like that….so unconnected, lacking feelings. Did she sense it too? I looked at her. She moaned and was smiling. Did she really love it, or was she just so in love with him, that she didn't even realize what was missing? Isn't that how I was when I met Rick? So in love, that I overlooked the bad sex? Yes, that's how it was. I didn't ever want to fall in love with a man and be fucked badly and deal with it just because of my feelings for him. No, I would not end up like that again. I decided I'd continue having sex on the first date, to make sure the man was passionate in bed. And then I went back to watching them.

He just fucked her liked that and then said he wanted to come on our faces. He pulled out of her and we lay on the bed near his hard cock, as he gave himself a few finishing strokes and his ejaculate shot out. We let him come on our faces and we both rubbed it in.

I let Bryce's ejaculate dry on my face and went upstairs to my room. I ran into Aiden. I wanted to see if he would think less of me for having cum all over my face.

"Aiden, I just had a threesome, and I have cum all over my face!"

His eyes lit up.

"Wow, that's so hot! Can I do that too?" And he smiled at me with so much love and affection in his eyes.

Wow, sweet! He didn't judge me or think it was gross I had another man's cum on my face? He adored me for it.

"Yes, and will you go down on me?" I asked him.

I was sure if any man could make me come, it was Aiden. He had almost killed himself because he had not licked pussy in four years. He probably loved it and was good at it and would do it long enough to finish the job.

"Yes!! Of course." His eyes lit up.

My heart skipped a beat and my clit felt tingly. He was going to give me an orgasm! Finally. My big day had come.

"Ok, let me just take a shower and I'll come right back," I told him.

"No, come dance first," he insisted and twirled me around.

There we danced to the DJ playing music, with Bryce's ejaculate dried on my face. Aiden was confident. He strutted and twirled me around. That was not the introverted depressed Aiden I had seen only the day before. Aiden was masculine, determined, and confident! I remembered that earlier that evening, he had intercourse with a woman, his first time having sex in years. I didn't know that getting sex could change a man so much and fill him with so much joy and confidence. He was a new man, and all because of sex. Then why did so many people think sex was bad?

I took a shower. My face was smooth and silky from the ejaculate. I came back to Aiden. He took me by the hand and led me to an empty room just off the main sex party room. He lifted me on a table and he proceeded to give me oral sex that would not stop. His tongue and hands were determined. I had not had an orgasm from a <u>man</u> going down on me since before I had been married, if ever. I really could not recall if it had ever happened. Every time I came close to coming during oral sex with a man, I started to think, *what if he didn't really like doing this? What if his tongue was tired? What if he thought I was taking too long? What if I couldn't come at all, even with his determination, then what did that mean to me sexually and my satisfaction with men?*

Aiden oral techniques were amazing. He had been licking me for a long time, and I was on the brink of an orgasm for about 30 minutes. I felt frustrated with myself that I couldn't come.

"Is your tongue tired?" I asked him.

"I love it," he said and he didn't even lift his face off my pussy to answer.

I could tell he meant it. My clit was hard and engorged, and I felt the hard ridge of my clit under his tongue. Yet I wasn't coming. I was so close and so turned on, so hard, and I couldn't come. I sank back into the table. I told him I had to stretch out and tense my legs. I repositioned myself and put my legs together and tensed them. Aiden just put his face right on my clit and spread my labia apart. I played with my nipples. And then it started. My orgasm grew from deep inside, and I knew it was inevitable. I could feel my orgasm building, and it grew and grew, and because he had been licking me so long and I was so aroused when I finally came about 15 minutes later, my orgasm was so strong and powerful and I erupted in a loud screaming roar that lasted for half a minute. Aiden kept licking me all the way through my orgasm. He kept stimulating me with his tongue but not right where I was sensitive, just next to that most sensitive spot so he could draw out my climax.

People streamed into our hideaway to see what had happened, and who was making all that noise. We just laughed happily, and then they left. I was so happy I could climax from oral sex, especially oral sex from a man. I kept thanking him over and over and over. Aiden was happy too, because he finally got to eat some pussy, and I'm sure it was very satisfying for him to have got me off, with that difficult history and all.

I gave him a blowjob, and when he got close to coming, I took his penis out of my mouth and let him ejaculate all over my face. He looked at me sweetly and rubbed in his cum. Then we hugged each other a long time and walked out.

Aiden was a changed man after that night. He was confident, masculine, and radiant! Before Zegg Forum the next morning, he asked me to share in the group what had happened. He needed that so much and I did it for him.

I got up in the circle. "Everyone here knows that I haven't been able to have an orgasm from oral sex by a man in over 30 years, and I didn't know if something was wrong with me. Last night, Aiden made me come from oral sex."

Everyone clapped. When Aiden got up, he did not say a word. He walked around the circle, and one by one, stopped for a second in front of each person, made eye contact, closed his eyes, held his hands together, and bowed. Nothing needed to be said. Sex healed and nourished him, and me. How could anyone say sex was bad or dirty?

I felt sexually powerful. I had repressed my sexual power, because I believed good girls don't show their sexual energy. It was a limiting belief that kept me from being fully expressed. The men at the retreat adored and desired us women, regardless of how many other men we had sex with or even if we said "no" to sex. I felt at home. I could be me. I didn't have to pretend. That freedom was priceless.

After the retreat, cunnilingus was top on my mind. Aiden, the man who got me off orally at the retreat, was the only <u>man</u> who gave me an orgasm in decades. Could other men make me come? What was my deal with getting oral, and why did I need to believe a man really liked doing it? Was it about feeling valued and loved? Why could men so easily send me penis pictures, and I was embarrassed to send pussy pictures? If I thought my pussy was beautiful, then I could send pussy pictures. But I didn't think it was beautiful at all. It had all those shades of pink and various folds and long inner labia lips, and didn't look like vulvas I saw in pictures. If I let more men go down on me, could I get more comfortable showing my pussy, and love it like I loved the rest of my body? If a man made me come, would that bring some novelty for my orgasms? Would I like him to make me come with his hands so he could be closer to me and kiss me, rather than with his tongue where is positioned far away from me? Answering those questions required getting more oral sex.

I only wanted to meet men online who loved giving oral sex. I updated the list of "6 things you cannot live without" on my online OKCupid profile to condoms, receiving oral sex, intercourse, meditation, trail runs, my children.

ANOTHER MAN MAKES ME COME FROM ORAL SEX

Carson, a 22-year-old business major who had just graduated from college, messaged me that he loved going down on a woman.

I met Carson for coffee at the Starbucks by the outlet mall. He was 5'10", blond, with a stocky strong build, and he was super sweet. He wore a jeans and a plaid shirt. We sat outside and drank our coffee. It was a little chilly that night, so I left on my jacket.

"So you like going down on women?" I asked, eager to listen to his voice and watch his body language to gauge his enthusiasm for oral sex.

He had already written to me he liked it. I wanted to be sure.

"I love eating pussy….pleasing a woman and making her come," and his face lit up.

"Yeah?"

"I can't get enough of it. I just love pussy."

His enthusiasm was obvious, so I invited him over before we even finished our coffee.

We were naked and in my bed within minutes of entering my apartment. I lay back on my bed so he could go down on me. I looked at Carson as he came on the bed, buried his head in my thighs, and tongued me. He looked up at me as he licked me. I watched the tip of his tongue flick across my swollen clit. Seeing his tongue action was hot, but I didn't ever stretch out my tongue when I gave a girl oral; I wanted to get really close, plus stretching out the tongue would make it get tired faster.

"Press your face right up against my pussy," I suggested.

He did. He put his lips on my vulva lips and tongued me deliciously. I spread my legs wide and lifted them up playfully and watched his face buried between my legs. He was good at that! I lay back on the pillow and closed my eyes. I moaned louder and harder. He put a finger inside my vagina, and moved it rapidly. I didn't want all that movement.

"Slow movement please with the fingers. I like them as a backdrop, else they overpower everything because it feels so good and I can't feel what you're doing on my clit," I told him.

He followed my directions. I fantasized someone was watching me. I didn't know if it was good or bad for me or my arousal and our connection for me to fantasize about some other person in the room, but I needed a way to build my arousal. I just didn't think I could come from just him and me in that room. I didn't have him near my face to look at or kiss, and the bedroom was dark and I couldn't see him well. I didn't feel like making the eye contact with him as he was going down on me, we just didn't have that kind of connection. I let myself fantasize.

His tongue was sensual and he built me up slowly. I worried if he could keep going or if he would get tired and stop right before I came. I didn't feel secure in that so I was afraid to let go. I didn't trust he would keep going no matter what. I also worried as I got close to coming he would switch spots and I'd miss my buildup and have to work so hard to get it back, as had happened so many times before. Maybe I thought too much. But he was a master at tonguing me. He kept the same steady pace and within seconds I was again convinced he would not let up. I let go mentally. I put my legs down, spread apart.

Max licked me for what seemed at least 20 minutes. I decided that was a long time, and then I became self-conscious about how long it took me to come. I thought I should hurry up and come to spare him the work of getting me off. I never considered he enjoyed the process, I believed he was just after the result: my orgasm. But just because I thought so and believed so, didn't mean it was true. I really didn't know what he wanted. I couldn't relax and enjoy it anymore, because I thought he was tired.

"Is your tongue tired?"

He grabbed my thighs tighter, and looked up at me with a smile.

"Not at all! I <u>love</u> this."

I sensed his enthusiasm and only then did I let go and go back into my body. I wished I could relax into my pleasure, regardless of whether his tongue was tired or he was enjoying himself. But I could not. Was something wrong with me for needing to think my partner enjoyed himself? It didn't matter then. His determined tongue slid all over my clit. He spread my outer lips and got his tongue right on my clit and I gasped. A deep pleasure wave built up deep within my body. I felt hotter, my pussy got even wetter.

Carson felt I was close to climax. He put his finger inside me and held it. That, I liked.

"I need to put my legs closer together and tense them to come."

We repositioned, and he found a way to keep his tongue on my clit. Circles and waves of pleasure came from my clit and filled my body. My breathing quickened and I moaned louder and louder, until my moans became a distraction.

I wanted to be silent. I had to stop moaning right before I came, forget everyone around me, and get lost in myself. When I was younger I moaned non-stop whenever I was stimulated during sex as a signal to the man that I liked it so he'd stay on the same spot, but the performance always ended in hyperventilation. I became more comfortable sexually over the years, so I could say what was so at the moment.

"Stay right there, that's awesome, don't move from that spot. I'm going to stop moaning and just be quiet and focus," I told him.

He said, "hmm" to indicate his understanding. I let go completely and trusted my body, the moment, and him. My orgasm started deep in my body and spread out in a rolling wave all over my body. I grimaced and moaned loud and louder, and for a long time...... "aaaaaaahhhh" with my swollen hard clit right in his face. I felt my left toes curl. He kept tonguing me until I pulled away.

I sat up and laughed, happy in my orgasm and afterglow, thrilled that a man had made me come. Whew, there was nothing wrong with me after all. I did like men; I didn't have some deep-seated block against them getting me off. Why couldn't my husband do that?

I was soaking wet and warmed up, ready to be fucked hard and deep. I got out a condom, unrolled it on his hard cock, and we fucked until he came inside me. There was nothing special about the way we fucked. He wasn't exciting in bed, even though he got me off. Carson didn't have anything besides the good oral technique and a hard cock.

After all that, I had to admit I wasn't really that much into getting oral sex, because when the man was at my pussy, I missed kissing him, looking at him, and feeling his chest on mine. I just wanted a man to start there, so I knew he loved my pussy.

The second time we saw each other, even though he got me off orally, I gave him a B.

CHALLENGES: MEN AS OBJECTS, AGE, SHAME, ACCESS TO GOOD SEX

November came. Oral sex was off my checklist. I was open to meeting all kinds of men. Mostly I wanted sex from men, but other times, especially when I got attached to a man after sex, I also wanted a boyfriend.

That first week in November, I met Tommy, the 21-year-old skater/surfer introduced in the opening chapter of this book. How could I fall for a man so much younger? I didn't even know anything about him.

Some of my friends said I was going about it all wrong, and that I would never get a relationship by dating men so much younger and starting with sex. Why not? Since I didn't like older men, why date them? Since I wanted mostly sex, why not start with that? Why did they give me advice based on what <u>they</u> wanted?

"I always have sex on the first date, because if the sex isn't good, there's no reason to have a second date," I told my friends.

"But the sex gets better with time," my friend Tina said.

"I'm afraid to count on that. I don't want to have feelings for a man who is terrible in bed. I need to check him out in the bedroom first," I insisted.

All I wanted from a man was sex. I didn't need a man to take me places, comfort me, or give me advice. I could get those needs met myself or with my friends. The only need I wanted met by a man was sex, passion, and connection. If I liked him after sex, I wanted to see him again and possibly date. The relationship would be mostly about lots of hot sex, and include sleepovers, good conversation, and sometimes spending time outdoors and going to dinner or shows. And that's it. I wanted to live alone and have time to myself.

Was it selfish to treat men as sex objects, as hard cocks, to fuck them and leave when I was done? Or rather, to make love to them, which is what I did. Could a relationship really never come from that, as some of my friends said? Why didn't other women hookup like I did? Maybe women who got drunk a lot did that. But sober?

And other days I wanted that feeling I got when a man curled up behind me in the middle of the night and wrapped his body around me to fall asleep. And then I cried for strong arms to hold me. I made myself wrong for that. I thought I 'should' be happy alone. Was my yearning for connection and love 'wrong'? Why couldn't I get a boyfriend?

And the next day I woke up and it was all okay. I jumped out of bed and went for my run.

I admired my toned curved body, which was slim but not skinny. I loved looking at myself in the mirror. I was beautiful. I loved the softness and expressiveness of my face, how I could radiate laughter and the depth of sadness and tears. The more I looked in the mirror, the more I liked my body and me, myself. I took more selfies and put them on Facebook. At first, I took the selfies in private, but then I challenged myself to do it in public. Why did I feel ashamed to admire myself? Someone had told me it was 'vain' and wrong and I believed them. Forget it! Admiring and loving myself made me happy and I did it more.

But did the men see that? I knew men loved my body, but I didn't have that same feeling about them loving my face. I had wrinkles and my eyes sometimes looked puffy. Would the young men think I was old and unattractive? It wasn't just an issue I had with the younger men...when I dated men my age, I thought they preferred younger women, women without wrinkles.

I knew mentally it was just in my head, and the men thought I was beautiful. Their cocks were proof enough. They also took me to dinner, beach walks, or coffee. Once I asked a 19-year-old man if he thought I was old, and he kissed me in a busy parking lot and said other men were just jealous of him and wished they could have me. The age issue was mine, and I knew it.

But why did they like older women? Did they have a mommy issue? Did they not get enough attention from their moms? I asked each young man why he liked an older woman, and the answer seemed more to indicate a man's maturity rather than neediness. Usually they said it was hotter, it was easier, they didn't have to woo/dine a girl over multiple dates in the hopes of having sex...but the #1 reason they give me was they had priorities/goals, which took time that a girlfriend would compete with, and they just wanted to hookup. I hoped I would not fall for one of these guys.

My other insecurity was shame about having had so many penises in me. Would the men I met disrespect me, as my parents, and perhaps society had taught me? My experience showed otherwise. Most men said they loved a woman who was confident and owned her sexuality. Women were drawn to me. Again, the shame was just in my head.

Why was it so difficult to get sex, and especially good sex? Much of the sex I had was mediocre, and men were not available when I wanted them. The young men I saw had roommates and didn't want to invite me over, so I had to invite them over when my kids were not here.

HE MADE NO SOUND

I felt lonely for a boyfriend, and I sought my peace in mediation and being outdoors. Fortunately, near my home I had a choice of trails, eucalyptus grove, and of course the beach. When I felt lonely, I went to these places, sometimes with a coffee, other times with just a water bottle. Usually I went alone, other times with my daughter. I walked and I sat.

I liked all my walks, except for the nighttime walks alone on the Oceanside pier, which brought out in me a romantic longing to be with a man. The beautiful lights from the shore, the moon up above…it brought out feelings in me that I didn't have before the walk. Maybe I shouldn't walk alone in the moonlight? I thought of taking a vacation, but not alone, no, not alone. Vacations required a lover. I didn't want to travel anyway.

I stopped by at Rick's house after work to see Wilson and Christine. Our black lab ran out as soon as I opened the door. I called him back in, and he came. I had trained him, and he always came for me. I gave him a snack. All they had to do was give him a snack every time he came. But they didn't. Sometimes I thought he ran out just so he could be called back in and get the snack. Smart dog. I went into Wilson's room, sat on his bed and petted his cat as we talked. Wilson smiled when he saw me.

"When are you coming over again, honey?" I asked.

"Sunday. I'm so busy with school, homework, and gym on school days, and its so much work to carry all my things over."

"Yeah, I know. Would it help if we got you a second set of books from school, so at least you didn't have to bring all that?"

"No, that's okay. The other thing is that since you live further from my school I have to get up 20 minutes earlier and spend double on gas."

"I'll give you gas money."

I handed him $60 and he smiled. He wanted to come over. He was just trying to make it all work too. I missed him, and yet I had the apartment to myself, so I had sexual freedom.

Had I been married, I would have fucked my husband several times a week, deep and hard, and it would have been a successful marriage and everyone would have been happy. But I was single, so fucking became something for which I was judged. And of course the kids didn't like it, when there were so many men. I wished one of the men would stick. I wanted a boyfriend many times. And then other times I didn't.

I always liked tall blond men. Caden was a 6'3", skinny, 19-year-old marine from Kansas, stationed at Camp Pendleton. He didn't show up for our coffee date. I had never been stood up for a date, so I waited 20 minutes. Then I texted him that I would have appreciated a cancellation and left. He never replied and I wrote him off as a flake.

Three days later he sent me a text, saying that he had just got his phone back after it had been taken away from him after inspection for having whiskey in the barracks. In addition to this punishment, they also gave him three days of house arrest. I thought it was hilarious and it explained why he couldn't meet me or message me to cancel our date. I still wanted to meet him because he looked so sexy in his pictures, so we set up another coffee date at the same Starbucks.

Caden arrived on time. He was tall and skinny, just as in his pictures. His blond hair was completely shaved, and he had a lot of acne. He did not make eye contact when he or I talked, and he only talked to answer a question. He told me he had never had sex sober. He had always been drunk. He seemed like a sweet kid that had never learned to be comfortable with himself or in social situations. I admired him for having the courage to meet up with me at all. He was probably just super horny.

I thought he just needed some love. I wanted to get him to relax and open up, and I wanted to show him how good sober sex could be. I could inspire him to not drink so much. All he had to do was provide me with a hard cock that I could ride for a long time. I invited him over to my apartment.

We drove to my apartment complex. I met Caden at the mailboxes and we walked up together. Did he look at my ass while he walked behind me up the stairs? I went into the kitchen and offered him something to drink.

"Hey, do you want some tea or water?"

He did not. He just stood there in the kitchen. He didn't make any moves on me, so I invited him to sit with me at my dining room table to talk. He sat upright and perfectly still, and did not say a word. It was really awkward. I needed to initiate, that was clear. I walked over to him and leaned over to kiss him. He refused to kiss me. He just sat there. Whenever a man refused me in some way I would keep an upbeat mood. Sometimes I would say something.

"I usually like to start out with kissing. It's fine you don't want to kiss. You are always at choice. Hmmmmm....let's see."

I was trying to figure out how to get myself turned on and start some kind of sexual interaction.

"Would you like to lie down and I can give you a massage?"

I thought the massage would arouse him and once I had him in my bed, he would take charge. He agreed to the massage. He removed his clothes while I got some oil. I sat on his buttocks, spread the oil on my hands, and slowly rubbed his back. I loved giving massages. He was completely quiet. He did not make a sound. I could not tell if he enjoyed the massage. He lay still, perfectly still.

I wanted to see if he was aroused, so I asked him to turn over. His penis was hard. I looked at his face to make a connection before I touched him again. His eyes were closed. He laid perfectly still, his arms out to his side. He looked like a corpse except that he was hard. There was no way I could ride him like that. And he had not even tried to touch me once. I wasn't sure what to do next with that naked man in my bed.

I decided to give him love by giving him a blowjob, and show him a taste of sober sex. Gently, I moved down his torso to his scrotum. He was freshly shaved. Completely hairless. Why did young men shave off all their pubic hair? I inhaled deeply and licked his balls ever so softly. I loved the smell of his scrotum.

"You smell good!" I told him.

He did smell good. Of course they all did. Balls smelled sweet and musky. I looked at him and he had not moved. I was sure my next move would get a reaction. I stuck out my tongue and glided it slowly from the base of his shaft to the head of his penis. I lingered at the ridge. Most men let out a moan when I did that. I listened for a reaction, a gasp, words. Still, nothing.

I wondered whether he was alive. His penis was erect, so he had to be alive. But I wanted to be sure. I looked at his chest, and it barely rose and fell. His neck artery was pulsing. I felt relieved. I wanted to just get him off and get him out of there. I sucked his cock. He came suddenly in my mouth, without warning, while he lay perfectly still with his eyes closed. There was no moaning, no quickened breath, no clenching of legs, no flinching.

As soon as Caden came, he said he had to go. He didn't care if I came or not. I reassured him it was fine and that he was always at choice. I reminded him that he had sober sex and it had felt good. He hurriedly left. I never talked to him again.

"SIT ON MY FACE"

It was early December, and the Christmas buzz was on. The kids and I talked about whether to go to the Nutcracker, Handel's Messiah, or both. Rick called and asked what I had planned for Christmas. I had no plans. I didn't want any plans. I never enjoyed the heavy holiday meals or the shopping for more stuff. Sending out cards was a chore. All that was left were the tree and decorations, and I didn't want the hassle. I told Rick he could have the kids for Christmas. I decided to just ignore Christmas that year and see how that felt.

I was back to looking for men who liked giving oral sex. Jackson, a 22-year-old economics student, sent me an online message saying 'I love eating pussy'. He was 6'1", with a bright smile and blond hair, so I was definitely interested.

We met for coffee in Encinitas on a Saturday afternoon. We both ordered lattes and sat inside to talk.

"So, you like older women?"

"Yeah, I do. I don't like girls my age."

That's hot," I told him.

I asked him if he was into oral sex.

"Yeah, I love going down on women, having a girl sit on my face. I don't like intercourse."

The face sitting part got my attention! I needed some healing in that regard. I still didn't feel like I deserved a man to "do the work" to "give" me an orgasm. I didn't feel comfortable asking to sit on a man's face or have him go down on me until I came. Most men and women sucked at giving oral sex and I dealt with whatever I got and I didn't know how to change that. Could I give better instructions, but how? I had tried that with my husband and it didn't work. I had a long way to go in asking for what I wanted.

One of my guy friends told me to ask for what I wanted

"Do you think a guy is going to kick you out of bed if you tell him what you like?" he asked.

"Haha, not really, but maybe he'll think I'm weird or demanding," I said. "Besides, it's not fair of me to ask a man to spend 30 minutes making me come when he doesn't even know me or love me," I said.

"Men are lucky to get pussy. You're giving a man something very valuable. Of course you should be satisfied!"

"Really? I see it the opposite way, that the man is giving me something very valuable. I'm lucky to get a good man with a hard cock that delivers good sex! That's hard to find."

Besides, I honestly didn't know what I wanted him (or her) to do differently. I couldn't see what the man was doing with his tongue on my clit, so I couldn't correct him. Men who needed direction often lacked sensitivity on their tongues and all the direction in the world could not infuse someone with passion and sensuality.

"Most guys have no idea what they're doing down there and would like a little input anyway," he continued.

Sitting at coffee with Jackson, I realized I had a safe space to ask for exactly what I wanted, face sitting and all. He told me he didn't like intercourse, and that he loved going down on a woman.

"It takes me a long time to come." I waited for his answer.

"Oh, I love doing it. I could do it for hours."

Hmmm....I imagined him licking my clit for hours and I got turned on.

"I have fantasies. I'm into BDSM and kink," he said.

"Oh, I'm not into that."

"I like sensuous play, like being bathed in a tub and then toweled dry."

"Oh, that arouses you?"

"Yes, it doesn't make me hard but it turns me on."

"Well, how do you like to orgasm then if you don't like intercourse?"

"Oral sex."

"Wow, that sounds amazing and fun! I miss giving my kids baths, and I miss having hugs, so your timing is perfect!"

Jackson came over that afternoon. As soon as he was in my apartment, I could only think of sitting on his face and coming. Knowing that he was kinky and pursued his fantasies, and his fantasy and turn-on was being in my pussy turned me on! I didn't have to worry about him doing me a favor going down on me. He wanted to!

We didn't kiss. Neither of us wanted to.

"Take off your skirt and panties," he instructed.

He lay down on the floor in my living room.

"Come here, sit on my face."

Wow. Sit my pussy and my clit on his face. Fucking turned me on! I had wanted to do that in my marriage, but had not dared to ask except one time at the end, and then I felt guilty for it. This guy got turned on by it. What would it feel like to sit on a man's face and know he was turned on by it?

I walked over to him, stood with one foot on each side of his face, and lowered myself down on him.

"Here, position me where you want me."

I didn't want to smother him.

"You're fine right there."

And he stuck out his tongue and the second it hit my clit I shuddered. He licked me softly, all over, rolled his tongue alongside and over my clit and I started moaning. He flicked his tongue lightly side to side and my arousal built quickly. I sat down with just a bit of pressure on his face, and stuck my swollen hard clit in his face, in his mouth.

Could he tell how turned on I was, by how big and hard my clit was? Is that how men felt when they pushed their hard dicks into my mouth? Sometimes when I masturbated I pretended I had a penis and it was big and hard and all the girls could see how turned on I was. Clits were smaller and we women didn't go around exposing our swollen clits, but why not? I wanted my arousal to be seen. Dare I tell him about that? Could I ask him to suck on my big hard clit? No, I was embarrassed. Maybe he didn't notice, because it was small. But I was hard and swollen. Could he tell? His technique with face sitting was amazing.

"I want to lay on my back, my legs are tired."

He laid me on my back and he wouldn't let up from licking my pussy and my clit. As I got closer to coming, he focused more on that very hard ridge, little circles, held my legs tight and then I knew it was coming...it started deep inside me, my legs trembled, it built up, my breathing quickened, my nipples got harder, my toes curled, and then a loud moan and roar and I came all over his face. I didn't have anything coming out like a man did, but I imagined myself coming all over his face and it excited me.

He was hard. He really didn't want to fuck. I gave him a blow-job while I looked him in the eyes and he came in my mouth.

That was fun! I couldn't wait to try bathing him. We made a date for him to come back the next day.

"BATHE ME"

Jackson, the man who liked kink and face sitting, came back the next day. I gave him a bubble bath. He took off his clothes and got in the tub. I washed him gently with a washcloth. I felt warm inside, pampering a man like that. He liked it so much. I washed him, washed his hair, squeezed out the washcloth and let the warm water run all over him. I wished I had a rubber duck. Did he like toys too? Did he maybe have a fantasy of being in a diaper, because I had heard of that too, or was I giving him all he wanted?

"Here, I'll dry you off."

He got out of the tub, and I wrapped a towel around him and dried him off. His penis was soft. I didn't understand how it turned him on exactly.

I went down on him first, so he could get off right after his bathing fantasy. Then he went down on me again and afterward we talked for about an hour.

"I just don't like intercourse," he told me.

"I see," I said.

I didn't know what else to say. Did he have an emotional issue; was he abused or molested as a child? I did not want to judge him or make him feel wrong for his preference.

"I'm really into kink," he said and took out his phone. He showed me pictures on tumblr of penises pinched by safety pins and tightly bound with rope and other painful images.

"Oh my god, that looks painful!" I gasped.

I was shocked by what I saw. How did people get turned on by being in all that pain, and wasn't it dangerous to their genitals? They could cut off circulation.

"Yes, and that's the turn-on. Once I pinched myself for so long and I cut off my circulation, but it came back." He actually got turned on by it.

It seemed like so much effort had been put into creating the pain. Why? It was interesting and it wasn't up to me to understand.

He showed me images of women sitting on men's faces, which turned me on immensely.

"Oh my god, that is so hot! I want to do that!!"

I felt flushed and my clit started throbbing, which surprised me because I had just come. In one image, a man lay on the floor and a woman in a red dress and high heels just sat on his face. So dominant, like she totally deserved it. Damn, I deserved it too. Why had I gone all those years never doing that? The face sitting pictures turned me on, and I made a tumblr account and subscribed to those pictures.

Jackson and I never saw each other after that but we stayed friends on FB.

FELL FOR A MAN I NEVER MET

I had heard of people who fell for each other online without ever having met, and women who were swindled out of money by men they met in faraway places. I myself had received messages from men in other states, who told me how beautiful I was, and how they couldn't wait to meet me. I always deleted them. The ploy was to get the woman hooked, then say he (or she for lesbians) needed money to get out of whatever country they made up to be stuck in. Usually the sum was thousands of dollars. I always shook my head. I was a logical grounded woman. There was no way I'd start an online conversation or search for any man outside of my own city.

I certainly would never ever fall for someone online, someone I had never met. I didn't even message much. I went right for the coffee meeting, so I could get to know them in person.

One morning, I browed through pictures on OKCupid, when a 28-year old blond haired man, tan, with a big smile and broad strong shoulders, appeared in the side bar. I was smitten. He looked so much like Rick when I met him, and I liked those blond haired men. He lived in Seal Beach and worked for the Navy. He was from out of town, but only by about an hour. I clicked on his profile. Fuck. Hot pictures. He lay on a boat in his bathing trunks. He had toned calves, light blond hair, a firm stomach, aviator glasses, and dimples. All I could picture was myself riding him. I got all warm in my pussy and also in my heart. He looked like a man I would want as a boyfriend. He touched a place deep inside of me where my dreams and fantasies lived.

I sent him a message, and mentioned the distance, and held my breath. Within minutes, he replied.

"Well, hello there beautiful. You're not that far away. I'd love to come see you."

My heart skipped a beat. I wanted to know more about him. I asked him how tall he was and what he did for work. He told me his name was Danny, he was 6'1" and his job in the Navy. We kept messaging each other. He said he was looking for a relationship. He was going to come see me in two days. I was so excited!

He messaged me the morning of our meeting. Something had come up at work and he couldn't come. We texted each other for days on end, and kept rescheduling our dates. He had a second job on the weekends so he could make his alimony and child support payments, so he had little free time. Sometimes we talked on the phone. I started getting more feelings for him, and we had not even met. I fantasized about him, mostly about riding his cock, but also of him kissing me and telling me I was beautiful. I imagined him in bed with me, with that perfect strong lean tan body, that sensuous face and blond curly hair that evoked images of romantic novels.

I still missed having a man in my bed. My hookups didn't spend the night. Danny evoked in me moods of romance, being held at night, and being made love to. He brought out feelings in me I wanted to feel. And I liked to feel, and I thought I would meet him any day, so I let it all happen. And then I realized I had fallen for a guy I met online. I was not like those women I had considered weak and gullible. I was humbled. We texted and when he didn't reply for a few days, I felt sad. I kept going online to see if he was online. He was. Why was he online and not texting me? Why couldn't he make time to see me, and why didn't he let me come to see him?

Our almost-relationship had two disagreements that we patched up. It felt so real. Then after a couple weeks it all sizzled out. He stopped contacting me. I was devastated and I cried over him for about a month. Sometimes I cried because I had felt there was a real connection between us, and other times it felt like I was crying over a fantasy of who he was because I certainly didn't know him. But my heart was still broken. And then, with the passage of time, I forgot all about him.

About four months later I contacted Danny online just to see how he was doing. He said his work schedule had freed up and he drove out one morning to see me. He was heavier than in his picture and not as handsome. He said he had gained weight. Our conversation did not flow as I had imagined it would. He was clumsy in bed and came quickly. I did not feel an emotional connection and I didn't like that he came first. I never wanted to see him again and he probably felt the same way, because he never contacted me again either.

I MADE LOVE TO HIM WITH MY STRAP-ON

My last few hookups had left me emotionally depleted. I was very sad that particular day. I had met a single dad the evening before, who met all my criteria and was amazing in bed. He didn't contact me since our date, and I was heartbroken. I just wanted someone to hold me.

In the mail that afternoon I received an offer for 50% off a massage at a spa near my home. I decided that was just what I needed. I hadn't had a massage in over a year. I made an appointment for that evening.

I was still filling out the paperwork, when the muscular male massage therapist in his mid-30's came out. He was around 6'1", burlier and bigger than the type I usually went for. He looked like a cuddly bear. He smiled at me and looked back at his forms. I could sense I was about to get playful with him. Anything could happen in that room. I smiled under my breath. He called my name and said he was Walter, and asked me to follow him to the massage room.

"Wow, you're really muscular," I told him as I followed him down the hall. I felt sexy and powerful to flirt with him so openly. He turned around and flashed me a smile.

In the massage room, I got under the sheets and waited for him to come in. He pulled down the sheet and put his warm oily hands on my back. I had an intense feeling of pleasure. He moved his hands up and down my back in firm strokes. He asked what I wanted massaged in the one hour we had.

"Can you increase my massage time to 2 hours?" I asked him.

"Yes, let me let the front desk know," he said and left.

When he came back in and shut the door, I let go into a deep relaxing massage. I fell asleep. He worked on my entire body with his strong hands. I forgot all about the last guy I was sad over.

"Your skin is really soft," he told me.

"Oh, thank you," I said. It was a huge compliment. I didn't put on any lotion. I used to years before because it often felt dry, but since I started taking cod liver oil, I no longer needed the lotion.

After the massage, as he walked me back to the front desk, I stopped him and whispered so nobody could hear.

"Hey, do you want to go out sometime? Can I have your number?"

"Sure, hold on," he said quietly.

He went into the staff room and came back with his business card. He had written his cell phone number on it. He didn't want any of the staff to know he gave his contact info to a client.

As soon as I got out to my car, I texted him. He called me right away. I invited him to come over to my apartment for dinner. I wanted company, not just a fuck. He said he would bring a bottle of wine and be there by 9pm. That just felt really good. I was even in the mood for a sleepover.

Walter and I went through a bottle of cabernet sauvignon at dinner, and I only drank a glass. He told funny stories and I laughed. I could tell he was lusty, because he told me so many sex stories. A good fit. Sitting across from him at dinner was very comforting. I really had missed out by just hooking up with men. I remembered what I had with Rick, and our dinners together. And my divorce, which was about to be final. I talked with Walter about everything and he liked me and he cared. He was easy to talk to. He said I was beautiful and he talked about other activities we could do together. He cared about things I told him about. We discussed STDs and he told me he had not had any sex since he had been tested six months earlier. I decided to use a female condom with him.

Walter kissed me as we cleaned up after dinner. He was so passionate and he turned me on with his kissing. I loved getting lost in his big burly arms. I liked teddy bear guys when I was younger. We left the dishes for later and went in my bedroom to fuck.

Walter went down on me because he liked a woman to come first. Like most men, Walter wasn't super good at oral on me, so I masturbated to come. I was super wet and still turned on and I climbed on top. Walter held me real tight and kissed me sweetly while I rode him. He put his finger near my ass and I didn't stop him. He kept going, and I moaned louder, a signal to him I liked it. He stuck his finger deep in my ass as I rode him. I hoped he would let me do the same to him. And I wanted to.

I climbed off him to go down on him. He let me put my finger deep in his ass while I sucked his dick. Since he liked it so much, I told him about the strap-on I had never used.

"Use that on me," he said.

That surprised me. Most men loved a finger in their ass, but they didn't go around asking to be penetrated with a dildo. He was actually more fun than I thought.

"Yes! Awesome. I'd love to," I told him.

I wasn't aroused by the idea of fucking a man in the ass, but I was excited to try something new and to get a chance to finally use the harness I bought to fuck a woman. I got my harness and dildo out of my closet. I put on the harness and made sure it was snug. Then I pushed the dildo through the opening of the harness. I admired myself in the mirror.

"Look at my cock," I said as I admired and stroked my dildo.

Walter said he wanted me to fuck him doggy style. He got on all fours. I knelt behind him. My dildo was at the level of his ass. I got myself into my male energy mindset. I imagined the dildo was my dick. I looked down at my dick and Walter's round bottom, and in that instant I realized the importance and significance of what I was about to do. I felt honored he trusted me to penetrate him in his most vulnerable spot. I also felt the responsibility and pressure to perform. I wanted him to enjoy my actions and be impressed by my sexual abilities. I also felt love, because I was making love to him. Could I put my love into my cock? There were so many thoughts and feelings whirring through me in that moment.

He trusted me and I had to make the penetration feel good. I rubbed lube on my penis and around his asshole. I pushed the tip of my dick gently on his asshole. I hoped it felt good. I made sure it was really lubed up, and I pushed a little harder until the tip of my cock penetrated his rectum. He let out a moan. I felt powerful to be able to please a man in that way.

Slowly, I pushed my cock in barely a little deeper, and he let out another moan. I pulled out slowly, and he moaned again. With each stroke, I gave him another quarter inch of my dick. Slowly, gently, and then I was in almost all the way. He moaned so loud. He rocked back on my dick and I gave him all of it. I was really sliding and getting into a rhythm. Walter moaned louder.

My heart flowed with love as I slid my cock in and out of his tight asshole. I wasn't fucking him. I was making love. My eyes welled up with tears. I wanted to make him feel even better. I thought of what else I could do. I got into a performance mindset. His pleasure seemed to be completely in my hands. I reached around to stroke his penis. I rubbed my hands on his bottom, penetrating him, in and out, in and out, giving him pleasure, nice and slow. He moaned and rocked with my motion.

And then he had enough and asked me to come to him. He fucked me with his beautiful wide cock for about ten minutes and then he came inside me. When he pulled out I noticed the female condom had slipped, so his ejaculate was inside of me also. I wasn't worried about getting pregnant; I was just worried about getting an STD. I took comfort in knowing he had not had any sexual partners since he was STD tested and I believed him. I was disappointed I had pretty much had sex without a condom, when I thought I had a condom. I saved that for men who I thought could turn into a relationship. I had to be more careful next time I used a female condom.

Then we fell asleep in each other's arms. I didn't have feelings for Walter, but he nourished me deeply. He was just what I needed on a day when I felt so hungry for connection. The next morning we had sex again. He left after breakfast and said he would be back.

I SQUIRTED

I saw Walter three more times. In one of our sessions, Walter talked about squirting. He found it so hot, as most guys did. I told Walter I never squirted. I didn't want to. I did not see the appeal of it. I had friends who squirted and every man they were with had thought it was hot. Every man I was with thought it was hot. The whole thing annoyed me. It seemed to be to be such a performance function, and so messy.

Walter was an expert at fingering me. I got lost in myself and I couldn't get enough. That evening he fingered me deeply, fast, and suddenly I saw streams of liquid squirt out of my vagina. It was not drops, it was squirts.

"Oh my god, I squirted," I cried out.

I was completely surprised and also elated, because I had never squirted and thought I couldn't. I had never wanted to because it just looked messy and like a performance. I looked at Walter. He smiled proudly. Apparently, he was pleased with himself. What was the point of squirting? I didn't have an orgasm with it and we had made a mess. I never wanted to squirt again.

"Please don't do that again," I told him.

Walter drank three bottles of wine that night. I didn't like being around all that drinking, and I didn't want to date a massage therapist because I liked career men with a good income and upward mobility, and I didn't have feelings for Walter either.

"I really like you," he kept telling me.

I didn't feel the same. I had to tell him.

"I don't feel the same way about you," I said.

"Wow. Oh wow," he said and looked sad.

"I have to be honest," I explained.

"I was looking for a reason to stay in San Diego. I thought you could be that reason," he said.

He spoke softly. I remembered clearly the sadness of wanting someone who did not want me. But I didn't feel sad. I just wanted him to leave.

"Look, I like you, I want to keep seeing you, I thought we had something here," he said.

"I'm sorry, I just don't feel the same way."

I didn't want to see him anymore. Walter and I ended it then. He moved to Washington and got a job working as a physical therapist. He texted me nine months later to wish me a happy thanksgiving and then I never heard from him again.

CHAPTER 14

SINGLE DADS

DIVORCED

R ick and I went to the courthouse to finalize our divorce. It was easy. We had made a list of all we owned, and what each of us had in our possession. Rick took steps to split our retirement accounts so half would go to me. We didn't have any court orders or agreements. Wilson would keep coming and going as it made sense and he liked, hopefully every other week with each parent.

Around that time, maybe because of the divorce and family life on my mind, I was tired of the young guys. I wanted to date men with children still at home, because it was deep in my heart to be a part of family life again. Rick told me to put that in my dating profile, and I did.

It was easy for me to love other people's children. My son's girlfriend lived with us for one year after high school, and I treated her and loved her like my own daughter. I loved hosting our exchange students, and enjoyed all the slumber parties and play parties when my kids were little.

I started looking online for men over age 40 who also had children.

MECHANICAL SEX

I was excited to finally meet a handsome man my age online. Bill was a 49-year-old executive recruiter who lived downtown. He was 5'10", fit, with an active lifestyle and twin boys in middle school. We met for coffee.

I immediately felt comfortable around him. The way we acted at coffee felt familiar. We both had been in long marriages and had children. He grabbed our coffees, I took the napkins. He threw away the cups, I pushed in the chairs. Each of us knew it took two to make something work. We both had experience caring for a spouse and children, we were both givers. It felt nourishing to me. I was really curious how the sex would be.

I followed him in my car back to his condo. I parked on the street, and followed him in.

He offered me wine. I didn't like that, because I liked to have sex sober. Why did he need wine?

He set his glass on the coffee table and invited me to sit on the sofa.

He turned on the TV. I didn't watch TV. I didn't come over to watch TV, I came over to connect and kiss and fuck. Why did he need to turn on the TV? He sat and watched the TV. Why did he do that? Why didn't he put on music and look at me?

Bill kissed me. His kisses did not turn me on. There was no passion in his kiss. It was just a motion he made with his lips.

I was curious though. Here was a single dad my age. Maybe the sex would be amazing.

He took off my clothes in the living room and invited me to sit on the sofa. His touch lacked passion. It seemed mechanical. I wasn't turned on. I wondered how many other naked women he'd had on that sofa, and why he didn't invite me into the bedroom, where we would have soft sheets and a warm blanket and so much room to romp around. The sofa was narrow. What about our juices? Wouldn't they stain the sofa? And how many other naked women had been on that sofa, and did he clean it regularly? He went down on me, and he was a little too rough so I asked him to stop. Maybe I could liven things up with my good blowjob. I went down on him, but since I was a bit turned off by the loud TV and the sofa, I wasn't really into it. I didn't ask him to turn off the TV or take me into the bedroom, because I wanted to experience how different men had sex. If the sofa and TV were his way, then let me have it. I wasn't looking for a boyfriend. I was looking for experiences.

Then he fucked me on the sofa with just his penis going in and out, nothing more. No feelings, no connection. Just our bodies. It felt mechanical, like we were just two dolls. I considered he had been single several years and had probably had his share of heartbreaks and disappointments in love. Even if at one time he was open hearted and passionate, all those disappointments over time could have shut him down. Sex could have become just physical for him, just another routine. One woman tonight, a different woman a different night.

It hit me that I could be on the track to turn out just like him!

If I kept having sex with so many men, a day would come where the next guy would be just a motion to me. How long could I be innocent and playful and fresh in my hookups, if I did that for years?

No, I had to end my hookups or cut back. I had to leave periods of time in between, so each man felt new and special, and not like another body for the night.

And I thanked him for that lesson.

ROCKED MY WORLD IN BED

I met Blake on OKCupid. He was 42 years old, 6'1", slender, with blond hair and blue eyes. He was fit from surfing and running. He was an electrical engineer who also designed products for his startup, had three children in elementary and middle school, and had been divorced about two years. Since he was so good-looking, I asked him if he was a womanizer. He replied that he was busy with work and had 50% custody of his children, and rarely dated. He sounded perfect, and I was smitten with him before we even met.

We originally planned to meet for coffee, but I wanted to try something different. His profile said he liked outdoor activities, and I did too. I suggested a beach walk late morning. I arrived first. He sauntered up to me, his hands in his pocket, which I found odd. He seemed nervous. I almost wanted to leave, because his lack of confidence was a turn-off, but I didn't leave because I liked to give guys a chance, in case they were just nervous. That was definitely the case with him.

We walked in the sand and talked. I found him interesting, and I could relate to him. He seemed like a dad from my kids' school or soccer games. He talked about his children, marriage, career, and running. I liked his story, and we kept walking for some time. It was getting chilly. I said I was cold and he gave me his jacket to wear. I liked wearing a man's jacket, but it didn't mean anything. I was not that into him.

We walked back to the stairs. I wondered why a good-looking successful man such as he was, wanted to date an older woman. He surely could get women his age or younger. I was sure that all men liked younger women. Why was he with me? Did he just like my sexy OKCupid profile that showed my bubble butt in a bikini and stated I loved sex? Of course, his age profile for women was set to ages 35-52.

"Don't you prefer younger women?" I asked him.

"I like older women because they know what they want. Also, younger women want children and I don't want anymore children," he told me.

I was reassured. I was surprised though that a younger man would find me attractive. All those TV ads and society had convinced me that youth was 'in', and women all around me were talking about plastic surgery and Botox and skin peels to look younger. It never occurred to me that a man as hot as he was would find a natural-looking older woman desirable.

We stopped and sat on a rock and touched each other under our clothes. He put my hand inside his pants and I felt how hard he was.

"I can stay hard for hours," he told me and we both laughed.

He wanted to come over right then, but I wanted to go back to work. I really wasn't that much into him. I told him we could get together another time. I thought of having sex with him sometime, just to try out that age group. I hadn't been with a man that old in awhile. Would he be more experienced? Would the sex be different? Would he have erection problems, would he connect well, what would it be like?

He came over the next evening, freshly showered, wearing a black V-neck cashmere sweater, his blond locks showing off his handsome face, and I just about melted.

"You're so handsome!" I looked up and flirted with him.

He smiled down at me. Damn, he was charming! Was that good-looking man really in my kitchen? Would he come back again? I could look at him for hours!

I made us a snack and tea, and we sat at my table and talked for about half an hour. He told me about his kids, work, and the last woman he dated.

"I looked at your Facebook," he said.

So he was interested in me? Or just curious? I had not thought to look at his. I put the dishes away. Blake followed me into the kitchen. He grabbed me tight and kissed me. I melted into him. We kissed tenderly and I opened my eyes and looked up him. My heart opened in wonder at his beauty. I could have looked at him every day for the rest of my life. He lifted my dress, unsnapped my bra, leaned down, and circled my nipple with his tongue. I went wild.

"Oh my god….oh my god….," I whimpered. He leaned down and sucked gently on my nipple. He smelled so good too. Then he reached into my panties and my very lubricated cunt. I went weak in the knees and held onto him. What was he doing to me?

"Let's go in my bedroom." I could barely get out the words.

I quickly went into my bedroom, and for some reason, I pulled back my down blanket. Usually I had sex on top of my covers. Blake felt like a man to be with under the covers, not on top. I jumped in bed and watched him undress. Fuck, he was gorgeous. His body was lean and toned, just the way I liked, and his cock was hard. Hard for me.

He got into bed and kissed me tenderly and nibbled on my lip. A moan escaped my mouth. *Take me.* I leaned forward and kissed him harder and pushed my tongue firmly into his mouth. He got more turned on and kissed me back hard and fingered me. I lay on the pillows and pulled him on top of me, and clutched my arms tightly around his neck. I let him finger me on and on; I just loved it so much. Then he went down on me. Good man. He sucked my labia and then flicked my clit with his tongue. Little flicks, softly. Then circles. He spread my outer lips apart with his thumbs so he could get really close. Fuck, it felt amazing! I looked down at the beautiful sight. My pussy swelled with excitement. He could definitely make me come if he kept going long enough. But I wanted to pleasure him and ride him.

"Come here."

He lay down and I went down on him. I looked at his beautiful hard cock. He didn't have my favorite shape, but he was extremely hard and so fucking handsome to look at. I gave him good head like I always do to men, and then I laid on him and kissed him. I ground my pussy on his pubic bone.

He looked at me tenderly, turned me over on my back, and then slid his cock in. That was my favorite position when Rick and I had made love. I didn't think Blake had feelings for me, and he

probably treated all women in the same way, but the way he tenderly made love to me, and thrusted in me, felt like he was making
love to his wife.

"I can stay hard for hours," he reminded me.

"Yeah, that sounds amazing," I said.

"I have to confess and tell you that I don't come from intercourse," I announced.

I wondered how he would respond. He understood right away.

"Here, let's do this," and he gently moved me on top.

When he said "let's" I felt a warm feeling come over me. Let's?
That word packed so much meaning and turned me on. It wasn't
just him or me, it was <u>we</u>. He was going to show me something that
seemed hot. But mostly, he was suggesting something in answer
to my lifetime insecurity of not coming from intercourse. Did he
have a way I could come from intercourse? My head was spinning.

"Some women can come by riding on top and rubbing their clit
here," and he pointed to his pubic bone.

"Wow, I want to try that!" I was excited. I got on top of him.

"How do I position myself?" I wasn't sure how to rub my clit on
his pubic bone.

"Every woman fits differently," he said.

We moved around on the bed and experimented. I lay on top
and rubbed my clit on his pubic bone while I rode him, but I didn't
fit right. My clit was not rubbing on anything and I wasn't stimulated there.

"Can we move into a position so I can masturbate while you're
inside me?"

"Sure. Here, I have an idea."

I loved that he had so many ideas on how I could come. Finally,
a man that took me to new places! He stood on the edge of the
bed and asked me to scoot down so he could be inside me while I
lay on my back, facing him. My legs were hanging off the bed, so
I stretched them out and supported them against the wall behind

him. He slid his hard cock into me, went in and out a few times, and watched me rub my clit.

"Could you hold still?" I wasn't sure if he'd lose his erection if he stopped thrusting.

"Yes." He looked at me tenderly.

He stood still and barely moved. He looked at my legs, while I looked at his high cheekbones, blue eyes, blond hair and tan face, and rubbed my clit in circles. He whispered some words and stood still like that, and that was his mission, be still so I could take my time. Looking at his face aroused me. I didn't have to fantasize! I could just look at his face. I kept my eyes on him as I rubbed myself, getting more and more turned on, with his hard cock perfectly still inside me. I felt my pussy grip his cock. It was my signal I was closer to coming. I was super wet. He whispered more hot talk that I couldn't make out, which turned me on even more. I was more and more aroused and my orgasm was building without a fantasy at all.

I looked at him as I rubbed and an inevitable orgasmic wave grew from my depths and it was powerful and couldn't be stopped. I kept rubbing and looked at him, and I knew it was coming and then it did. I looked at him as my pussy gripped and pulsed on his cock. I hoped he could feel every throb of my vagina engulfing his cock, and hoped he was impressed with how long and tight my contractions were. *Look at me coming. Look at me.* But he didn't. He looked at my legs. He let himself feel a couple contractions, and then he started moving inside me and filled me with his hardness while I rode my orgasm to the end.

"Wow, thank you," I whispered as I looked at him. "I have never come before with a guy inside me, except maybe once a long time ago. That was awesome, thank you."

He smiled. He was so charming, handsome, and sexy! I liked him and I was excited I came with a man's penis inside of me, so I could share my orgasm with my lover and not have it all alone every time.

I was all wet and warmed up and he put on a condom, and rode me hard and fucked me until he came.

"Thanks for making sure I came first," I told him.

"Ladies first," he answered.

"I love that! It makes so much sense for the woman to come first."

He held me while I laid on him and we talked. After about half an hour, he got dressed and then he left and said he would be in touch. I went to sleep happily.

After that first date, I kept thinking about him. I built him up in my mind as I relived the key sexual moments. I also wanted to know more. How did he become interested in surfing? How did he become interested in engineering and what were his design ideas? How was his relationship with his children? What were their evenings like? I was definitely interested in him and hoped I could see him again.

About a week after we met, Blake texted me. It was 9 p.m. He wanted to see me and I definitely wanted to see him again. We talked on the phone and decided that I would drive to his place in Encinitas.

"I don't want just sex. I want more. If I come over, I want to spend the night," I told him.

"Sure, you can stay the night," he said.

To me, that meant he also wanted more than sex. But I really didn't know, because I didn't ask him what he wanted.

From the moment I walked in the door at his house, I was laughing. He was funny and charming, as he cleaned up the evidence of his children's visit from the past week. I sat down and looked at a book on the coffee table. There was a thick book, a biography on Napoleon Bonaparte, and some westerns. I asked him how he became interested in history. He walked over to me, sat right across from me, and told me he fell in love with history in 8th grade. His main interest was Roman history.

He brought me some leftover chicken he had made for his kids, and sat on the sofa. He was cute, offering me leftover chicken and nothing else with it. I liked how it was all so real. We ate, and then I straddled him. We kissed on the sofa and he unbuttoned my blouse and lightly touched my nipples and drove me wild.

Blake asked me to follow him into the bedroom. I took my purse with me. I had brought female condoms to use. I checked my phone for messages, and when I came in, he was naked in bed. Was he going to be passive or were we replicating married sex? I lay on top of him and we kissed.

"Sometimes it takes me a long time to come," I said.

"A woman's orgasm is a delicate thing," he said.

And with that, he gave me permission to be <u>me</u>, to take my time. I immediately relaxed and trusted him.

We started out in missionary position. He entered me gently and moved slowly. His warm body felt strong on top of me. Then a new feeling appeared. It was in my body but not in my genitals. It was in my heart. Was I falling for him? Would I cry over him as I had over other men? *Please no god, no more attachment, no more crying, please no.* Did he feel it too? And if he did, could I let myself feel it?

"I'm afraid I could be falling for you, and I don't want to."

"That is always a risk. Thank you for telling me how you feel."

What did that mean? Did he like me too? I pushed those thoughts aside and focused on his thrusting cock, and then I noticed the feeling in my heart was gone. I looked if the female condom was still in place. I no longer saw it sticking out, which meant it had slipped and was not serving its purpose. We needed to use a regular condom or none at all. I asked Blake about his sexual history, and he said he had been STD-tested a month ago and had sex only with one woman since, and he had used a condom. I took the female condom out and slipped his cock inside me. Oh wow, he felt so much better skin on skin.

We turned around and I got on top. The room was semi dark and his eyes were closed.

"Let's turn on the light so I can see," I requested.

Blake turned on the lamps on his nightstands. His eyes were closed as I rode him.

"Here, look at me," I whispered.

He opened his eyes. He was so handsome! I liked riding him and looking at his handsome face. As I rode him, he pulled back his legs and bent his knees.

"If someone walked in now, they'd think you were fucking me," he laughed

So hot! I looked down, and indeed it did. I kept riding him as his legs were pulled up and if someone only saw our torsos and legs it looked like I was fucking him. But what did he mean and want? Did he want me to fuck him with a strap-on? Or was he just having fun moving his body? Was he bisexual and like men? His sexy idea turned me on.

He turned over and got on top again. He ground on top of me, his heavy breathing in my ear, and his erection felt strong and demanding. He pushed deep inside of me with each deep short thrust. I liked those short pulses deep inside, pushing next to my cervix, so deep, deep, deep.

Blake asked me to touch myself as I rode him. I said it would be easier if I lay on my back. I rubbed on my clit in circles. Blake came near me so I could touch his penis. I kept rubbing my clit. It felt good. Blake put his penis near my mouth, and I sucked on his head like a lollipop. I didn't care how weird it looked. I got into a rhythm sucking his head. I recalled seeing a man suck on a woman's tits at a sex party, just like that. He was sucking on her tits like he was a little baby. It didn't look weird at all, so I figured I didn't look weird either. Sucking on Blake's penis head like that as I masturbated was deeply arousing. As I got close to coming, Blake quietly and slowly moved off the bed and slowly inserted his cock into my pussy. It was a brilliant move! His slow move ensured I didn't lose my inner focus while masturbating. He was definitely experienced. His limber body and sexual intuition gave him movements that I did not ever consider.

I felt stuck though in my buildup. I was masturbating but I wasn't moving the action forward. He noticed and brought his cock back to my mouth. I closed my eyes and masturbated and sucked on his cock as he watched.

"You're so sexy," he whispered.

Somehow, those words released any inhibition. I let go mentally and while I suckled on his cockhead, my body responded. My orgasm came within minutes. I was soaking wet, not from squirting, but from being so turned on. I looked at his penis after I came and he was rock hard. I liked that he was turned on by me.

I asked him where he wanted to come. He wanted oral sex. I loved a man to come inside me, yet I also loved making a man come in my mouth. I moved down. I licked his balls and penis slowly at first, and then I started to suck while twisting my hand in circular up and down motions on his shaft. I sucked hard while playing with just the opening of his asshole. As he breathed harder and his legs tensed up, I moved faster. His breathing became louder and faster and almost scared me a little. His legs were tense, so tense, and I felt his contractions and warm liquid shoot in my mouth. He moaned so hard and fast, I was worried he could pass out. He moaned and fell back in exhaustion. It took him well over one minute to catch his breath.

Blake tried clumsily to hold me. Didn't he know how to hold a woman, or did he not like me enough? It didn't matter. I knew how to hold someone and I enjoyed doing so. I wanted to give back because he had done so much for me. I asked him to turn on his side and I held him in a spoon. It was very awkward, because he didn't engage with me at all. He just lay there. We fell asleep.

I woke up with daylight and felt aroused. I pressed my body against his and rubbed on him and he waited until he was hard, then he turned around on his back. He kept his eyes shut and let me ride him. I was getting a little bored just riding him like that while his eyes were closed and he was just lying there. So I tried different positions. I went into reverse cowgirl, but I was bored there also.

He came inside me, and then I just wanted to get up. After the sex there was nothing between us. He did not show any interest in me or ask to cuddle. I couldn't tell if he didn't connect with anyone at all, or if he just didn't like me in that same way. He got up to make us tea and I got dressed and made his bed. I came out to the kitchen and my tea was ready. He had that post sex happy glow.

"I'd like to see you again but nothing exclusive. I still want to have sex with other guys," I told him.

"Keep me as another horse in your stable," he smiled.

Was he glowing because he liked me, or just because of all the post-sex hormones? Was that 'horse in the stable' comment a good thing to say and what did he mean exactly? We drank our tea and then it was time to leave. Blake grabbed his jacket and walked me out to my car.

"I won't call you. If you want to see me again, you call me," I told him.

A couple days later, as I kept replaying the lovemaking scenes in my mind, I liked him more and more. By the end of the week, I was deeply attached. I imagined myself making dinner for his boys. Maybe I would end up moving in with them and I'd have my career and we'd have family dinners and go to soccer games. Maybe I would have a do-over on my sexless marriage. I forgot how he kept his eyes closed, and that I couldn't wait to leave after we were done with sex, and that he didn't reply to my messages. I just remembered he took me to new places sexually, his funny stories, and how I felt happy just looking at him. I knew he didn't have his kids that weekend. Of course we could have more hot sex. I had told him I wouldn't contact him again, but I changed my mind.

"I really like you and I'd like to see you tomorrow," I texted.

"Busy tonight, but looking forward to seeing you again," he texted back.

All I heard was *busy*. I didn't listen to the part that said he looked forward to seeing me again. I heard busy, and I was mad. How could he not want to see me again right then? Why didn't he suggest an alternate date? We had great sex. Didn't he want more? Didn't he want to see me again right away because it was all so awesome? Maybe I was too much woman for him, too open and honest, and he couldn't handle me. What other reason could there be? He didn't say when he'd want to see me again, so I didn't like that at all. It sounded like he was just putting me off. My friend Ally said the 'horse in the stable' comment was a bad sign and made him think he was just another fuck. Should I be ashamed of fucking so much? Over the next week, I sent him about ten text messages saying how much I wanted to see him, asking when I could see him, and telling him how wonderful the sex was. He did not reply to any of my texts. Maybe I chased him away with all that neediness.

I thought about Blake constantly. I was sad, and sometimes I cried. I heard songs on the radio that reminded me of him, and I cried. I went to sleep and sometimes I cried. At work, I was sad. I worked on changing my thoughts, and not thinking of him. I deleted his messages and his contact from my address book. I remembered the last four digits of his number so I could know it was him in case he ever called or messaged me.

I tried to push my sad feelings away. I "knew" being sad was "bad", so I kept working on getting rid of it. I had some solid techniques but none worked anyway. So I felt bad about myself for being sad.

Six weeks later he texted me when he was horny. I went back to his place and spent the night. By then, I was less interested. I messaged him a few times after that, and sometimes he replied, and then he stopped replying. I never saw him again.

HIS ED

Dwight and I met for coffee and had a great conversation. He was extremely attractive and fit, with a flat stomach, and a successful career. His kids were in college. Maybe my friends were right, that sex should be saved for the second or third date if I wanted a relationship, so I didn't have sex with him on the first date.

For our second date, I wanted to go for a walk on the beach or coffee, but he wanted to meet for drinks. I did not want to meet for drinks. Men who wanted to drink were a turnoff. I had the image of bar fly and womanizer in my mind. I really preferred a man who wanted to walk on the beach or do an outdoor activity, meditate, or go to a vegan restaurant. Yet I also wanted to be flexible and open to new experiences. I agreed to meet him for a drink.

We ordered cabernet sauvignon and a cheese plate. We talked about our work, and I asked him if he had erectile dysfunction (ED). I still had a fear that men over 50 had ED, and I didn't want to be anywhere near a man who had that. I still had a bad taste in my mouth with it, from my marriage.

"Oh, you have nothing to worry about in that department," he assured me.

His gray hair made him seem old and thus more likely to have ED, so when we walked out to my car, I asked him again if he had ED. He reassured me he did not.

"Well, do you want to come over? You can spend the night," I invited him.

"Sure!"

Dwight came over and he asked for more red wine. That was a turn-off, since I rarely drank myself and I didn't like to be around people who did. I poured him a glass of red wine, and we talked in the kitchen. He told me he had a few different ladies he saw for hooking up. He was handsome and fit, so I could imagine women sought him.

He didn't turn me on, but I was curious to try sex with an older man. We took off our clothes and lay on my bed. There was nothing romantic about it. He lay on his back, and I had my first look at his penis. I was used to seeing hard cocks, some so hard it touched the man's stomach. This was not the case here. Dwight's penis was soft like a washcloth or a noodle. What a disappointment!

I didn't like a soft penis at all. I wanted him rock hard so I could ride him. He was useless to me. Maybe I could get him hard. I licked his balls and licked and sucked his penis until eventually he was a little erect and then he came in my mouth. He never was hard enough to ride. We fell asleep together. The next morning, I wanted to have sex with him again.

"Oh, I have such a headache!" he said.

I didn't have any medication at home, not even Tylenol, since I didn't get headaches.

"I'll go to the store and get you some ibuprofen," I offered.

"No, no, I'll go home," he said.

"Why weren't you hard last night?" I asked.

"It was the red wine," he said.

Why the fuck did he drink red wine if he knew that would prevent him from getting hard? He hurriedly got dressed and left. I wondered if he left so fast because he knew he couldn't get hard that morning either.

We texted a few times. He wanted me to come over later that day. He said he would be hard and we could try again. I texted him to ask what time would work. I told him I only wanted to see him if he could be hard for sure. He did not reply to that text and I never heard from him again.

It was March. The birds chirped, and days were longer. Wilson came over every other week, and he started bringing his cat. Christine and Wilson were close, so when she spent the night, they would both crawl into the double bed together. I loved walking into their room in the morning, seeing them together in one bed, and I felt happy that my children were close and loved each other. Matt was busy with school and work, and I saw him less. He loved cooking and I did not, so he came over with groceries, cooked us a meal, and cleaned up after dinner. On the off weeks, the kids called just to hang out. Usually they wanted to go for a smoothie or coffee. Other times, they wanted to come over to play piano or use my juicer. They would call first, to make sure I was home and did not have any man over.

"Dad never buys any fruit," they'd say as they devoured all the grapes. But at least their dad cooked and I did not.

Work was picking up and I got involved in new projects and had more responsibility. I asked for an increase in my hourly rate, and I got it. My company was pleased with my work. Specifically, my curiosity, loyalty, and how smart I was.

CHAPTER 15

"KISS ME AND LET ME FLY"

I t was May. A year had gone by since I moved into my apartment. I was excited to go to a connection event in Encinitas that morning. The event would feature eye gazing and authentic communication. I was in a mood to look sweet and motherly, not single and sexy as I usually did. I put on my Hudson straight leg jeans, a beige long silk top and a cardigan that flowed halfway down my legs, flat shoes, and my hair in a ponytail.

Some of my friends went too, and we planned to go to dinner afterward. In our first exercise, we were to become curious about others. We walked around in a circle, bumping into each other. First we bumped feet, then hips. I noticed him right away: a lean man, about 6'2" in a red shirt, in his early 30's. He came toward me. I bumped against his hip and laughed and looked up. He smiled down at me. Wow! I felt warm in my heart. I immediately liked his tall strong body and handsome face.

"Can I give you a hug?" I asked playfully.

"Yes."

I hugged him, and he put his arms around me. I grabbed him tightly and buried my head in his chest. His strong body turned me on and made me feel protected. I didn't worry if he liked older women. I just assumed he would like me, since he had come over to me.

"You're so strong! I like tall lean guys, and I love younger men!" And I beamed him a huge smile.

"Oh, you do?"

'Yeah. I'm Schahrzad by the way."

"I'm David."

I liked meeting a man I was attracted to in person. It was new. I had met all the other men online. The men were often nervous when we met, so I had to be patient and give them a few minutes to relax so I could see their true personality. I felt a physical, but not romantic, attraction to the men I invited over. I had sex with them because I was horny, or curious about something. But there, with David, I had attraction and feelings. I liked how it all happened so naturally.

We sat down for our next exercise. David sat next to me and handed me his business card. I felt a thrill inside my heart. He was flirting with me, and he made the first move! In my entire single life the past 15 months, no man had come on to me or asked me out. I liked being pursued, especially by a hot guy.

I kept my eye on him during the workshop and he did the same. We partnered in an eye gazing exercise in which we had to show our partner regret we felt over something. He showed his feelings through his eyes, and I did the same. I felt so close to him.

In another exercise, Partner A asked Partner B "what is love", letting Partner B answer. After three minutes, we switched. David came to me for the exercise. He kept asking me what is love, and each time I answered. Hugs, children, god, happiness, hugs, pain. He nodded. He understood. I felt closer to him.

In the last exercise, we walked around a circle and handed out red beads to other participants while saying "I love you". I gave a red bead to David while I said it. I didn't love him, but it was fun to say.

I liked the exercises, and how they built our intimacy and closeness. After the event ended, I looked for him, so I could invite him to join my friends and me for dinner.

"Do you want to come with us to dinner?" I asked.

"I'm so tired. I'm just going home to sleep," he said.

But he just stood there and looked at me and didn't seem like he was about to go anywhere, so I suggested dinner and a sleepover at my house.

"Really? That sounds awesome," and he smiled at me.

I couldn't believe my good fortune. I was so excited. I hoped he wouldn't change his mind.

I met him outside at my apartment complex, and that's when we kissed. There were neighbors all around and he didn't care and he kissed me. He wasn't embarrassed to kiss someone as old as me in public? Why was I so insecure about my age around men I liked?

We went into my kitchen and I made dinner for us: a salad, lentil soup from the night before, and a cheese and bread plate, and water. Over dinner, we talked about our sexual history. I had been STD tested just two weeks before, and he had not had sex at all since his last STD test eight months earlier, so we decided we wouldn't use a condom. I put away the dishes. He was so fucking handsome and manly! I was wet and turned on just looking at him.

He sat on the sofa. I playfully came over and straddled him. His erection pressed into me. I wrapped my arms around his neck and looked in his beautiful brown eyes.

"You're so handsome!" I felt happy just looking at him.

I leaned forward to kiss him. We started with soft kisses, but as I rubbed on him and got turned on, we kissed harder. My panties felt soaked, and the room felt hot. I explored his mouth with my tongue, in rhythm with my moans, as I ground harder on his erection. He must have got more turned on from that, because he picked me up and carried me into my bedroom and laid me on my bed. I laughed with joy.

David got on top of me and kissed me gently. He wrapped his warm lips around mine, and tugged on my lips. I returned his playful kiss. Then he undressed me and went straight for my pussy. That's what I wanted. Oral sex wasn't my favorite, but I liked a man starting there, so I knew he loved my pussy.

David's tongue explored my outer and inner lips and my clit, and then he sucked on my clit and made circles with his tongue. I loved what he was doing.

"Wow, that feels amazing1"

I let myself be spoiled. For maybe five minutes. I still had that thing about men going down on me too long unless they totally loved it.

I asked him to lie on his back so I could please him and explore his cock. I licked his balls as I held them gently in my hand. I gently put them inside my warm mouth. He moaned. I explored his perineum and ass with my tongue, flicking it all around. I ran my tongue up his shaft, then sucked on just the ridge of the head of his cock, and suckled on the head. Then I took it all in. I put his head in my mouth and wrapped my lips tight around his cock and pushed down, then up, …down and up, four fast strokes. Then slower again. I was getting turned on doing it, and I knew he loved it. David raised his head and looked at me and watched me take his cock in and out of my mouth. I was moaning too, and wanted him inside me.

I scooted up and lay on his warm strong chest, and we kissed. I felt so happy looking at his face. He so beautiful! His hard cock pressed on my pubic mound as I ground on him. I was so wet and turned on.

We looked at each other. Slowly, he pushed the tip of his cock head inside me with his hand, while he looked deeply into my eyes. I gasped. Out again. Still looking at me, he pushed in deeper, so half his head was in me. I moaned as he stretched me wide. *See me, see my pleasure.* Out again. Slowly, while we eye gazed, he went in deeper and then out, in10-second strokes, deeper each time. He looked in my eyes and searched for my reaction. He was totally in control. It was the hottest thing I had ever done.

I got lost in my moans, his hard cock, and his beautiful eyes. His pleasure didn't show. I wanted to lose myself in him emotionally, but I couldn't. I didn't know if he blocked himself from having feelings, or if I blocked him somehow. I wanted so much to feel him in my heart but I couldn't. The extra emotional connection would have deepened the experience for me. I was still turned on though. I moved my hips too and rode his cock the way it felt good for me for what seemed like at least ten minutes. I was soaking wet. I wanted more, more of him.

"Stick your finger in my ass," I whispered.

He reached his arm around and slid his finger in my ass. A deep wave of pleasure washed over me from my bottom. I rode him like that, with his finger in my ass, and then he picked me up and laid me on my back. He lay down next to me and then he tenderly brought my knees to my chest. It was really comfortable. I had never been positioned like that. David reached over and cradled me with his arms. I felt deeply protected and loved. He slid his cock inside, while he looked at me. He just fucked me in that position, and I got lost again, in him and his cock and my moans. Then he got on top of me in the missionary position and gave me some deeper thrusting. Everything he did felt so good. I felt a little guilty for just being able to lie there while he did all the work, but it all felt so good and I liked how he took charge. He was really sweaty. I felt his warm breath in my ear.

"Let's give me a break," he said.

He lay next to me. He slid his fingers easily and slowly to the depths of my pussy, deep inside my body, and held me. He gave me that steady pressure, without moving. Damn, that felt good! It felt so much better than having those fingers moving around. I loved that deep steady connection.

"You should touch yourself," he said sweetly.

Gladly. His fingers glided across my nipples, and sent boosts of stimulation to my clit. I closed my eyes and rubbed my clitoris while he fingered me and played with my nipples.

"You're such a good girl to touch yourself for me."

That turned me on even more and I felt something building deep within my body. I looked at him. And then it came, from deep within. My orgasm swelled out in a big wave, it pulsed out larger and larger and larger, the wave got bigger and along with it my moan became a roar, and my roar became a scream. I gave in to it and let it be. I knew the neighbors would hear but I didn't care, I screamed long, deep, and loud, in tandem with the strong pleasure wave that washed over me. My orgasm lasted at least thirty seconds. It was the most intense orgasm I ever had! I looked at him and saw he was rock hard.

He got on top, and slid his erection in me. I was wet and could take it deep, so I grabbed his ass with both hands and pulled him rhythmically toward me, and back and forth. I wanted him as deep inside as I could.

"Deep, deep, deep," I whispered to him. "Let me have it deep!"

That turned him on. He had to slow down a bit. He kissed me tenderly and then he nibbled on my ear lobe and pressed his warm tongue inside my ear. It drove me wild!

"Yes, yes, yes." I didn't even know I loved having that done!

"Go deep again, let me have all of your cock, deep." He went faster and then he moaned and came inside me. We held each other and fell asleep together.

He got up during the night to get something out of his car while I slept. He could have just left but he came back. We woke up and fucked again and then I hoped he could stay and talk.

"Do you want some coffee?" I asked him in the morning.

"No, I have to be somewhere at 9am," he replied.

I hoped he would ask me to go with him to wherever he was going.

"I'll see you again," he said.

"That's what they all say."

David texted me that he got home safely. I didn't ask him to do that, and no other man had done that. He texted me the next day and asked if he could see me a few days later. I wasn't attached to him, but I did look forward to having more good sex wit him. I also felt respected that he set our dates up ahead of time, and didn't just call at the last minute when he was horny.

He came over and the sex was amazing. After we made love, I asked him a question.

"What do you like about older women?"

"They know what they want."

He didn't stay the night, but after that, we texted and messaged each other more. As I replayed key moments of our time together, I grew more attached. I sent him sexy pictures, and he was replying with messages which made me feel desired.

"You're distracting me with that nice ass," he messaged me. He asked if he could see me again early the following week. That seemed so far away. I counted the days.

I looked out the kitchen window when I saw him walk up the stairs to my apartment. I was washing dishes in my pencil skirt, silk blouse, high heels, and apron, He looked up. When our eyes met, his face turned red. I knew then he had at least some feelings for me.

"Come on in," I yelled out.

He came into the kitchen, walked up behind me, and gave me a kiss. I turned around and saw his smiling face. He looked happy to see me. I felt happy too, to have David there in my kitchen. He pulled up a chair and we talked while I finished washing the dishes. I dried my hands and went over and smiled at him.

"I want to dance for you."

I put on music. He sat on my living room sofa, legs apart, leaned back, with his hands on his hips. He was so handsome. I felt so happy having him there, full of anticipation of what would and might be about to unfold between us. I stood there, in front of him.

"I'm a little shy, but I just want to show you….," my voice trailed off.

"Show me what you've got?" his eyes twinkled.

"Yeah."

I smiled at him, and began to move to the music, for him, for me, and for us. He watched, enjoyed, and savored me. I loved dancing for him, and having him watching and wanting me. I danced over to him and straddled his lap while kissing him. He put his arms around me and we held each other. Then he moved my legs to the side, gathered me up, and carried me to my bed.

I wanted him inside me and he wanted that too. We skipped the oral. I climbed on him and he let me. I looked down on him and slid his cock inside with my right hand. I was soaking wet. He slid right in. I fucked him and then I got so wet that he didn't feel so good anymore. I needed more friction and I told him. He laughed. He liked how wet I was. I sat up and slowed the pace. We just looked at each other again, as I moved my hips slowly side to side. I looked in his eyes. I wanted to feel him in my heart, but I didn't. I still couldn't feel him, which was different from what it had been with other men.

David smiled at me, then he turned me on my back and into the cradle position. Our eyes locked together. He gently and slowly probed the opening of my sex with his cock.

"Do it," I said, as I looked him in his eyes. I wanted him to enter me.

"Yes?" he asked and moved his cockhead toward my ass. Did he think I wanted him to fuck me in the ass? I didn't ask for that, but I was going to let him if that's where he was headed.

"Don't we need lube?" I asked.

He just kept looking at me and slid his cock further in my ass.

"We don't need lube?" I asked again.

He didn't answer. He looked at me tenderly. Slowly, he pushed his cock against my ass. He pushed without going in, and he looked at me, and it seemed he was waiting for a reaction. I felt safe and loved.

"I trust you," I whispered and looked at him.

And then my entire lower pelvis relaxed and opened up. My ass, my pussy, my heart, it was all one and it was open. We looked into each other's eyes. Nobody blinked. And as he looked at me, he pushed his cock slowly into my ass. David slid about half an inch further with each thrust. I was soaking wet. We didn't need lube.

Then his cock was all the way inside my ass, and he moved in and out while I moaned with pleasure. My moans were deep and guttural. How did my moans just come out of me and change with what was happening in my body? I just let it all happen. He fucked me in the ass. So hot!! And then he took his cock out and slipped it back into my vagina. I wondered if he hadn't read that was against sanitary sex rules. It was supposed to be a no-no to go from anus to vagina without washing first. But I trusted him and I didn't want to break the flow of our connection by getting up to wash. I didn't know if what we did was safe, but I wanted to just enjoy it all.

I masturbated to come, and then we fucked longer until he came inside me. I lay on his chest and was quiet for about two minutes so he could stay attentive to his orgasm and refractory period.

"I noticed I came first every time we were together. I liked that," I told him.

"I love giving women orgasms and I like the woman to come first," he said.

He left and an hour later he texted me that he was home, and may not have time to see me again before his vacation.

Over the next few days, as I replayed key moments of our time together, I grew more attached to David. I liked him for more than sex. David led a purpose-filled life, and his happiness came from his actions. I wanted what he had. I wanted to be happy without dating or a man, and I wanted a purpose that inspired me.

I had a huge crush and thought of him constantly. Did David want me too? I had to tell him how I felt, and find out if he felt the same. I texted him that I couldn't wait to see him again.

"Kiss me and let me fly," he replied.

Really? I fought back tears. Did he mean fly away for good, or fly away and come back for more kisses between flights? What did he mean?

I called him and we talked for about 30 minutes. I told him I had feelings for him. David said he didn't feel the same way. He said he was sorry he hurt me, and his focus was advancing his career and finding a wife. He wanted a family. He also said he didn't like a woman who had sex with so many men.

"When you meet a man you like, date him for 4-6 weeks before you have sex. Get to know him. It makes the sex so much better."

I was definitely out. I was the girl who fucked him the first day. That's not the kind of girl he wanted. He didn't date girls like me....girls who hooked up when they felt like it and had a long list of lovers. He just happened to meet me and like me. But how was I going to hold off on sex for one date, let alone dates spanning 4 – 6 weeks, when sex was the first thing I wanted?

I understood all his reasons for not wanting me. But maybe he would change his mind, because our connection had been so awesome? Sadly, David never called me back to say he changed his mind. Not that day or the next day or the next or the next.

He gave me a nice ending, so why was my heart breaking? Maybe I was too harsh when I judged guys who ended it by ignoring or blocking me, because telling me all the reasons and thirty minutes on the phone didn't make the ending any easier or stop my heart from breaking. I cried over him for almost three months.

CHAPTER 16

"WHAT WOULD YOUR LIFE BE LIKE IF YOU WERE SINGLE FOREVER?"

David and I practically made love. I felt secure around him and I trusted him. Sex like that was rare to find. If I couldn't have him or someone I felt that way about, I didn't want to have sex at all.

To get a good man like David, I couldn't go around having sex whenever I wanted it. I made a decision to be abstinent. It wasn't that hard at first, because I didn't want other penises in me, and I was too sad to go out anyway.

I reconnected with myself. What was it that I really wanted when I wanted him? I wanted his joy. His joy came from following his purpose. I wanted that too: a purpose or mission so great it would fill me with joy and transcend my *need* for a man. Some people said that nobody really needed a mission and that the joy of life was living in the moment. I disagreed. I kept looking for my purpose and mission.

I loved cycling as a child, and had wanted to do it again for years. I asked my friend to take me out a bike ride, to see if I still liked it. We cycled down the coast highway. On my bike, pedaling fast with wind blowing through my helmet, I felt free, powerful, and self-expressed. I bought a used bike and bike rack for my car, and I took my coastal bike ride on weekends. It was my time.

I had lunch with a friend, and she said, "You should write a book." It wasn't the first time I heard it. Several friends had coaxed me since earlier in the year to write a book about my sex life, but I always brushed it aside. I never had a desire to write a book.

That time, at lunch, I listened. The book was the mission I had been seeking. Yes. I had a story to tell. I sat down and started writing. I bought a legal pad and took it to a coffee shop and wrote the story about David, through streams of tears at first, and then later it got easier. For ten months, I wrote down the stories of some, but not all, of the women and men with whom I shared my heart, mind, and body.

Around my sixth week of abstinence, my friend Paula Padmakshi asked me, "What would your life be like if you never found a man, if you were single forever?"

Paula had been a great inspiration to me. She was powerful and self expressed. I was in her women's group that summer when she asked that questions. A new door opened up: a door to be me. I could be single forever, so why would I want to be abstinent or be anything at all, so a "good" man would like me? I would have all the sex I wanted, if that's what I wanted. I wasn't going to change for some man to come along and possibly like me. Any man, who was right for me, would like me the way I was.

It was September 2014. I ended my abstinence and went on Tinder. I met a 24-year-old artillery officer who rocked my world in bed. He liked me too and said he would spend the night and date me when he got back from a month in the field. I was excited. I had fucked marines or former marines before, but had never paid any attention because I had been anti military most of my life, so I basically overlooked that they were in the military. That man ignited in me a new type of lust. Marines were all I wanted and dated from then on. They were fit, sensitive, passionate, and manly. Why had I not discovered Tinder or marines before? I sent him texts showing all my love for him, and then his texts stopped, and when he came back six weeks later, he didn't want to date me anymore. I sobbed over him for a month.

I made a few decisions after that. I was not going to cry over men anymore. I closed down a little bit. I stopped being so open during sex. I used less eye contact. I got attached less often, and when a guy I liked ended it, I wasn't quite as sad.

I also had that insatiable hunger for marines. Where did that come from? And why didn't I ever see them around anywhere? Could I meet them anywhere but Tinder?

EPILOGUE

S hutting down my feelings was against everything I wanted to be! I wanted to be more and feel more, and there I was, feeling less. Sex wasn't as much fun when I held back emotionally. I wanted my sex with feelings, or not at all. I changed my online profile and looked for men to date, rather than men to hookup, but I was still starting with sex when I met them. I had made my dating all about what I didn't have in my marriage, not about what I wanted.

What did I really want? I wanted a man who asked me out instead of just coming over. I wanted him to say in the morning, "What are you doing later today?", instead of leaving and maybe texting me a couple days later. I wanted a man who told me how he felt and dealt with relationship challenges with a hunger for personal growth, instead of avoiding and withdrawing. I had to stop with the young men. I set my minimum dating age to 28.

In March 2015 I met the last guy who broke my heart. We started with a hookup on a day I was horny and we liked each other and then one morning after I texted him he blocked me. What had happened? Did I need to learn something, and what? Did I fall really short somehow, or was he just not right for me? I cried over him for two months, but not as much as I had cried over other men. I made a decision. I didn't want to date any more men who treated me as disposable and ended our relationship by blocking me. I didn't want to cry over men anymore at all. I had to make a change. I didn't know what. I took a break from dating.

There was more. I talked about dating and sex everywhere, even at work. In January 2015 I was put on notice at my job that I was to cease from discussing my "sexual experiences, preferences or likings in person, in social settings" with clients, colleagues, or on my work FB account. It was clear I couldn't publish and promote a sex book while I had a professional job. I needed more time to write anyway, so I quit my job. I needed cash so I got a job as a nude stripper. Then, I had no jobs at all and worked full-time on my book and two weeks later, voila, this book was done.

I had left my marriage to be more, and feel more. I accomplished that. I still didn't have the experience of making love, of being able to let go and cry while I made love, and to discover more of my emotional side. That was something I could look forward to.

But most important, I had discovered me. All those tears, all that discomfort, all those risks I took – they shaped me to completeness and purpose. I was comfortable and happy alone. If I ever got into a relationship, I wouldn't need to be afraid of a man leaving me, because if he did, I still had myself. It was the first time in years I felt complete.

I am thinking about a next project. A sequel called "The Dating List"? No, please no, no more men I like who don't feel the same.....no more lists.

I could be a national spokesperson for masturbation. I am a big fan of masturbating, and I do like shining a light on taboos. Hmmmmmm........

May 24, 2015.

ABOUT THE AUTHOR

 **Schahrzad Morgan**'s friends coaxed her to write a book about her sex life. She has a B.S. in Computer Science from the University of Nebraska - Omaha, and an MBA from Arizona State University-West. She was born in Düsseldorf, Germany, in 1961, and moved to the U.S. at age 9. She loves running hilly trails, playing piano, Transcendental Meditation, younger men, asking questions, and of course, sex. She and her children live in San Diego, California. This is her first book.

www.thef-cklist.com

Photography by Kondor Imaging
Cover Design by Laura Rapalski

Printed by CreateSpace, An Amazon.com Company
Available on Kindle and other devices